VIETNAM'S FOREIGN POLICY
UNDER *DOI MOI*

ISEAS YUSOF ISHAK INSTITUTE

The **ISEAS – Yusof Ishak Institute** (formerly Institute of Southeast Asian Studies) is an autonomous organization established in 1968. It is a regional centre dedicated to the study of socio-political, security, and economic trends and developments in Southeast Asia and its wider geostrategic and economic environment. The Institute's research programmes are grouped under Regional Economic Studies (RES), Regional Strategic and Political Studies (RSPS), and Regional Social and Cultural Studies (RSCS). The Institute is also home to the ASEAN Studies Centre (ASC), the Nalanda-Sriwijaya Centre (NSC), and the Singapore APEC Study Centre.

ISEAS Publishing, an established academic press, has issued more than 2,000 books and journals. It is the largest scholarly publisher of research about Southeast Asia from within the region. ISEAS Publishing works with many other academic and trade publishers and distributors to disseminate important research and analyses from and about Southeast Asia to the rest of the world.

VIETNAM'S FOREIGN POLICY UNDER *DOI MOI*

Edited by Le Hong Hiep
& Anton Tsvetov

ISEAS YUSOF ISHAK
INSTITUTE

First published in Singapore in 2018 by
ISEAS Publishing
30 Heng Mui Keng Terrace
Singapore 119614

E-mail: publish@iseas.edu.sg
Website: <http://bookshop.iseas.edu.sg>

ISEAS Library Cataloguing-in-Publication Data

Vietnam's Foreign Policy under *Doi Moi* / edited by Le Hong Hiep and Anton Tsvetov.
1. Vietnam—Foreign relations—20th century.
2. Vietnam—Foreign relations—21st century.
3. ASEAN—Membership.
4. Vietnam—Foreign relations—South China Sea.
5. South China Sea—Foreign relations—Vietnam.
6. Vietnam—Foreign economic relations—European Union countries.
7. European Union countries—Foreign economic relations—Vietnam.
I. Le, Hong Hiep, editor.
II. Tsvetov, Anton, editor.
DS556.57 V661   January 2018

ISBN 978-981-4818-14-8 (soft cover)
ISBN 978-981-4818-15-5 (E-book PDF)

Typeset by International Typesetters Pte Ltd
Printed in Singapore by Markono Print Media Pte Ltd

CONTENTS

LIST OF TABLES

LIST OF FIGURES

LIST OF ABBREVIATIONS

ADB	Asian Development Bank
ADMM	ASEAN Defence Ministers' Meeting
AEC	ASEAN Economic Community
AFTA	ASEAN Free Trade Agreement
AIIB	Asian Infrastructure Investment Bank
AMF	ASEAN Maritime Forum
AMM	ASEAN Ministerial Meeting
ARF	ASEAN Regional Forum
APEC	Asia-Pacific Economic Cooperation
ASEAN	Association of Southeast Asian Nations
ASEM	Asia Europe Meeting
ASW	anti-submarine warfare
BIMSTEC	Bay of Bengal Initiative for Multi-Sectoral Scientific, Technological and Economic Cooperation
BJP	Bharatiya Janata Party
BRI	Belt and Road Initiative
BTA	Bilateral Trade Agreement
CNRP	Cambodia National Rescue Party
CPP	Cambodian People's Party
CPV	Communist Party of Vietnam
CSIS	Centre for Strategic and International Studies

DOC	Declaration on the Conduct of Parties in the South China Sea
DRV	Democratic Republic of Vietnam
DTTI	Defence Technology and Trade Initiative
EAEU	Eurasian Economic Union
EAS	East Asia Summit
EEZ	exclusive economic zone
EU	European Union
EUVFTA	European Union–Vietnam Free Trade Agreement
FDI	foreign direct investment
FON	freedom of navigation
FTA	free trade agreement
GDP	gross domestic product
GSO	General Statistics Office
GSP	*Generalized System of Preferences*
IFI	international finanical institutions
ILO	International Labour Organization
IMF	International Monetary Fund
IORA	Indian Ocean Rim Association
JICA	Japan International Cooperation Agency
JICPAC	Joint Intelligence Centre Pacific
KPRF	Communist Party of the Russian Federation
LEMOA	Logistics Exchange Memorandum of Agreement
LMC	Lancang–Mekong Cooperation
LPRP	Lao People's Revolutionary Party
MFN	Most Favoured Nation
MGC	Mekong-Ganga Cooperation
MOFA	Ministry of Foreign Affairs
MOU	Memorandum of Understanding
NEA	Naval Engagement Activity
NPE	Normative Power Europe

OCED	Organisation for Economic Co-operation and Development
ODA	Official Development Assistance
ONGC Videsh	Oil and Natural Gas Corporation Videsh
PNTR	Permanent Normal Trade Relations
POW/MIA	Prisoner of War/Missing in Action
PRC	People's Republic of China
RCEP	Regional Comprehensive Economic Partnership
SIPRI	Stockholm International Peace Research Institute
SLOC	sea lines of communication
SOE	state-owned enterprise
SOM	Senior Official Meeting
SPS	Sanitary and Phytosanitary
TBT	Technical Barriers to Trade
TPP	Trans-Pacific Partnership
TRA	Trade Related Assistance
TSIA	Trade Sustainability Impact Assessments
UN	United Nations
UNCLOS	United Nations Convention on the Law of the Sea
UNCTAD	United Nations Conference on Trade and Development
UNSC	United Nations Security Council
USSR	Union of Soviet Socialist Republics
VCG	Vietnam Coast Guard
VPA/FLEGT	Voluntary Partnership Agreement on Forest Law Enforcement, Governance and Trade
WB	World Bank
WTO	World Trade Organization

ACKNOWLEDGEMENTS

Six out of twelve chapters in this edited volume (Chapters 3, 4, 6, 8, 11 and 12) are based on papers presented at the Vietnam Forum 2016 on "Vietnam's Thirty Years of *Doi Moi* and Beyond" organized by ISEAS – Yusof Ishak Institute on 7–8 April 2016. The conference was sponsored by the Konrad-Adenauer-Stiftung (KAS), which also funded the publication of this volume.

The authors of the above chapters would like to thank the participants and attendees at the conference for their comments and suggestions which contributed to the improvement of their final papers.

The editing of the volume was initially conducted by Le Hong Hiep. He would like to thank Mr Tan Chin Tiong, former Director of ISEAS – Yusof Ishak Institute, and Mr Daljit Singh, Senior Fellow and Coordinator of ISEAS' Regional Strategic and Political Studies Programme, for their encouragement and guidance throughout the whole process. Anton Tsvetov later joined Le Hong Hiep as a co-editor and helped with the initial review and editing of five chapters. Hiep would like to thank Tsvetov for his timely help, without which this book project may have been delayed.

This edited volume is a joint effort of all the contributing authors. The editors are thankful to them for their cooperation and patience.

Some of the chapters are based on the respective authors' previous research. Specifically, Carlyle A. Thayer's Chapter 2 is based on the paper titled "Vietnamese Diplomacy, 1975–2015: From Member of the Socialist Camp to Proactive International Integration" that he presented at the International Conference on "Vietnam: 40 Years of Reunification, Development and Integration (1975–2015)" organized by Thu Dau Mot

University on 25 April 2015; Chapter 5 is based in part on a working paper written by Thuy T. Do during her visiting research fellowship at the Japan Institute of International Affairs in 2014; and Hoang Hai Ha's Chapter 12 is based on her PhD study titled "Analysing Normative Power Europe through Trade and Development Cooperation Policies towards Vietnam" that she undertook at Sant'Anna School of Advanced Studies, Italy, and Ghent University, Belgium. The views and opinions expressed in all chapters of this book are those of the respective authors and do not necessarily reflect the views of their institutions.

Finally, the editors and contributing authors are grateful to two anonymous reviewers for their valuable comments and suggestions that have helped to improve the manuscript, and to Anh Pham, Dickson Yeo, and Tran Chi Trung for their comments and ideas about the book cover design. They would also like to thank the editors at ISEAS Publishing for their generous and efficient assistance during the production of this book.

ABOUT THE CONTRIBUTORS

Rajeev Ranjan Chaturvedy is a researcher at the Institute of South Asian Studies (ISAS), National University of Singapore. Prior to joining ISAS, he was heading Foreign Policy Division at the Federation of Indian Chambers of Commerce and Industry. He was a Global Emerging Voices Fellow in 2013; Young Strategists Forum Fellow in 2012; a 2009 Professional Development Award recipient at the Canadian International Development Research Centre in Ottawa. Before going to Ottawa, he worked with the Indian Council for Research on International Economic Relations and the Indian Pugwash Society. Rajeev was also part of the "Nuclear Cluster" at the Institute for Defence Studies and Analyses. Rajeev has authored a number of academic and policy papers and frequently comments on Indian foreign policy issues in the media.

Vannarith Chheang is Vice-Chairman of the Cambodian Institute for Strategic Studies and a Board Member and Senior Fellow at the Cambodian Institute for Cooperation and Peace where he previously served as the Executive Director from 2009 to 2013. He was a Lecturer of Asia Pacific Studies at the University of Leeds from 2013 to 2016 and was also Visiting Fellow at the ISEAS – Yusof Ishak Institute (Singapore), China's Institute for International Studies (Beijing, China), Nippon Foundation's Asian Public Intellectuals (Tokyo, Japan), the Institute for Developing Economies (Chiba, Japan), and East-West Center (Washington D.C., USA). Chheang also served as a technical adviser to the Cambodian National Assembly in 2011 and assistant to

Cambodia's Defence Minister from 2011 to 2012. He was honoured as a Young Global Leader by the World Economic Forum in 2013.

Julia Luong Dinh (aka Dinh Thi Hien Luong) is a Senior Research Fellow and a Lecturer at the Institute of Foreign Policy and Strategic Studies, the Diplomatic Academy of Vietnam. Dinh earned her doctoral degree from the University of Sydney in 2016. She was awarded the Ushiba Memorial Fellowship for ASEAN Researchers under the auspices of the Japan Association for Promotion of International Cooperation to conduct her research project on Japan's role in the building of East Asian Community in Chiba (Japan) between 2007 and 2008. Her research background and interests include Chinese foreign policy, power politics, regionalism, international relations theory and practice in East Asia.

Thuy T. Do is a Senior Lecturer at the Department of International Politics and Diplomacy, the Diplomatic Academy of Vietnam. She obtained her doctoral degree from the Department of International Relations, Australian National University in 2016. She has been awarded visiting research fellowships at the S. Rajaratnam School of International Studies (2008), East-West Center (2010), and the Japan Institute of International Affairs (2014). Her research and teaching interests include international relations theory, East Asian international relations, Asia-Pacific security, and Vietnam's relations with the major powers. She has published widely in Vietnam and abroad on these topics.

Hoang Hai Ha is a Lecturer at the Faculty of History, Hanoi National University of Education. She earned her bachelor's degree from Hanoi National University of Education in 2006 and Master's degree in European Studies from Maastricht University in 2008. She started a joint doctoral programme in International and European Politics sponsored by Sant'Anna School of Advanced Studies (Italy) and Ghent University (Belgium) in 2012 and received her doctoral degree (cum laude) in 2015. Her current research focuses on international relations and foreign policy of Vietnam. She is the author or co-author of some articles published on *International Relations, Asia Europe Journal*, and *Contemporary Politics*.

Le Hong Hiep is Fellow at the ISEAS – Yusof Ishak Institute, Singapore, and Lecturer at the Faculty of International Relations, Ho Chi Minh City University of Social Sciences and Humanities. Hiep earned his PhD in Political and International Studies from the University of New South Wales, funded by a Prime Minister's Australia–Asia Award. Before becoming an academic, he worked for the Ministry of Foreign Affairs of Vietnam from 2004 to 2006. Hiep's scholarly articles and analyses have been published, among others, in *Contemporary Southeast Asia, Southeast Asian Affairs, Asian Politics & Policy, Korean Journal of Defence Analysis, ASPI Strategic Insights, ISEAS Perspective, American Review, Project Syndicate, The Straits Times, The Diplomat,* and the *East Asia Forum.* His book *Living Next to the Giant: The Political Economy of Vietnam's Relations with China under Doi Moi* was released by ISEAS Publishing in December 2016.

Phuong Nguyen is an Associate Fellow with the Chair for Southeast Asia Studies at Centre for Strategic and International Studies (CSIS), Washington D.C.. In this role, she leads the Chair's research team, writes on Southeast Asia, U.S. foreign policy toward ASEAN countries, and China's peripheral diplomacy. Nguyen is a co-author of *Building a More Robust U.S.–Philippines Alliance* (August 2015), *Southeast Asia's Geopolitical Centrality and the U.S.–Japan Alliance* (June 2015), *Thailand in Crisis: Scenarios and Policy Responses* (July 2014), and *A New Era in U.S.–Vietnam Relations: Deepening Ties Two Decades after Normalization* (June 2014). She is a co-editor of *Examining the South China Sea Disputes* (November 2015) and *Perspectives on the South China Sea: Diplomatic, Legal, and Security Dimensions of the Dispute* (September 2014). Her work has also been published in *East Asia Forum, Yale Global, World Politics Review, Nikkei Asian Review, The Straits Times, Bangkok Post,* and *Business Insider.* Nguyen holds an M.A. in Asian Studies from the School of International Service at American University in Washington, D.C. She speaks fluent French and Vietnamese.

Carlyle A. Thayer is Emeritus Professor, The University of New South Wales at the Australian Defence Force Academy, Canberra. Most of his academic career has been spent teaching in a military environment: The Royal Military College-Duntroon (1979–85); Australian Defence Force Academy (1985–2010); Asia-Pacific Center for Security Studies,

Honolulu (1999–2002); Centre for Defence and Strategic Studies, Australian Defence College (2002–4); and the Australian Command and Staff College (2006–7 and 2010). In 2005 he was appointed C. V. Starr Distinguished Visiting Professor at the School of Advanced International Studies, Johns Hopkins University in Washington, D.C. In 2008 he was appointed the Inaugural Frances M. and Stephen H. Fuller Distinguished Visiting Professor at the Center for Southeast Asian Studies, Ohio University, Athens, Ohio. Professor Thayer was educated at Brown (1967), and received an M.A. in Southeast Asian Studies from Yale (1971) and a PhD in International Relations from the Australian National University (1977). He is the author of over 500 academic publications, including: *The Vietnam People's Army Under Doi* (1994); *Beyond Indochina*, Adelphi Paper 297 (1995); *Vietnam People's Army: Development and Modernization* (2009); and *Southeast Asia: Patterns of Security Cooperation* (2010). He is currently Director of Thayer Consultancy that provides political analysis of current regional security issues and other research support to selected clients.

To Minh Thu is currently a researcher at the Diplomatic Academy of Vietnam, where she studies economic and international integration issues. From 2013 to 2016, she was a Research Fellow at the Center for Policy and Economy, the Mitsubishi Research Institute in Tokyo. Thu earned her Master's degree in International Economics from Massey University and her PhD in International Public Policy and Economics from Osaka University. Thu's research interests include regional and Vietnam's economic integration, ASEAN Economic Community building, regional economic cooperation, and assessing economic integration using computable general equilibrium (CGE) models. Her recent projects include an assessment of Vietnam's deeper trade liberalization (using CGE model), and the enhancement of the textile and garment industries in Vietnam in the context of TPP and Vietnam–EU FTA.

Nguyen Thanh Trung earned his PhD from the Hong Kong Baptist University. He is currently serving as the Head of the Faculty of International Relations, University of Social Sciences and Humanities in Ho Chi Minh City. His research interests focus on comparative politics and international relations, with a particular emphasis on international security, China, and Southeast Asia. He has contributed commentaries and analyses to the *IAPS Dialogue, The Asia Maritime Transparency Initiative, The Diplomat,* and *The International Policy Digest.*

Anton Tsvetov is an expert at the Foreign Policy and Security Division of the Center for Strategic Research (CSR), a Moscow-based think-tank. He holds a BA in Area Studies and an MA in Russian Foreign Policy and Diplomacy. His research interests include international relations and great power politics in Southeast Asia, Russia's policies in Asia, and Vietnamese politics and political economy. He publishes on these topics in academic journals, analytical outlets and the media. His most recent publication is "After Crimea: Southeast Asia in Russia's Foreign Policy Narrative", *Contemporary Southeast Asia* 38, no. 1 (2016).

Dang Cam Tu joined the Diplomatic Academy of Vietnam in 2000 and is currently serving as Deputy Director General of the Institute for Foreign Policy and Strategic Studies (IFPSS) at the Academy. Tu earned her PhD in Politics and International Relations from the University of New South Wales in 2011. She is a member of several major research and education projects at both institutional and national levels. She is also a member of major research and think-tank networks in the Asia Pacific. Her main areas of research and publications include international relations in Southeast Asia and the Asia Pacific, ASEAN, and Vietnam's foreign policy and relations with important partners in the region.

Ha Anh Tuan is a Senior Research Fellow at Bien Dong Maritime Institute, the Diplomatic Academy of Vietnam. Tuan earned his PhD in Politics and International Relations from the University of New South Wales in 2014. He has authored or co-authored a number of book chapters and journal articles on the South China Sea disputes, including "Vietnam's Regional Security Challenges" (2016), "Navigating through Troubled Waters: A Vietnamese Perspective on Sino–Vietnamese Relations in the South China Sea" (2016), and "ASEAN and the Disputes in the South China Sea" (2012). Tuan is also a frequent commentator in Vietnam's news media.

Nguyen Vu Tung is President of the Diplomatic Academy of Vietnam (DAV). From July 2010 to January 2014, he was Deputy Chief of Mission at the Vietnam Embassy in the United States. His previous positions include Director General of the DAV Institute for Strategic Studies and Foreign Policy and Institute for East Sea Studies. Tung earned his MA in Laws and Diplomacy (MALD) from the Fletcher School of Law and Diplomacy in 1998 and his PhD in Political Science from Columbia University in 2003. His main areas of teaching, research, and publications include international relations theories, international relations in Southeast Asia and the Asia Pacific, Vietnamese foreign policy and relations with the United States, China, and ASEAN.

Truong-Minh Vu is Director of the Center for International Studies (SCIS) at the University of Social Sciences and Humanities in Ho Chi Minh City. His research interests include international and strategic relations of Southeast Asia. His scholarly articles and analyses have been published in *The National Interest, The Asan Forum, Revista Brasileira de Política Internacional, Global Asia, East Asia Policy, ASIEN, The German Journal on Contemporary Asia, The Asia Maritime Transparency Initiative* and *RSIS Commentaries*. He is co-editor of the book, *Power Politics in Asia's Contested Waters: Territorial Disputes in the South China Sea* (2016).

Part I

Analytical and Historical Framework

1

Introduction: The Making of Vietnam's Foreign Policy under *Doi Moi*

Le Hong Hiep

Since Vietnam launched its economic reforms under *Doi Moi* in 1986, foreign policy has been an essential tool for the ruling Communist Party of Vietnam (CPV) to facilitate the implementation of its domestic agenda. As the CPV considers foreign policies as the extension of domestic ones, the Party has consistently sought to make use of external relations to enhance the country's national security and prosperity, and, ultimately, to strengthen the Party's rule. Understanding Vietnam's foreign policy is therefore necessary for one to fully appreciate the transformations that Vietnam has undergone since the adoption of *Doi Moi*.

   This chapter serves as a background for readers to understand the making of Vietnam's contemporary foreign policy before examining its various aspects in subsequent chapters. The chapter first provides an overview of key drivers, objectives, principles, and actors involved in the making of Vietnam's foreign policy. It then assesses transformations in Vietnam's foreign policy under *Doi Moi* by examining major political and policy documents released by the CPV and how these changes have been translated into

3

actual developments of the country's foreign relations. Finally, the chapter discusses several contemporary foreign policy challenges that Vietnam is facing before providing a summary of the book's structure.

The Making of Vietnam's Foreign Policy

Unlike democratic countries where government changes may lead to foreign policy shifts, Vietnam's foreign policy is fairly stable thanks to the continuity maintained under the country's one-party system. As "the force leading the state and society", the CPV single-mindedly dictates Vietnam's foreign policy, and the country's foreign policy is therefore also the foreign policy of the Party. On the one hand, the stability and predictability in Vietnam's foreign policy lends it credibility, and thus the international community's confidence in its external commitments. On the other hand, the convergence of national interest with the CPV's interest in foreign policymaking renders it impossible to determine how much each weighs in the country's actual policies. In certain cases, the Party's ideological considerations and regime security concerns may interfere to dictate the country's foreign policy in ways that cannot be fully accounted for by national interests (see, for example, Co 2003; Hiep 2013*a*).

Balancing between national interests and regime interests therefore remains one of the major challenges for the CPV in terms of foreign policymaking. Developments in the country's foreign policy over the past three decades, however, show that pragmatic considerations of national interests have now become the most important factor shaping the country's foreign relations. To be more precise, while the CPV's ideological considerations still matter in certain cases, their importance in the making of Vietnam's foreign policy has somewhat declined. Such a shift started when *Doi Moi* was accelerated in the late 1980s and early 1990s (Palmujoki 1999; Thayer 1994*a*), and became more pronounced since the early 2000s. The evidence for this trend can be found, among others, in Vietnam's hardened stance towards China over the South China Sea disputes as well as its rapprochement with the United States in recent years.

At its twelfth national congress in 2016, the CPV stated that it sought "to carry out a foreign policy of independence, sovereignty, multilateralization and diversification of relations, proactive and active international integration; to firmly maintain a peaceful and stable environment, create favourable conditions for national construction and defence; and to elevate

Vietnam's status and prestige in the region and the world" (CPV 2015). According to the Party, such a foreign policy would be conducted on the fundamental principles of "international law, equality and mutual benefit", and "independence, autonomy, peace, cooperation and development". It should also be noted that Vietnam has long maintained the non-alignment principle in its foreign policy, which is embodied in the so-called "three no's principle". Specifically, Vietnam will not seek military alliances, will not allow foreign bases on its soil, and will not use relationship with one country against another (Ministry of Defence 2004, p. 5).

As the CPV dominates Vietnam's political system, the country's foreign policy is made at its discretion. Most important foreign policy decisions will be made collectively by the Party's Politburo. However, to enhance the legitimacy of its decisions, the Politburo may table certain important issues to the Party's Central Committee for discussion and decision through voting. For example, at its fourteenth plenum in January 2016, the CPV's Eleventh Central Committee voted to endorse Vietnam's ratification of the Trans-Pacific Strategic Economic Partnership Agreement (TPP). The collective making of Vietnam's foreign policy has both pros and cons. While the practice ensures a high level of consensus among the party leadership and the bureaucracy, and thus the prospect of smoother implementation of major decisions, it also obscures the accountability of decision makers, especially when such decisions lead to devastating outcomes. Following the end of the Vietnam War in 1975, for example, Vietnam missed several opportunities to normalize its relations with the United States due to its insistence on U.S. war reparations as a condition for normalization. The decision later proved to be a miscalculation, and the delayed normalization with Washington put Hanoi in a disadvantaged strategic position in dealing with Beijing as well as the Cambodian issue. However, no specific leader was held accountable for such an outcome.

The decisions made by the Party's Politburo and Central Committee, however, are normally based on inputs and policy recommendations provided by relevant ministries. Depending on the issue in question, one of the ministries will act as the coordinator in charge of collecting recommendations from other ministries to shape the Party's position on the issue. For example, issues related to foreign trade will normally be coordinated by the Ministry of Industry and Trade (MOIT), defence issues will be handled mainly by the Ministry of Defence (MOD), while the Ministry of Foreign Affairs (MOFA) will take care of general diplomatic relations with foreign countries as well as international organizations.

Among ministerial agencies involved in Vietnam's foreign policymaking and implementation, the MOFA is the key actor. The Ministry was established on 28 August 1945 with about 20 staffs (MOFA 2015, p. 33). By 2015, the Ministry had evolved into a full-fledged and modern agency of about 2,400 employees, most of whom are well-trained professional diplomats. Under the Ministry, there are currently 31 functional departments and a network of 71 embassies, 22 consulates-general, and 4 permanent missions to international organizations (MOFA 2015, p. 362). Unlike other ministries, the MOFA does not operate a vertical system of local units. However, it is in close contact with departments of external affairs of provinces and municipalities in certain functional areas, especially border, economic and protocol affairs.

In terms of policymaking procedure, the MOFA normally has to draw on consultations with various governmental organizations, such as other relevant ministries, intelligence agencies, the military, and the CPV's Commission of External Affairs.[1] Depending on the issues under consideration, the list of stakeholders may be expanded. For example, when it comes to South China Sea issues, the Ministry normally has to consult PetroVietnam and the Directorate of Fisheries, especially for technical inputs. In other cases, the Ministry's policy recommendations are based on in-house research and analysis done by its own experts, including those working at the Diplomatic Academy of Vietnam, the training and research arm of the Ministry.

As the CPV exercises collective leadership, individual diplomats and policymakers tend not to play a prominent role in the making of Vietnam's foreign policy. However, in the earlier stages of the republic, due to the nascent nature of the state apparatus in general and the MOFA in particular, some individual leaders did play an essential role in the making and conduct of Vietnam's foreign policy. For example, President Ho Chi Minh, who also acted as the first foreign minister of the Democratic Republic of Vietnam (DRV), was the architect of the republic's foreign policy in the period 1945–46 as well as during the First Indochina War. During the Second Indochina War, other individuals such as General Secretary Le Duan also played an important role in shaping the DRV's foreign policy (Nguyen 2012). After the wars, and especially since *Doi Moi* was adopted in 1986, the Party gradually returned to the collective and consensus-based foreign policymaking model, with individual leaders having a less decisive role.

As such, foreign ministers are just part of the Party's innermost foreign policymaking circle, although ministers who are also Politburo members normally wield greater influence on the policymaking than those who are not.

That said, when it comes to controversial or divisive issues, some researchers have argued that Vietnam's foreign policy are sometimes negotiated between two competing camps within the Party: conservatives and reformists (see, for example, Vuving 2004). As most important decisions are made collectively by the Politburo and the CPV Central Committee, it is difficult to identify and measure the relative weights of the two camps in the outcome of any particular policy debate. However, the labels "conservative" and "reformist" may still be useful to describe certain segments of high-ranking party officials who favour specific policies. Accordingly, conservatives tend to consider the preservation of regime security as the top foreign policy mandate. Therefore, they typically take a cautious approach to economic liberalization and favour stronger ties with China over Western countries. In contrast, reformists seek further economic liberalization and stronger relations with the West — although ideally at minimum risk to regime security. So far, while conservatives seem to be more influential when it comes to ideological and internal security matters, reformists seem to take the lead on the economic front, especially when the CPV is feeling the pressure for further reforms to buttress the country's economic performance — the vital basis of the Party's legitimacy (Hiep 2012). This explains some of Vietnam's recent bold foreign policy decisions, such as the embrace of the TPP which requires Vietnam to allow the establishment of independent labour unions.

The Evolution of Vietnam's Foreign Policy under *Doi Moi*

Since 1945, Vietnam's foreign policy has evolved through different phases corresponding to developments in the country's internal conditions. The country's foreign policy objectives are therefore shaped and implemented mainly in accordance with its domestic goals. For example, during the early years of the republic, its main diplomatic goals were to gain international recognition and to prevent France from re-colonizing the country. During the two wars against France and America, Vietnam's diplomacy focused on mobilizing international support for its war efforts in order to unify the country and to re-establish peace. After 1975, Vietnam's diplomatic efforts turned to mobilizing international resources to facilitate the "building of socialism" across the whole country and to end its international isolation and economic embargo, especially after Vietnam sent its troops into Cambodia to unseat the Khmer Rouge regime in late 1978.

Since 1986 when the CPV adopted market-based economic reforms under the banner of *Doi Moi*, Vietnam's foreign policy has again taken a decisive turn as the Party sought to create favourable external conditions and to attract foreign resources for the cause of *Doi Moi*. Towards these ends, Vietnam had to undergo a major foreign policy overhaul, which required the Party to reform its foreign policy thinking. The exercise, however, proved to be a lengthy and onerous one.

Prior to the CPV's sixth national congress in 1986, the Party had long shaped its worldview through the ideological prism (see, for example, Palmujoki 1997, 1999; Porter 1980, 1990; Thayer 1984). Such ideological considerations remained prevalent in the foreign policy sections of the CPV's political reports to its sixth national congress in 1986. They were also translated into practical terms. For example, at the congress, the CPV stated that it considered Vietnam's relationship with the Soviet Union as the "cornerstone" in the country's foreign policy; strongly supported "the heroic struggle of the people and the working class in advanced capitalist countries", and expressed its deep sympathy and solidarity with national liberation movements in Africa, Latin America, and elsewhere (CPV 2006, pp. 434–39).

However, the CPV's ideology-based foreign policy proved to be detrimental to Vietnam's national interests. In the Cold War context, the CPV's emphasis on relations with the socialist bloc obviously narrowed Vietnam's relations with Western and non-socialist countries. Meanwhile, Vietnam's prolonged engagement in Cambodia since the late 1970s, which was based partly on the CPV's wish to establish a friendly communist state in Cambodia, turned out to be an economic and political suicide pill for Vietnam. The undertaking of the "international duty toward Cambodian people", as the CPV maintained, put excessive strains on Vietnam's war-torn economy. The policy also caused Vietnam to suffer from widespread international diplomatic isolation, which laid tremendous obstacles to Vietnam's efforts to revive its moribund economy.

Until the late 1980s, Vietnam remained heavily dependent on socialist countries, especially the Soviet Union, for its foreign economic exchanges.

By 1986 when *Doi Moi* was adopted, socialist countries accounted for 83.3 per cent and 67.1 per cent of Vietnam's imports and exports, respectively (Mya 1993, pp. 214–25). Such a heavy dependence on socialist countries for external trade not only limited Vietnam's ability to increase its total foreign trade turnover, but also exposed the country to serious risks that might disrupt its economic development. For example, in 1991 when the Soviet Union disintegrated, Vietnam's trade with the socialist bloc contracted dramatically, forcing Vietnam to increasingly look to non-socialist countries for substitute imports as well as export outlets.

Consequently, by the late 1980s, the CPV's top priority was to open up and diversify the country's external relations in order to take advantage of foreign resources, such as markets, capital and technologies, to boost economic growth. Toward these ends and despite its official rhetoric, by around its sixth national congress in 1986, the CPV began to step up efforts to retune the country's foreign policy towards the "diversification and multilateralization" of international relations beyond ideological considerations. On 9 July 1986, for example, the CPV Politburo passed Resolution No. 32 that sought to articulate changes to Vietnam's foreign policy. The top foreign policy objective identified by the Resolution was to "combine the strength of the nation with that of the time; take advantage of favourable international conditions to build socialism and defend the nation; and *proactively create a stable environment to focus on economic development* [emphasis added]" (Nam 2006, p. 26).

Despite these efforts, no major advance in Vietnam's foreign relations was made within the first few years after the CPV's sixth congress, mainly due to the adverse Cold War environment, and especially Vietnam's prolonged military engagement in Cambodia.

It was against this backdrop that in 1987, the CPV Politburo secretly adopted Resolution No. 2 to bring about more radical strategic adjustments to the country's security and foreign policy directions. Most importantly, the Resolution stated that Vietnam would completely withdraw its forces out of Cambodia and Laos, and to reduce the country's standing army to save resources for economic development efforts (Thayer 1994*b*, 1995). Soon after that, the CPV Politburo adopted Resolution No. 13 dated 20 May 1988 on "Tasks and Foreign Policy in the New Situation", which stressed that the top objectives of Vietnam's foreign policy would be to assist the stabilization of the political system and to facilitate the country's economic renovation. The

Resolution emphasized the policy of getting "more friends, fewer enemies" [*thêm bạn bớt thù*]. It also called for diversifying the country's foreign relations on the principle of national independence, equal sovereignty and mutual benefits, and set some specific foreign policy goals for the country, including the resolution of the Cambodian issue, diplomatic normalization with China and the United States, and improving ties with ASEAN, Japan and Western countries. Resolution No. 13 has therefore been considered as a landmark in the reform of the CPV's foreign policy thinking and a foundation for the country's later policy of diversifying and multilateralizing foreign relations (Hung 2006, p. 14; Nam 2006, p. 27).

At its seventh national congress in 1991, the CPV reaffirmed the overall foreign policy objective of maintaining peace and expanding its foreign relations to facilitate domestic development. It also declared that Vietnam would "diversify and multilateralize economic relations with all countries and economic organizations". More importantly, it was at this congress that the CPV officially departed from its traditional ideology-based foreign policymaking in favour of a more pragmatic approach. Specifically, it officially stated that Vietnam wished "to be friend with all countries in the world community" (CPV 2010, p. 403) and sought "equal and mutually beneficial cooperation with all countries regardless of differences in socio-political regimes based on the principles of peaceful co-existence" (CPV 2010, p. 351). This pragmatic approach to foreign policymaking was maintained and further developed by the CPV in its subsequent congresses. For example, at its ninth congress (2001), the Party reaffirmed that "Vietnam is willing to be a friend and a reliable partner of countries in the world community, striving for peace, independence and development". Such a slogan has since become the standard summary of Vietnam's foreign policy.

The pragmatic nature of Vietnam's new foreign policy under *Doi Moi* is also reflected in its economic focus. Accordingly, promoting international economic cooperation and integration has been identified as a key foreign policy task in various official documents of the Party. For example, in March 1989, the Party's Central Committee adopted a resolution in which the MOFA was demanded to decidedly shift its focus from political to politico-economic diplomacy. At its eighth congress in 1996, the Party embraced the policy of "building an open economy which is integrated with the region and the world" and "to accelerate the economic integration process". Five years later, the CPV Politburo adopted Resolution

No. 7 dated 27 November 2001 on Vietnam's economic integration, outlining specific measures to facilitate the country's "active integration" into the global economy. At its eleventh congress in 2011, the CPV's foreign policy guideline expanded the scope of international integration to cover not only the economic realm but also integration in other fields. Two years later, the CPV Politburo adopted Resolution No. 22 to further detail the comprehensive international integration called for in the guideline. It also links Vietnam's international economic integration with its efforts to restructure the economy.

Under these foreign policy shifts, Vietnam's external relations expanded rapidly. By 2016, the country had established diplomatic relations with 180 countries and secured membership in most major international and regional institutions. Vietnam has also sought to deepen ties with important countries. By 2016, Vietnam had established "special partnership" with Laos, and strategic partnerships with Russia (2001), India (2007), China (2008), Japan, South Korea, Spain (2009), the United Kingdom (2010), Germany (2011), Italy, Thailand, Indonesia, Singapore, France (2013), Malaysia and the Philippines (2015).[2] It also entered into comprehensive partnership with South Africa (2004), Chile, Brazil, Venezuela (2007), Australia, New Zealand (2009), Argentina (2010), and the United States (2013).

Vietnam's policy of proactive international integration also helped to mobilize valuable external resources to turn the country into an economic success story. Between 1990 and 2014, Vietnam enjoyed an average annual growth rate of 6.8 per cent and reached the low middle income status in 2009. The poverty rate also declined significantly, from 58.1 per cent in 1993 to 11.1 per cent in 2012. Expanded foreign trade and foreign investment have played an essential role in this process. By 2014, for example, the total registered FDI stock into Vietnam amounted to US$290.6 billion. In the same year, the country's two way trade turnover reached US$298 billion, equivalent to 160 per cent of its GDP (GSO 2015). As such, Vietnam has become one of the most outward-looking economies in the region.

In sum, *Doi Moi* has served as the single most important driver of transformations in Vietnam's foreign policy over the past three decades. As the country sought to create a favourable external environment and mobilize foreign resources for its economic development, diplomacy has become an essential tool. Foreign policy breakthroughs, such as the diplomatic normalization with China and the United States or the accession to ASEAN and WTO, have indeed contributed to Vietnam's economic success as well as its enhanced international standing. Nevertheless, there remain significant foreign policy challenges that Vietnam needs to overcome in the coming decades. Among them, managing the South China Sea disputes and handling the relationships with China and other major powers, especially the United States, emerge as the two most challenging ones.

Vietnam's Major Contemporary Foreign Policy Challenges

Managing the South China Sea Disputes

The South China Sea plays an important role in Vietnam's national defence as the long coastline makes the country vulnerable to seaborne attacks. Similarly, Vietnam would come under significant strategic constraints if it lost control over both the Paracels and the Spratlys. The sea is also essential for Vietnam's economic well-being. In 2010, for example, PetroVietnam's revenue, which was generated mainly from the company's operations in the South China Sea, accounted for 24 per cent of Vietnam's GDP (*Ha Noi Moi* 2011). The sea also brings Vietnam other significant economic benefits, such as fishery, tourism, maritime transportation and port services. In 2007, the CPV Central Committee passed a resolution on "Vietnam's Maritime Strategy Toward the Year 2020" which set the target for Vietnam to generate 53 to 55 per cent of its GDP and 55 to 60 per cent of its exports from maritime economic activities by 2020 (Dang Huong 2012).

Nevertheless, Vietnam is now locked into two increasingly heated disputes over the South China Sea. The first is related to the competing sovereignty claims over the Paracels and the Spratlys. While the Paracels dispute is mainly between Vietnam, China and Taiwan, the Spratlys row involves also the Philippines, Malaysia, and Brunei. The other dispute is related to conflicting claims regarding maritime boundaries in the sea. Claimant states' activities to enforce their claims have recently stoked up tensions in the region. Some notable developments include China's placement of the giant oil rig *Haiyang Shiyou* 981 in Vietnam's proclaimed exclusive economic zone (EEZ) in May 2014, and China's construction and militarization of seven artificial islands in the Spratlys since 2014.

Vietnam is of the view that the South China Sea disputes should be solved peacefully on the basis of international law, especially the 1982 United Nations Convention on the Law of the Sea (UNCLOS). However, given the complex nature of the disputes as well as the unwillingness of China to have the disputes addressed through legal avenues, Vietnam has also resorted to other measures to manage the disputes. Specifically, in its dealing with China, Vietnam has adopted a hedging strategy composed of four major components: economic pragmatism; direct engagement; hard balancing; and soft balancing (Hiep 2013*b*). Accordingly, while Vietnam has tried to promote economic cooperation and political engagement with China to boost mutual trust and cooperation, it has also pursued a "hard balancing" strategy against the latter through its military modernization programme. At the same time, Vietnam has also sought to "soft-balance" against China through deepened ties with other powers as well as regional multilateral arrangements, especially ASEAN.

The key challenge for Vietnam is how to simultaneously achieve the two goals: adequately protecting its national interests in the South China Sea while maintaining peace, stability and a friendly relationship with China. Given the economic and strategic importance of the South China Sea to its well-being, Vietnam will not be able to bow to pressures from China, Hanoi's main antagonist in the disputes. Rising nationalism in Vietnam means that bowing to China's pressures will do irreparable damages to the CPV's political legitimacy. Therefore, on occasion, Vietnamese leaders have managed to speak up against China and emphasized Vietnam's determination to protect its interests in the South China Sea. For example, in a press conference in the Philippines during the *Haiyang Shiyou* oil rig crisis in 2014, then Prime Minister Nguyen Tan Dung condemned China's actions and stated that Vietnam would not trade its sovereignty and territorial integrity for an "illusionary friendship". On the other hand, due to the geographical proximity and the power asymmetry between the two countries, Vietnamese leaders are aware that Vietnam cannot afford a hostile relationship with China. Moreover, as China is an important trade partner for Vietnam, a broken relationship will also hurt Vietnam's economic interests. Therefore, given the contradicting nature of the two goals, handling the South China Sea disputes and China's growing maritime assertiveness will likely remain a key challenge for Vietnam in the years to come.

Balancing between China and the United States

In 1995 when Vietnam normalized its relations with the United States, it was the first time that Vietnam had enjoyed normal relations with all the major world powers. Although Vietnam emphasizes a non-alignment policy and wishes "to be a friend and a reliable partner of countries in the world community", balancing between the major powers has been a key challenge for the country's foreign policy. This is particularly the case since the late 2000s when strategic rivalry between China and the United States started to intensify.

China's phenomenal rise since the late 1970s has presented the United States with a dilemma. While the sheer size of the Chinese economy and the deep economic interdependence between the two countries make it necessary for Washington to maintain a peaceful and stable relationship with Beijing, the latter's rise in terms of hard power and its strategic ambitions have also alarmed policymakers in Washington. In particular, China's rapid military build-up and its assertiveness in maritime disputes with neighbouring countries threaten to unravel the regional order and stability underpinned by Washington's strategic preponderance. In response, the United States has adopted a two-pronged strategy to deal with China. On the one hand, the administration of President Barack Obama announced the "strategic rebalance" to Western Pacific by shifting 60 per cent of its naval capabilities to the region. On the other hand, the United States led negotiations to establish the TPP which involved eleven other countries on the Pacific Rim but excluded China. By late 2017, although the Trump administration has withdrawn the United States from the TPP and nominally cancelled the rebalancing strategy, the U.S. economic and military engagement with the region remains rather robust.

At the same time, Washington also seeks to strengthen bilateral relations with its traditional allies as well as emerging partners, including Vietnam. Broader frameworks for bilateral strategic cooperation have been set up with the two sides concluding a Memorandum of Understanding on defence relations in 2011. In 2013, the two countries established a comprehensive partnership. In July 2015, CPV General Secretary Nguyen Phu Trong paid a historic visit to Washington, and in May 2016, President Barrack Obama visited Vietnam, during which he fully lifted the longstanding lethal weapon sales ban on Hanoi. As argued by Phuong Nguyen in Chapter 3, these developments have significantly strengthened the strategic trust between the two former enemies.

The strengthened relationship with the United States was a logical development in Vietnam's foreign policy as it brings Vietnam additional leverage to deal with China's increasing pressures in the South China Sea. Nevertheless, in the context of intensifying U.S.–China strategic competition, Hanoi's endeavours to deepen ties with Washington may be interpreted by Beijing as Hanoi being recruited into the U.S.-led efforts to contain China rather than merely a move to address its grievances in the South China Sea. As such, how far and how fast Vietnam should promote its relations with the United States in order to strengthen its strategic position in the South China Sea while not overtly offending Beijing becomes a fundamental puzzle that Vietnamese strategists have to solve.

Indeed, balancing between the great powers is not a new challenge to Vietnam. During the Cold War, after the split between China and the Soviet Union, Vietnam's balancing act between the two antagonistic powers became increasingly precarious, and its decision to side with the Soviet Union in the late 1970s adequately contributed to the downward spiral in Sino–Vietnamese relations and partly accounted for China's decision to invade Vietnam in early 1979. The 1979 war was brief but extremely costly for Vietnam, and not only in terms of casualties. Aside from maintaining incessant armed harassment along the Sino–Vietnamese border in the 1980s, China also pursued a policy of isolating Vietnam diplomatically and providing aid for the Khmer Rouge's warring efforts in the Cambodian conflict to exhaust Vietnam economically. Vietnam's attempts to diversify foreign relations during the early phase of *Doi Moi* also witnessed limited success, mainly due to China's obstructions.

The current regional strategic context is far different from that of the 1970s and 1980s, but bitter memories of the 1980s are still well alive, and Vietnamese policymakers are prudent not to be caught in another great power game. While trying to forge a stronger relationship with Washington to resist China's pressures in the South China Sea, Vietnam still wishes to maintain a delicate balance between Beijing and Washington due to China's strategic importance to Vietnam's peace, stability and prosperity. The real challenge lies in the fact that China has consistently and coercively pressed its claims in the South China Sea at the expense of Vietnam as if Beijing was of the conviction that Vietnam could not escape its shadow. Such calculations by Beijing tend to gradually push Vietnam's strategic patience to its limit, by which Vietnam may have to consider a trade-off between an amicable relationship with Beijing and its enhanced capabilities and strategic position to defend its vital interests in the South China Sea by aligning itself more closely with Washington.

That said, the best policy option for Vietnam in the foreseeable future remains walking a fine line between China and the United States. China's growing assertiveness in the South China Sea and the intensifying strategic competition between the two superpowers will make Vietnam's task ever more challenging. However, at least for the time being, a decisive shift in its balance between the two powers still proves too risky and unfeasible for Hanoi. As such, the challenge for Vietnam in managing its relations with the two superpowers will continue to feature high on its future foreign policy agenda.

Structure of the Book

Vietnam's contemporary foreign policy is both a by-product of and a major contributor to the success of *Doi Moi*. Fundamental shifts in Vietnam's foreign policy thinking and thus its diplomacy in the late 1980s and early 1990s were born out of Vietnam's desperate need to break out of international isolation and to create a favourable external environment conducive to its domestic economic reforms. At the same time, the economic success of *Doi Moi* over the past three decades has also facilitated Vietnam's efforts to "diversify and multilateralize" its foreign relations as other partners in the international community become more interested in the country, both economically or strategically. Vietnam's foreign policy has also embraced an increasingly outward-looking vision under *Doi Moi* by expanding its focus from mainly securing an external environment favourable for its socio-economic performance and regime security to pursuing active and comprehensive international integration into the global community. During this process, Vietnam's foreign policy becomes increasingly pragmatic as ideological considerations have generally receded to take a back seat in the policymaking process.

As Vietnam expands its foreign relations, however, it also finds itself faced with new-found challenges. Apart the South China Sea disputes and the triangular relationship with China and the United

States, it also has to manage increasingly complex relationships with other major powers, as well as its Southeast Asian neighbours. At the same time, it has to address issues related to its deepened international economic integration, which presents Hanoi with opportunities for economic development but also subjects the country to increasing external pressures.

In order to analyse the multiple aspects of Vietnam's foreign policy under *Doi Moi*, this book is divided into three parts, covering the overall background of Vietnam's foreign policy over the past three decades, its key international relationships, as well as topical issues that matter most to the country. The first part, including the current chapter and Chapter 2, presents an overview of Vietnam's foreign policy under *Doi Moi* and serves as the analytical and historical framework for the whole book. The second part is comprised of seven chapters examining Vietnam's bilateral relationships with its most important partners, namely the United States, China, Japan, India, Russia, Laos, Cambodia, and ASEAN. In the final part, the book examines two key issues in Vietnam's contemporary foreign policy: the South China Sea disputes and Vietnam's integration into the global economy under *Doi Moi*.

In Chapter 2, Carlyle A. Thayer presents a broad overview of the evolution of Vietnamese diplomacy from 1986 to 2016. After highlighting the seismic shifts in Vietnam's foreign policy after its adoption of *Doi Moi*, the chapter assesses the implementation of Vietnam's foreign policy of "diversifying and multilateralizing" its external relations and becoming "a friend and reliable partner" to all countries during the period 1991–2005. The chapter also analyses Vietnam's proactive international integration, including the pursuit of strategic partnerships with the major powers and regional states, in the period 2006–16. Thayer concludes that Vietnam has been able to make successful major strategic adjustments in its foreign policy to safeguard its sovereignty and national independence while promoting its prosperity over the past three decades.

In Chapter 3, Phuong Nguyen examines the evolution of strategic trust in Vietnam–U.S. relations by looking into both the institutional and agency-level factors that helped or impeded bilateral strategic trust, and thus the pace of rapprochement between the two former enemies. Towards this end, Nguyen analyses four major phases of bilateral ties from the early days of *Doi Moi* in 1987 until 2016. The author concludes that the two sides, driven by their strategic and economic interests, were able to move the relationship forward by narrowing down areas of distrust at each stage of the relationship.

In Chapter 4, Nguyen Thanh Trung anh Truong-Minh Vu review Vietnam–China relations under *Doi Moi,* focusing on changes in bilateral ties after the 2014 oil rig crisis, an incident that sent bilateral trust to the lowest level in decades. By investigating Vietnam's domestic and foreign policy responses after the incident, the authors argue that the incident prompted Vietnam to step up its efforts to counter China's maritime assertiveness through four key measures: strengthening relations with the United States and other major powers; reducing economic vulnerabilities vis-à-vis China; stepping up naval and maritime law enforcement modernization; and relaxing control over anti-China nationalism. The authors predict that these initiatives by Vietnam, as well as corresponding reactions by China and other regional powers, may further complicate the future trajectory of bilateral ties.

The next three chapters examine Vietnam's deepening ties with its three key strategic partners, namely Japan, India and Russia. In Chapter 5, Thuy T. Do and Julia Luong Dinh review recent develop-ments in Vietnam–Japan relations and analyse the rationales for the two countries to lift their bilateral ties from mainly economic cooperation to a partnership of greater strategic focus. In Chapter 6, Rajeev Ranjan Chaturvedy looks into the drivers of the deepening partnership between India and Vietnam, especially the elevation of the India–Vietnam Strategic Partnership to a Comprehensive Strategic Partnership in September 2016. Meanwhile, Anton Tsvetov's Chapter 7 analyses Russia–Vietnam relations by assessing their recent history, contemporary state and future prospects. A common thread in the three chapters is that security and defence cooperation between Vietnam and the three powers have been deepened considerably in recent years due to the increasing convergence of their national interests, especially regarding the South China Sea. However, while Vietnam's strategic ties with Japan and India have been built on strong foundations and enjoy bright prospects, Hanoi's future strategic ties with Moscow remain uncertain, mainly due to Russia's limited interest in the South China Sea and its warm ties with Beijing.

Chapters 8 and 9 address Vietnam's relations with its Southeast Asian neighbours. In Chapter 8, Vannarith Chheang argues that Vietnam is gradually asserting its leadership role in the Mekong subregion by tightening its traditional ties with Laos and Cambodia. The chapter also assesses the achievements, challenges, and remaining issues in Vietnam's relations with the two neighbours, especially against the backdrop of China's rising influence in Southeast Asia. Meanwhile, in Chapter 9, based on Vietnam's diplomatic archive and interviews with Vietnamese foreign policymakers and diplomats, Nguyen Vu Tung and Dang Cam Tu examine the link between Vietnam's pursuit of ASEAN membership in the early 1990s and its efforts to resist China's pressures in the South China Sea. The chapter contends that Hanoi did not seriously consider its prospective ASEAN membership as a strategic tool to counter China's expansion in the South China Sea because Hanoi realized that ASEAN was indeed not a military organization, and ASEAN members did not want to antagonize China by supporting Vietnam in the South China Sea disputes.

In Chapter 10, Ha Anh Tuan shows how Vietnam's perceptions of the South China Sea disputes and ASEAN's role in managing them have evolved over the past two decades. By dissecting Vietnam's South China Sea strategy since 2007, the author argues that Hanoi considers the South China Sea disputes as a highly complicated security issue that warrants a multi-faceted approach, which includes three main elements: improving relations with China, building up domestic capabilities to deter against hostile actions in the South China Sea, and engaging regional stakeholders, especially ASEAN, to play a more active role in managing the disputes.

The final two chapters analyse Vietnam's process of international integration under *Doi Moi*. In Chapter 11, To Minh Thu reviews the contextual and ideological drivers behind Vietnam's international integration policy. The chapter argues that Vietnam's international economic integration happened in parallel with its domestic transformation from a centrally-planned to a market-based economy. During this process, the economic thinking of the CPV gradually evolved to adapt to changes in the internal and external conditions, and to maximize the benefits that international integration could contribute to the Party's domestic agenda. Meanwhile, in Chapter 12, Hoang Hai Ha examines Vietnam's reactions to the European Union's diffusion of norms through trade. Using the EU–Vietnam Free Trade Agreement (EUVFTA) as a case study, the chapter argues that Vietnam imports norms diffused by the EU through the EUVFTA negotiations at various levels, depending on its perception of national interests as well as its political, cultural and economic background. Vietnam selects and adapts certain EU norms and values that help promote its economic development while rejecting those that Hanoi perceives as incompatible with its domestic interests and the CPV's political agenda.

NOTES

1. In the late 1980s and early 1990s, for example, the MOFA was marginalized and the CPV's Commission of External Affairs took a decisive role in the handling of Vietnam's relations with China and Cambodia (Co 2003; Elliott 2012, chapter 2).
2. Vietnam has upgraded its strategic partnerships with China, Russia and India into "comprehensive strategic partnerships".

REFERENCES

Co, Tran Quang. "Hoi uc va suy nghi: 1975–1991" [Memoir and Reflections: 1975–1991]. Unpublished manuscript, 2003.

Communist Party of Vietnam (CPV). *Văn kiện Đảng toàn tập* [Complete Collection of Party Documents]. Vol. 47 [1986]. Hà Nội: NXB Chính trị quốc gia [National Political Publishing House], 2006.

———. *Văn kiện đại hội đại biểu toàn quốc thời kỳ đổi mới* [Documents of National Congresses in the Era of Doi Moi]. Vol. 1. Hà Nội: NXB Chính trị quốc gia [National Political Publishing House], 2010.

———. "Dự thảo Báo cáo chính trị của Ban Chấp hành Trung ương Đảng khoá XI tại Đại hội đại biểu toàn quốc lần thứ XII của Đảng" [Draft Political Report of the Eleventh Central Committee to the Party's Twelfth National Congress], 15 September 2015. Available at <http://laodong.com.vn/chinh-tri/du-thao-bao-cao-chinh-tri-cua-ban-chap-hanh-trung-uong-dang-khoa-xi-tai-dai-hoi-dai-bieu-toan-quoc-lan-thu-xii-cua-dang-376284.bld> (accessed 17 November 2015).

Dang Huong. "Bien Đong và Chien Luoc bien Viet Nam den 2020" [The East Sea and Vietnam's Maritime Strategy towards 2020]. *VNEconomy*, 29 January 2012. Available at <http://vneconomy.vn/2012129112717475P0C9920/bien-dong-va-chien-luoc-bien-viet-nam-den-2020.htm> (accessed 12 March 2012).

Elliott, David W.P. *Changing Worlds: Vietnam's Transition from Cold War to Globalization*. Oxford: Oxford University Press, 2012.

General Statistics Office of Vietnam (GSO). *Statistical Handbook of Vietnam 2014*. Hanoi: Statistical Publishing House, 2015.

Ha Noi Moi. "Doanh thu năm 2010 cua Tap doan Dau khi: Dong gop 24% vao GDP cua ca nuoc" [PetroVietnam's 2010 Revenue Accounts for 24 per cent of GDP], 2011. Available at <http://hanoimoi.com.vn/Tin-tuc/Kinh-te/420974/dong-gop-24-vao-gdp-cua-ca-nuoc> (accessed 12 March 2012).

Hiep, Le Hong. "Performance-based Legitimacy: The Case of the Communist Party of Vietnam and *Doi Moi*". *Contemporary Southeast Asia* 34, no. 2 (2012): 145–72.

———. "Vietnam's Domestic–Foreign Policy Nexus: *Doi Moi*, Foreign Policy Reform, and Sino–Vietnamese Normalization". *Asian Politics & Policy* 5, no. 3 (2013*a*): 387–406.

———. "Vietnam's Hedging Strategy against China since Normalization". *Contemporary Southeast Asia* 35, no. 3 (2013*b*): 333–68.

Hung, N.M. "Thuc hien nhat quan duong loi doi ngoai doc lap, tu chu, hoa binh, hop tac va phat trien" [Consistently Implementing the Foreign Policy of Independence, Autonomy, Peace, and Development]. *Tap chi Cong san* [Communist Review] 17 (2006): 14–18.

Ministry of Defence. *Quoc phong Viet Nam nhung nam dau the ky XXI* [Vietnam's National Defence in the First Years of the 21st Century]. Hanoi: Ministry of Defence, 2004.

Ministry of Foreign Affairs (MOFA), Vietnam. *Bộ Ngoại giao: 70 năm xây dựng và phát triển (1945–2015)*. Hanoi: National Political Publishing House, 2015.

Mya, Than. "Vietnam's External Trade, 1975–91: A Survey in the Southeast Asian Context". In *Vietnam's Dilemmas and Options: The Challenge of Economic Transition in the 1990s*, edited by Than Mya and Joseph L.-H. Tan. Singapore: ASEAN Economic Research Unit, Institute of Southeast Asian Studies, 1993.

Nam, P.D. "Ngoai giao Viet Nam sau 20 nam doi moi" [Vietnam's Diplomacy after 20 Years of Renovation]. *Tap chi Cong san* [Commusit Review] 14 (2006): 26–30.

Nguyen, Lien-Hang T. *Hanoi's War: An International History of the War for Peace in Vietnam*. Chapel Hill: University of North Carolina Press, 2012.

Palmujoki, E. *Vietnam and the World: Marxist-Leninist Doctrine and the Changes in International Relations, 1975–93*. London: Macmillan Press, 1997.

———. "Ideological and Foreign Policy: Vietnam's Marxist-Leninist Doctrine and Global Change, 1986–1996". In *Vietnamese Foreign Policy in Transition*, edited by Carlyle A. Thayer and Ramses Amer. Singapore: Institute of Southeast Asia Studies, 1999, pp. 25–43.

Porter, Gareth. "Vietnam and the Socialist Camp: Center or Periphery?" In *Vietnamese Communism in Comparative Perspective*, edited by William S. Turley. Boulder: Westview Press, 1980, pp. 225–64.

———. "The Transformation of Vietnam's World-View: From Two Camps to Interdependence". *Contemporary Southeast Asia* 12, no. 1 (1990): 1–19.

Thayer, Carlyle A. "Vietnamese Perspectives on International Security: Three Revolutionary Currents". In *Asian Perspectives on International Security*, edited by Donald H. McMillen. London: Macmillan Press, 1984, pp. 57–76.

————. "Sino–Vietnamese Relations: The Interplay of Ideology and National Interest". *Asian Survey* 34, no. 6 (1994*a*): 513–28.

————. *The Vietnam People's Army under Doi Moi*. Pacific Strategic Paper 7. Singapore: Institute of Southeast Asian Studies, 1994*b*.

————. "Vietnam's Strategic Readjustment". In *China as a Great Power: Myths, Realities and Challenges in the Asia-Pacific Region*, edited by Stuart Harris and Gary Klintworth. Melbourne: Longman Australia, 1995, pp. 185–201.

Vuving, Alexander L. "The Two-Headed Grand Strategy: Vietnamese Foreign Policy since Doi Moi". Paper presented at the Vietnam Update 2004: Strategic and Foreign Relations, Institute of Southeast Asian Studies, Singapore, 2004.

2

The Evolution of Vietnamese Diplomacy, 1986–2016

Carlyle A. Thayer

This chapter presents a broad overview of the evolution of Vietnamese diplomacy from 1986 to the present. This thirty-year timeframe is divided into three parts. The first part highlights the seismic shifts in Vietnam's foreign policy after its adoption of *Doi Moi* in late 1986 until 1990. The second part assesses the implementation of Vietnam's foreign policy of "diversifying and multilateralizing" [*đa dạng hóa, đa phương hóa*] its external relations and becoming "a friend and reliable partner" [*bạn bè và đối tác đáng tin cậy*] to all countries during the period 1991–2005. The third part analyses Vietnam's proactive international integration, including the pursuit of strategic partnerships with the major powers and regional states, in the period 2006–16. This chapter concludes by noting that Vietnam has been able to make successful major strategic adjustments in its foreign policy to safeguard its sovereignty, national independence and territorial integrity over the past three decades.

Vietnam Joins the International Community, 1986–90

The year 1986 was a pivotal year in the evolution of Vietnam's domestic and foreign policy. Up until 1986, Vietnam had always regarded its relations with the Soviet Union and membership in the socialist camp as the cornerstone of its foreign policy.

Two major factors influenced Vietnam's decision to jettison outmoded Marxist–Leninist conceptions embodied in the "two world theory" that international relations were shaped and determined by the antagonistic contradictions between socialism and capitalism, or, more prosaically, as a struggle between friends and enemies and "who will triumph over whom" [*ai thắng ai*]. The first factor was Vietnam's mounting domestic socio-economic crisis due to the breakdown of its Soviet-styled central planning system. The second factor was external and arose from the "new political thinking" emanating from the Soviet Union under the leadership of Mikhail Gorbachev (Palmujoki 1997; Thakur and Thayer 1987).

Due to the confluence of these domestic and external factors, Vietnam turned from a foreign policy structured by ideological considerations to a foreign policy framework that placed greater emphasis on national interest and pragmatic diplomacy. Vietnamese analysts now stressed global economic forces and the impact of the revolution in science and technology as key determinants of international relations (Cam 1995; Khoan 1995). Vietnam's changed worldview emerged gradually and nested with remnants of Leninist ideology.

In other words, Vietnam's "two world theory" gave way to a view of an interdependent world (Palmujoki 1997). Fears of dependency and assimilation [*hoà tan*] gave way to a positive view of economic integration [*hội nhập*] that offered opportunities as well as challenges (Elliott 2012, pp. 99–100; 142–43). Vietnam's new worldview embraced comprehensive security over the much narrower military security. Nonetheless, a residue of the old worldview was reflected in the continual reference to the "threat of peaceful evolution" [*diễn biến hòa bình*] (see, for example, Kim Ninh 1998; Thayer 1999).

During the early years of *Doi Moi*, two key turning points marked Vietnam's new foreign policy orientation: Politburo Resolution No. 32 (July 1986) and Politburo Resolution No. 13 (May 1988).[1]

During 1985, Vietnam's economy deteriorated to such an extent that Vietnam faced a major crisis. At the same time, the Soviet Union became increasingly critical of what it viewed as Vietnam's misuse of its aid

(Thayer 1991; 1993, p. 197). In May–June 1986, the Central Committee of the Communist Party of Vietnam (CPV) held its tenth plenum. Following this meeting, the Politburo adopted Resolution No. 32 (32/BCT21) entitled "The Solution to the Cambodian Issue Must Preserve the Cambodian Revolutionary Gains and Solidarity Among Three Indochinese Countries" on 9 July 1986. Significantly, this resolution identified "peace and development" as the highest priority and laid the basis for "new thinking" in the conceptualization of Vietnam's national security policy (Minh 2012, pp. 56–57). According to a later account, Resolution 32:

> clearly set out guidelines and revised diplomatic policies, and moved toward a solution in Cambodia. The Resolution clearly stated:
> – The external mission of Vietnam is to have good coordination between the strength of the people and the strength of the time, to take advantage of favourable international conditions to build socialism and defend the Fatherland, proactively create a condition for stability and economic construction.
> – It is necessary to move proactively to a new stage of development, and peaceful coexistence with China, ASEAN, and the United States, and build Southeast Asia into a region of peace, stability and cooperation (Nam 2006, p. 26).

At its sixth national congress in December 1986, the CPV adopted the *Doi Moi* policy aimed at overcoming the domestic socio-economic crisis. General Secretary Truong Chinh's Political Report called for, *inter alia*, the expansion and heightening of the effectiveness of external economic relations as one of the means of addressing the domestic economic crisis (CPV 1991, pp. 659–64). In other words, Vietnam decided to open itself to foreign investment from non-socialist countries (Thayer 1987).

Vietnam also decided to liquidate the Cambodian problem by withdrawing its military forces (Thayer 1987, 1989). According to then Deputy Minister of Foreign Affairs Tran Quang Co (2003), "The period of struggle aimed at a total victory of the Cambodian revolution, under the illusion that the 'situation is irreversible,' had come to an end, and we had to acknowledge the reality of a step by step struggle to achieve a political solution for the Cambodian question."

On 20 May 1988, Vietnam adopted Politburo Resolution No. 13, "On the Tasks and Foreign Policy in the New Situation". This Resolution declared "economic weaknesses, political isolation, and economic blockade are major threats to our country's security and independence" (quoted in Tung 2004, p. 4).

Resolution No. 13 presented a new codification of foreign policy objectives that gave priority to "a strong economy, a sufficiently strong national defence, and expanded international cooperation" (quoted in Tung 2004, p. 4). Resolution No. 13 used the term "national interest" [*lợi ích dân tộc*] for the first time. The new emphasis was "to maintain peace, take advantage of favourable world conditions" in order to stabilize the domestic situation and set the base for economic development over the next ten to fifteen years.

Resolution No. 13 called for a multi-directional foreign policy toward the goal of having "more friends, fewer enemies" [*thêm bạn, bớt thù*]. It also stressed the need of not only resolving the Cambodian conflict but also normalizing relations with China and the United States, and strengthening ties with ASEAN, Japan, and European countries (Chuc 2004, pp. 4–7; Huynh 2004; Nam 2006, p. 27; Nien 2005, p. 30).[2]

With Resolution No. 13 signalling the abandonment of the "two world" view in favour of the concept of an interdependent world, Vietnam was now poised to shift from confrontation to accommodation in its foreign policy. According to one party official, Resolution No. 13 directed that a "comprehensive and long-term regional policy towards Asia and Southeast Asia" be drawn up "as soon as possible" (Cat 1996, pp. 28–29). Resolution No. 13 is now widely recognized as a major landmark in the transformation of Vietnam's external relations under *Doi Moi*.

In March 1989, the CPV Central Committee's sixth plenum adopted a resolution that "clearly pointed out the need to strongly shift the focus in foreign policy from political relations to political-economic relations" (Nien 2005, p. 31). Six months later, Vietnam unilaterally withdrew the last of its armed forces from Cambodia to improve its strategic environment and facilitate international economic integration. By that time, it was clear that socialist regimes in Eastern Europe were collapsing and that the Soviet Union was in crisis.

Diversifying and Multilaterializing Foreign Relations, 1991–2005

The year 1991 was another pivotal year in the evolution of Vietnam's foreign policy. The conflict in Cambodia was brought to an end in October through a comprehensive political settlement reached in Paris. The Soviet Union staggered through crisis before collapsing in December. In the midst of these developments, the CPV convened its seventh national congress in June 1991. According to the Political Report presented at the congress, Vietnam would now "diversify and multilateralize economic relations with all countries and economic organizations [...] and become the friend of all countries in the world community..." (CPV 1991, p. 134).

The Political Report also declared, "We stand for equal and mutually beneficial co-operation with all countries regardless of different socio-political systems and on the basis of the principle of peaceful co-existence." However, priority was given to relations with the Soviet Union, Laos, Cambodia, China, Cuba, other "communist and workers' parties", the "forces struggling for peace, national independence, democracy and social progress", India, and the Non-Aligned Movement. It was only at the end of this list that the Political Report set the objective:

> To develop relations of friendship with other countries in Southeast Asia and the Asia-Pacific region, and to strive for a Southeast Asia of peace, friendship and co-operation. To expand equal and mutually beneficial co-operation with northern and Western European countries, Japan and other developed countries. To promote the process of normalization of relations with the United States (CPV 1991, p. 135).

Vietnam reaped substantial foreign policy dividends following the Cambodian peace agreements. It succeeded in diversifying its foreign relations by moving from dependency on the Soviet Union to a more diverse and balanced set of external relations. In 1989, Vietnam had diplomatic relations with only twenty-three non-communist states. By the end of 1995, this number rose to 163.

In January 1994, the CPV convened its first mid-term party conference. General Secretary Do Muoi reaffirmed Vietnam's commitment to the broad outlines of economic and political renovation that emerged since the seventh CPV congress. The Political Report listed eight essential tasks to be carried out, including the expansion of Vietnam's external relations (*Nhan Dan* 1994). Priority was given to industrializing and modernizing Vietnam by mobilizing domestic and international capital. Media reports after the conference highlighted four dangers facing Vietnam: being left behind economically by regional countries; peaceful evolution against socialism; corruption; and deviation from the socialist path (CPV 2010, p. 524).

After the mid-term conference, Vietnam continued to pursue its open door foreign policy designed "to make friends with all countries". These efforts met with success. In 1993–94, the United States ended its long-standing objections to the provision of developmental assistance to Vietnam by the World Bank and International Monetary Fund, and gradually lifted restrictions on trade and investment in Vietnam. Vietnam thus became eligible for a variety of aid, credits and commercial loans to finance its development plans.

Vietnam's open door policy also resulted in membership in the ASEAN Regional Forum in 1994. More importantly, the following year Vietnam normalized relations with the United States, became ASEAN's seventh member, and signed a framework cooperation agreement with the European Union. For the first time, Vietnam had diplomatic relations with all five permanent members of the United Nations Security Council and, equally importantly, with the world's three major economic centres — Europe, North America and East Asia.

The next evolution of Vietnam's foreign policy came at the eighth CPV national congress held from 28 June to 1 July 1996. Delegates from Southeast Asia included, for the first time, representatives from ruling parties in Cambodia, Malaysia and Singapore.

The foreign policy section of the Political Report reflected the view of pragmatic policy practitioners. On "the characteristics of the international system", the Political Report noted that the "scientific and technological revolution was developing at an increasingly rapid pace, thereby accelerating various production forces and the process of globalisation of the world economy and social life" (*Nhan Dan* 1996). According to Vu Khoan (2006), "this was the first time we had spoken of globalisation and assessed that it was an objective trend."

The Political Report stressed the importance of relations with neighbouring countries and ASEAN by listing these relationships as Vietnam's top priority. It stated:

> To strengthen our relations with neighbouring countries and ASEAN member countries, to constantly consolidate our ties with traditional friendly states, and attach importance to our relations with developed countries and political-economic centres in the world while at the same time upholding the spirit of solidarity and brotherliness with developing countries in Asia, Africa and Latin America, and with the Non-Aligned Movement (*Nhan Dan* 1996).

In 1996, Vietnam participated in the Asia Europe Meeting (ASEM) for the first time. Two years later, Vietnam joined the Asia Pacific Economic Cooperation (APEC) forum.

The Political Report also juxtaposed the potential for conflict arising from competition in the areas of economics and science and technology with the potential for cooperation arising from peaceful co-existence between "socialist countries, communist and workers parties and revolutionary and progressive forces" and "nations under different political regimes" (*Nhan Dan* 1996).

The tension between conflict and cooperation between countries with different political systems was illustrated by Vietnam's negotiations with the United States for a Bilateral Trade Agreement (BTA) (Manyin 2005, pp. 5–6). Vietnam's policy elite was divided on the risks of exposing Vietnam to the forces of globalization. Consensus was finally reached at the tenth plenum of the CPV Central Committee held in June–July of 2000. The plenum resolved that in order to achieve the objective of industrializing and modernizing Vietnam by 2020, Vietnam had no choice but to step up the rate of economic growth, encourage more foreign investment, and continue regional and global integration. The tenth plenum gave its approval for the new trade minister, Vu Khoan, to go to Washington to sign the BTA. Key clauses in this agreement were phased in over a period from three to nine years. In 2001, the United States granted Vietnam temporary normal trade relations status on a year-by-year basis. For those in Hanoi seeking global economic integration, these were necessary first steps that Vietnam had to undertake in order to join the World Trade Organization (WTO).

In March 2001, Vietnam consolidated its ties with the Russian Federation, a "traditional friendly state", by signing its first strategic partnership agreement during the course of a visit to Hanoi by President Vladimir Putin (Thayer 2012*b*). This agreement set out broad-ranging cooperation in eight major areas: political-diplomatic, military equipment and technology, oil and gas cooperation, energy cooperation for hydro and nuclear power, trade and investment, science and technology, education and training, and culture and tourism. In July 2012, Vietnam and Russia raised their strategic partnership to a comprehensive strategic partnership on the occasion of a state visit by President Truong Tan Sang to Moscow (Thayer 2012*a*).

The centrepiece of the Vietnam–Russia strategic partnership is defence cooperation, including arms sales and the transfer of technology. In 2013, Russia and Vietnam established a Joint Working Group on defence cooperation and signed a five-year Memorandum of Understanding (MOU) covering annual defence dialogues, military technology, professional military education and training, assistance in weapons maintenance, joint venture service, and the sale of twelve Sukhoi Su-30MKs multirole jet fighters.

The Vietnam–Russia strategic partnership became the model for Vietnam's relations with the major powers and other important countries. The purpose of strategic partnerships is to promote comprehensive cooperation across a number of areas and to give each major power equity in Vietnam's stability and development in order to ensure Vietnam's non-alignment and strategic autonomy.

The ninth CPV national congress, held in April 2001, reaffirmed that "Vietnam wants to be a friend and a reliable partner to all nations" by diversifying and multilateralizing its international relations with priority on developing relations with "socialist, neighbouring and traditional friendly states" (Thayer 2002). More significantly, the congress set the goal of overcoming underdevelopment by the year 2010 and accelerating industrialization and modernization in order to become a modern industrialized state by 2020.

According to Vu Khoan (2006), the ninth congress identified two main measures to attain this goal, "first, perfect the regime of a market economy with socialist characteristics, and second, integrate deeper and more fully into the various global economic regimes. Integration into the global economy will tie our economy into the regional and global economies on the basis of common rules of the game."

In August 2001, Vietnam and the Republic of Korea raised bilateral relations to a Comprehensive Partnership in the 21st Century. In October 2009, this was raised to a Strategic Cooperative Partnership and the two sides agreed to cooperate in politics and security, judicial and consular relations, economics, trade, investment, development cooperation, science and technology, environment, and culture and education. Vietnam and South Korea regularly exchange high-level political and defence visits and hold annual strategic and national defence strategic dialogues (Giap, Que, and Duong 2011, pp. 12–13).

A Politburo resolution adopted in November 2001 sketched Vietnam's diplomatic strategy as follows:

> continue to strengthen relations with Vietnam's neighbours and countries that have been traditional friends; give importance to relations with big countries, developing countries, and the political and economic centres of the world; raise the level of solidarity with developing countries and the non-aligned movement; increase activities in international organizations; and develop relations with communist and workers' parties, with progressive forces, while at the same time expanding relations with ruling parties and other parties. Pay attention to people's diplomacy (Vu Duong Ninh 2002, p. 110).

In the course of multilateralizing and diversifying its foreign relations and becoming a reliable partner, Vietnam discovered that areas of friction arose with China, a socialist and traditional friendly state, and areas of convergence emerged with its former enemy, the United States.

The conundrum of how to reconcile these realities was resolved by the eighth plenum of the CPV's Central Committee that met in mid-2003. This plenum adopted a resolution that dialectically combined two opposing forces — cooperation and competition — in the concepts of "partners of cooperation" [*đối tác*] and "objects of struggle" [*đối tượng*]. According to the plenum's resolution, "any force that plans and acts against the objectives we hold in the course of national construction and defence is the object of struggle", and, "anyone who respects our independence and sovereignty, establishes and expands friendly, equal, and mutually beneficial relations with Vietnam is our partner" (quoted in Thayer 2008, p. 27).

The resolution concluded:

> with the objects of struggle, we can find areas for cooperation; with the partners, there exist interests that are contradictory and different from those of ours. We should be aware of these, thus overcoming the two tendencies, namely lacking vigilance and showing rigidity in our perception, design, and implementation of specific policies (quoted in Thayer 2008, p. 27).

The eighth plenum resolution provided the policy rationale for Vietnam to stiffen its stance against China over territorial disputes in the South China Sea that had been brewing since 1992 and to step up cooperation with the United States (Thayer 2005). After the plenum, Vietnam advised the United States that it would accept a long-standing invitation for its Minister of National Defence to visit Washington. Vietnam also approved the first port call by a U.S. Navy warship since the Vietnam War.

In December 2005, Vietnam became a founding member of the East Asia Summit and supported its expansion to include the United States and Russia who became members in 2010.

Proactive International Integration and Strategic Partnerships, 2006–16

The CPV convened its tenth national congress in Hanoi in April 2006. According to the Political Report, Vietnam will "carry out the foreign policy of openness, multilateralization and diversification of international relations. To proactively integrate into the international economy and, at the same time, expand international co-operation in other domains" (CPV 2015, p. 1195). After the congress, two inter-related themes became increasingly prominent in Vietnam's foreign relations: proactive international integration and the diversification and multilateralization of relations through strategic and comprehensive partnerships.

Proactive International Integration

The centrepiece of Vietnam's regional integration is ASEAN and ASEAN-centred multilateral institutions. Former Minister of Foreign Affairs Nguyen Dy Nien offered the assessment that Vietnam's foreign policy reached three peaks in 2006 — hosting the APEC summit, gaining membership in the WTO, and unanimous nomination by the Asia bloc for non-permanent membership on the United Nations Security Council (*VnExpress* 2006). In 2007, Vietnam was overwhelmingly elected by the UN General Assembly as a non-permanent member on the Security Council for a two-year period beginning in 2008. Before that, Vietnam became a founding member of the ASEAN Defence Ministers' Meeting (ADMM) in 2006. In 2010, Vietnam became a founding member of the ASEAN Maritime Forum (AMF) and hosted the inaugural meeting of the ADMM-Plus. The country also served as ASEAN's country coordinator for relations with the European Union from 2012–15.

In April 2013, the CPV Politburo adopted Resolution No. 22 on International Integration. It declared that, "Proactive and active international integration is a major strategic orientation of the Party aimed to successfully implement the task of building and protecting the socialist Fatherland of Vietnam" (CPV 2013). Resolution No. 22 underscored the need for Vietnam to

> Deliver on international commitments in parallel with proactive, positive participation in developing and making use of international rules and practices and participate in activities of the regional and international communities; proactively propose initiatives and cooperation mechanisms under the mutually beneficial principle; consolidate and enhance our country's position in the regional and international communities, actively contributing to the struggle for peace, national independence, democracy and social progress in the world (CPV 2013).

After Resolution No. 22 was issued, the cabinet adopted an action plan and the prime minister issued Directive No. 15/CT-TTg. This led to the establishment of the National Steering Committee on International Integration headed by the prime minister. Three major inter-agency steering committees were also set up, the first on international integration in politics, security, and national defence, the second on economic integration, and the third on integration in the areas of culture and society, science and technology, and education and training.

Strategic and Comprehensive Partnerships

After the tenth congress, Vietnam kick started its drive to transform bilateral relations into strategic and comprehensive partnerships. From 2006 to 2016, Vietnam established strategic partnerships with India (2007), China (2008), Japan, South Korea, Spain (2009), the United Kingdom (2010), Germany (2011), Italy, Thailand, Indonesia, Singapore, France (2013), Malaysia and the Philippines (2015). It also entered into comprehensive partnership with more than ten countries. As bilateral relations developed breadth and depth, several strategic partnerships have been upgraded and described as extensive, enhanced, comprehensive or comprehensive strategic cooperative partnerships.

The subsections below highlight some of Vietnam's key partnerships with the major powers and regional states established during this period. More detailed analyses of Vietnam's relations with these partners (except for Australia) can be found in subsequent chapters of the book.

Japan. In October 2006, Japan and Vietnam announced the intention to become strategic partners when Prime Ministers Shinzo Abe and Nguyen Tan Dung issued a Joint Statement Toward a Strategic Partnership for Peace and Prosperity in Asia. This document called for frequent high-level visits and exchanges of views and the establishment of a ministerial-level joint cooperation committee.

In November 2007, Nguyen Minh Triet became the first Vietnamese president to make an official visit to Japan. President Triet and Prime Minister Yasuo Fukuda issued a joint statement that included a forty-four point Agenda Toward a Strategic Partnership. The agenda was divided into seven substantive areas: exchanges, cooperation in policy dialogue, security and defence; comprehensive economic partnership; improvement of the legal system and administrative reforms; science and technology; climate change, environment, natural resources and technology; mutual understanding between the peoples of the two countries; and cooperation in the international arena (Thayer 2012*b*).

In April 2009, during CPV General Secretary Nong Duc Manh's visit to Japan, the two countries officially established a bilateral strategic partnership. In an effort to add substance to the partnership, the Japanese and Vietnamese defence ministers met in Tokyo in October 2011 and signed an MOU that included defence exchanges at ministerial, chief of staff and service chief level; naval goodwill visits; annual defence policy dialogue at the deputy defence minister level; cooperation in military aviation, air defence, humanitarian assistance and disaster relief; and personnel training including scholarships for defence personnel to study and train in Japan.

In March 2014, Vietnam and Japan raised their bilateral relations to an Extensive Strategic Partnership in an agreement running to sixty-nine paragraphs. As a follow up, CPV General Secretary Nguyen Phu Trong made his first official visit to Japan at the invitation of Prime Minister Shinzo Abe. At the end of their talks, the two leaders issued a thirty-one point Joint Vision Statement (Thayer 2014*b*). As demonstrated by Do and Dinh in Chapter 5, bilateral ties since then have further strengthened with a stronger emphasis on strategic dimensions.

India. In July 2007, India and Vietnam became strategic partners when their leaders adopted a Joint Declaration on Strategic Partnership that mapped out cooperation in five major areas: political, defence and security cooperation; closer economic cooperation and commercial engagement; science and technology cooperation; cultural and technical cooperation; and multilateral and regional cooperation (Thayer 2012*b*).

The election of Narendra Modi as Prime Minister in May 2014 injected new momentum into the strategic partnership between Vietnam and India. For example, President Pranab Mukherjee visited Hanoi in September and issued a joint statement with his counterpart President Truong Tan Sang that declared, "cooperation in national defence was an important pillar" in their strategic partnership (Thayer 2016). To underscore this point, Mukherjee announced that India offered Vietnam a US$100 million line of credit to facilitate defence procurement over the next fifteen years.

Vietnam's Prime Minister Nguyen Tan Dung made an official visit to India in October 2014 at the invitation of Prime Minister Modi who noted, "it is no surprise that Vietnam has been at the forefront or our efforts [to Act East]... We have a shared interest in maritime security, including freedom of navigation and commerce and peaceful settlement of disputes in accordance with international law" (Thayer 2016). In May 2015, Vietnam and India signed a Joint Vision Statement on Defence Cooperation for the period 2015–20. Vietnam is currently coordinator for ASEAN–India relations (2015–18).

China. In June 2008, following a summit of party leaders in Beijing, the two countries officially announced the establishment of a strategic partnership (Thayer 2012b).[3] A year later, it was upgraded to a strategic cooperative partnership, and in 2013, the relationship was elevated to a comprehensive strategic cooperative partnership, the highest designation among all of Vietnam's strategic partners.

As strategic partners, China and Vietnam have developed a dense network of party, state, defence and multilateral mechanisms to manage their bilateral relations, including a joint steering committee at deputy prime minister level.

Although economic and political ties have been robust, the South China Sea proves to be a constant irritant in bilateral relations that Vietnam attempts to manage through its policy of "cooperation and struggle". In 2014, however, a major crisis erupted when China placed the mega oil drilling platform *Haiyang Shiyou* 981 in Vietnam's exclusive economic zone (EEZ) accompanied by a mixed armada of military ships, coast guard vessels, tug boats and fishing craft that totalled over one hundred at the peak. During the months May–July, Vietnam's Coast Guard and other vessels were continually rammed and subject to blasts by high-powered water cannons. Vietnam embedded the foreign media on its ships to beam the "David versus Goliath" struggle to a world audience (Thayer 2014a).

The crisis ended in mid-July when China withdrew the oil rig (Thayer 2014c). The two sides rapidly moved to restore strategic trust after the exchange of high-level visits and the inauguration of an annual Border Defence Friendship Exchange at the end of 2014. In June 2017 the fourth border exchange was abruptly cancelled by China due to differences over Vietnam's resumption of oil exploration in its EEZ (Thayer 2017).

Australia. In September 2009, during the visit of CPV General Secretary Nong Duc Manh to Canberra, the Australian and Vietnamese deputy prime ministers signed a joint statement to raise bilateral relations to a comprehensive partnership. This statement highlighted six major areas of cooperation: political ties and public policy exchanges; economic growth and trade development; development assistance and technical cooperation; defence and security ties; people-to-people links; and global and regional agenda. In October 2010, Australia and Vietnam agreed to a plan of action to realize the comprehensive partnership for the years 2011–13 that has since been extended for another three-year period.

In March 2015, during the course of an official visit to Australia by Prime Minister Nguyen Tan Dung, Australia and Vietnam adopted a declaration on enhancing their bilateral relations (DFAT 2015). The two leaders pledged to step up cooperation in five areas: bilateral political and diplomatic relations; regional and international cooperation; economic growth, trade and industry development; development assistance and defence; law enforcement and security ties. The two sides also agreed to establish a strategic partnership in the future.

United States. In July 2013, during the state visit to the United States by President Truong Tan Sang, the two sides issued a joint statement raising their bilateral relations to a comprehensive partnership. The statement spelled out nine areas of cooperation: political and diplomatic relations; trade and economic ties; science and technology; education and training; environment and health; war legacy issues; defence and security; protection and promotion of human rights; and culture, sports, and tourism (The White House 2013).

In June 2015, bilateral defence cooperation witnessed another major advance when the defence ministers of Vietnam and the United States adopted the Joint Vision Statement on Defence Relations in Hanoi. The statement identified twelve areas of cooperation, including maritime security.[4] A month later, U.S.–Vietnam political relations were raised to a new level when President Barack Obama received CPV General Secretary Nguyen Phu Trong at the White House. The two leaders issued a joint vision statement that affirmed "their continued pursuit of a deepened, sustained, and substantive relationship on the basis of respect for the United Nations Charter, international law, and each other's political systems, independence, sovereignty, and territorial integrity".[5] As noted by Phuong Nguyen in Chapter 3, these developments demonstrate an enhanced level of mutual trust between the two former enemies and serve as a strong foundation for the future growth of bilateral ties, especially in the more sensitive areas of defence and security cooperation.

Deepening Strategic Partnerships

In January 2016, Vietnam's cabinet reviewed bilateral strategic and comprehensive partnerships with twenty-five countries and approved a policy document entitled "Overall Strategy for International Integration Through 2020, Vision to 2030" (*Nhan Dan* 2016). This document concluded that Vietnam had to make greater efforts to implement political commitments and to deepen cooperation under these agreements, including defence cooperation.

In 2016, Vietnamese diplomacy went into high gear to deepen its strategic and other partnerships. Newly elected Prime Minister Nguyen Xuan Phuc visited Russia and China in May and September, respectively (Thayer 2016, pp. 27, 35). In Moscow, Prime Ministers Phuc and Dimitry Medvedev reaffirmed "the continuation of co-operation in defence-security, particularly in military techniques" (*Viet Nam News* 2016*b*). In Beijing, Phuc and Premier Li Keqiang issued a joint communiqué stating that the two "leaders concurred in fostering cooperation in diplomacy, defence, security and law enforcement".

In 2016, Vietnam also hosted visits by the president of the United States, prime minister of India, and president of France. Vietnam also utilized ASEAN and APEC summit meetings to hold discussions with Prime Minister Abe.

President Barack Obama made an official visit to Vietnam from 23–25 May at the invitation of President Tran Dai Quang. In Hanoi, Obama announced the lifting of all restrictions on arms sales to Vietnam. The two presidents adopted a joint statement that set out six areas for cooperation: political–diplomatic, economic, people-to-people, security–defence, human rights and legal reform, and regional and global challenges. In particular, the two presidents "agreed to further enhance the U.S.–Vietnam Comprehensive Partnership, making it deeper, more substantive, and more effective in order to better serve the interests of the two peoples for peace, stability, and cooperation in the region and the world" (The White House 2016).[6]

In early September, during Indian Prime Minister Modi's official visit to Hanoi, he and his counterpart Prime Minister Phuc raised bilateral relations to a comprehensive strategic partnership (Thayer 2016, pp. 32–33). In Hanoi, Modi announced that India was extending a US$500 million line of credit to Vietnam for the purchase of defence equipment. In the same month, French President François Hollande also made an official visit to Hanoi where he met President Quang. The two sides announced their agreement "to develop a long-term vision for cooperation that could ensure their common interests". They also agreed to intensify strategic dialogues and military ties, and expand cooperation in the area of maritime safety and security (*Zing News* 2016).

Also during 2016, Vietnam exchanged visits by defence ministers with Russia, China and India, and hosted a visit by France's defence minister.

In March, Russia's Defence Minister Sergei Shoigu met with his counterpart, newly installed Minister of National Defence Ngo Xuan Lich, in Hanoi. Shoigu then visited Cam Ranh Bay. General Lich made his first overseas visit as defence minister to Moscow in April. Lich and Shoigu discussed fulfilling defence agreements already signed, mutual support in international forums, cooperation in military training, and further arms sales (Thayer 2016, pp. 27–28).

Also in March 2016, Vietnam and China co-hosted the third Border Defence Friendship Exchange that involved the reciprocal visits by their respective defence ministers (Thayer 2016, pp. 33–35). In August, Defence Minister Lich made his first official visit to China at the invitation of his counterpart. The two ministers discussed the fourth Border Defence Friendship Exchange to be held in 2017, and called for the continuation of high-level exchanges and defence strategic dialogues at deputy ministerial level, and annual defence exchanges, including naval port visits and exchanges by junior officers. The two ministers also witnessed the signing of an MOU on cooperation between the Institute for Military Strategy and China's Academy of Military Science (*Viet Nam News* 2016*a*). As noted above, the fourth border exchange was abruptly cancelled and then reinstated later in the year.

In June, India's Defence Minister Manohar Parrikar visited Hanoi for discussions with General Lich. Parrikar agreed to commence phase two of Indian assistance to the Information Technology and Foreign Languages Centre at the Signal Officers Training School in Nha Trang by funding the construction of a software park for the Vietnamese military. General Lich paid a reciprocal visit to India in December with a delegation comprising thirty persons, including the Deputy Chief of the General Staff and the commanders of the air force and navy. After talks, Parrikar and Lich witnessed the signing of an agreement on India's provision of basic and advanced training for Vietnamese Su-30 pilots and assistance in the repair and maintenance of this aircraft. In addition, an MOU on peacekeeping and an MOU on exchange of delegations were also signed (*Quan doi Nhan dan* 2016).

France's Defence Minister Jean-Yves Le Drian made an official visit to Hanoi in June 2016 for discussions with his counterpart, General Lich. The two ministers agreed to facilitate defence industry cooperation and to establish a strategic partnership in defence cooperation (Thayer 2016, p. 45).

Conclusion

This chapter presented an analysis of the evolution of Vietnamese foreign policy over the past three decades from the adoption of *Doi Moi* to the present. This analysis divided this evolution into three periods.

During the first period of evolution (1986–91), Vietnam's Marxist–Leninist worldview underwent a remarkable transformation from a framework of the globe divided into two hostile camps to a view of one global economy that offered Vietnam both opportunities and challenges. Two factors played a major role in this transformation — the failure of Soviet-styled central planning that induced a domestic socio-economic crisis, and the "new political thinking" emanating from the Soviet Union under Mikhail Gorbachev.

Vietnam's adoption of the view that there is a single world community and a unified global economy led it to develop a more positive outlook on global integration. Integration was no longer viewed as a process of assimilation but one of interdependence. Vietnam rejected the zero-sum view of the world divided into "friends and enemies" and sought to become friends with all countries.

At the same time, Vietnam adopted a comprehensive view of security that depreciated the relative importance of military power and elevated the salience of economic relations and science and technology. In order to operationalize this new worldview and end its international isolation, Vietnam took steps to extricate itself from the conflict in Cambodia.

Nonetheless, the residue of "old political thinking", especially in relation to the major powers, remained. On the one hand, some leaders of the CPV continued to view the United States with considerable suspicion. They feared that the United States aimed to overthrow socialism in Vietnam through "peaceful evolution" by advocacy of democracy, human rights and religious freedom. On the other hand, some CPV leaders still valued socialism as a shared ideology uniting Vietnam and China.

In jettisoning the view that the world was divided into hostile socialist and capitalist camps, Vietnam set the stage for developing economic relations with non-socialist states regionally and globally on the basis of national interests. Politburo Resolution No. 13 (May 1988) called for a multi-directional foreign policy in order to make "more friends, fewer enemies". This new orientation was only practical after a comprehensive political settlement of the Cambodian conflict was reached in October 1991. Additional impetus to open up resulted from the collapse of the Soviet Union in late 1991.

The second period of the evolution (1991–2006) was initiated by the CPV's seventh national congress that prioritized the development of economic relations with all states regardless of differing political systems and economic organizations. Yet, as demonstrated by the Mid-Term Party Conference in early 1994, Vietnam's leaders assessed that the country faced both internal and external dangers, including being left behind economically and the threat of peaceful evolution.

Subsequent CPV national congresses in 1996 and 2001 reaffirmed Vietnam's commitment to multilateralizing and diversifying external relations and becoming a friend and reliable partner of all countries around the world. This strategy was aimed at assisting Vietnam's development through international integration while preserving its socialist-oriented market economy.

During this period, Vietnam normalized relations with China, Japan, the European Union, the United States and joined ASEAN. Vietnam soon discovered that the residue of old ideological thinking had to be modified to take into account differences in interests with socialist China and the growing convergence of interests with the United States. Toward this end, Vietnam opted to cooperate with both as long as they respected Vietnam's interests, and to struggle against infringements on its national interests and sovereignty.

The third and most recent period of Vietnam's foreign policy evolution (2006–16) witnessed Hanoi's increasing efforts to multilateralize and diversify its external relations and to proactively integrate into the global economy. During this period, Vietnam forged strategic and comprehensive partnerships with the major powers and then regional states. It also sought to add more substance to its key partnerships, especially with Japan, India and the United States, by stepping up defence cooperation with these states. After the twelfth CPV national congress in 2016, Vietnam successfully added further depth to these partnerships through intense diplomatic efforts.

The analysis in this chapter illustrates that four major themes have shaped Vietnam's diplomacy over the past three decades of *Doi Moi*: diversification and multilateralization of external relations; defending national interests through struggle and cooperation; pro-active international integration; and maintenance of independence, sovereignty and strategic autonomy. As a result, Vietnam is increasingly viewed by the international community as a valued strategic partner that positively contributes to the region's prosperity and security.

NOTES

1. Key VCP Politburo resolutions relating to Vietnam's external policies in this period, such as Politburo Resolutions No. 32 (1986), No. 2 (1987), and No. 13 (1988), have not yet been made public.
2. The call for normalizing relations with China was remarkable given that two months earlier, on 13 March 1988, Chinese naval forces attacked Vietnamese ships in waters around Fiery Cross and Johnson South Reefs and occupied these and other features (Hayton 2014, pp. 81–84).
3. For an overview of Vietnam's policy towards China since 1986, see Hiep (2017, pp. 40–64).
4. Full text of the statement can be found at <http://photos.state.gov/libraries/vietnam/8621/pdf-forms/usvn_defense_relations_jvs2015.pdf>.
5. Full text of the statement can be found at <http://www.fetp.edu.vn/en/news-events/fuv-news/usvietnam-joint-vision-statement/>.
6. On 31 May 2017, President Donald Trump received Prime Minister Phuc at the White House. After the meeting, they released a joint statement reaffirming their commitment to enhance the comprehensive partnership reached between the two countries in 2013.

REFERENCES

Cam, Nguyen Manh. "Gia tri lau ben va dinh huong nhat quan". In *Hoi nhap quoc te va giu vung ban sac*, edited by Bo Ngoai Giao. Hanoi: NXB Chinh tri quoc te, 1995, pp. 223–30.

Cat, Nguyen Huu. "Viet Nam hoi nhap vao khu vuc vi hoa binh va phat trien". *Nghien Cuu Dong Nam A* (February 1996): 28–29.

Chuc, Chu Van. "Qua trinh doi moi tu duy doi ngoai va hinh thanh duong loi doi ngoai doi moi". *Nghien Cuu Quoc Te* 3 (2004): 3–11.

Co, T.Q. "Hoi uc va suy nghi: 1975–1991" [Memoir and Reflections: 1975–1991]. Unpublished manuscript, 2003.

Communist Party of Vietnam (CPV). *7th National Congress Documents*. Hanoi: Vietnam Foreign Languages Publishing House, 1991.

————. *Van kien dai hoi dai bieu toan quoc thoi ky doi moi* [Documents of National Congresses in the Era of Doi Moi] (Vol. 1). Hanoi: National Political Publishing House, 2010.

————. "Nghi quyet so 22-NQ/TW ngay 10/4/2013 cua Bo Chinh tri ve hoi nhap quoc te", 10 April 2013. Available at <http://dangcongsan.vn/tu-lieu-van-kien/van-kien-dang/van-kien-bo-chinh-tri-ban-bi-thu/nghi-quyet/doc-2925201511520646.html>.

————. *Eighty-five Years of the Communist Party of Viet Nam (1930–2015): A Selection of Documents from Eleven Party Congresses*. Hanoi: The Gioi Publishers, 2015.

Department of Foreign Affairs and Trade (DFAT). "A Declaration on Enhancing the Australia–Vietnam Comprehensive Partnership", 15 March 2015. Available at <http://dfat.gov.au/geo/vietnam/pages/a-declaration-on-enhancing-the-australia-viet-nam-comprehensive-partnership.aspx>.

Elliott, David W.P. *Changing Worlds: Vietnam's Transition from Cold War to Globalization*. Oxford: Oxford University Press, 2012.

Giap, Nguyen Hoang, Nguyen Thi Que, and Nguyen Van Duong. *Quan he Viet Nam-Han Quoc tu nam 1992 den nay va trien vong phat trien den nam 2020*. Hanoi: NXB Chinh tri Quoc gia, 2011.

Hayton, Bill. *The South China Sea: The Struggle for Power in Asia*. New Haven and London: Yale University Press, 2014.

Hiep, Le Hong. *Living Next to the Giant: The Political Economy of Vietnam's Relations with China Under* Doi Moi. Singapore: ISEAS – Yusof Ishak Institute, 2017.

Huynh, Luu Doan. "Vietnam–ASEAN Relations in Retrospect: A Few Thoughts". *Dialogue + Cooperation* 1 (2004): 23–31.

Khoan, Vu. "Mot so van de quoc te cua Dai hoi VII". In *Hoi nhap quoc te va giu vung ban sac*, edited by Bo Ngoai Giao. Hanoi: NXB Chinh tri quoc gia, 1995, pp. 71–76.

———. "Tich cuc va chu dong hoi nhap kinh te quoc te". *Tap chi Cong san 119* (2006).

Manyin, Mark E. "The Vietnam–U.S. Normalization Process". *CRS Report IB98033*, 17 June 2005. Available at <https://www.fas.org/sgp/crs/row/IB98033.pdf>.

Minh, Pham Quang. *Chinh sach doi ngoai Doi Moi cua Viet Nam (1986–2010)*. Hanoi: NXB The Gioi, 2012.

Nam, Phan Doan. "Ngoai giao Viet Nam sau 20 nam doi moi" [Vietnam's Diplomacy after 20 Years of Renovation]. *Tap chi Cong san* [Commusit Review] 14 (2006): 26–30.

Nhan Dan. Political Report of the Seventh Communist Party of Vietnam Central Committee delivered by General Secretary Do Muoi at the opening of the Midterm National Party Conference at Ba Dinh Conference Hall, Hanoi, 20 January 1994.

———. "Du thao Bao cao Chinh tri cua Ban Chap hanh Trung Uong Dang Khoa VII trinh Dai hoi lan thu VIII cua Dang", 10 April 1996.

———. "Chien luoc tong the hoi nhap quoc te den nam 2020, tam nhin 2030" [Overall Strategy for International Integration Through 2020, Vision to 2030], 10 January 2016. Available at <http://www.nhandan.com.vn/chinhtri/item/28490602-chien-luoc-tong-the-hoi-nhap-quoc-te-den-nam-2020-tam-nhin-2030.html>.

Nien, Nguyen Dy. "Chinh sach va hoat dong doi ngoai trong thoi ky Doi Moi". *Tap Chi Cong San* 17, no. 740 (2005): 31–37.

Ninh, Kim. "Vietnam: Struggle and Cooperation". In *Asian Security Practice: Material and Ideational Influences*, edited by Muthiah Alagappa. Stanford, CA: Stanford University Press, 1998, pp. 445–76.

Ninh, Vu Duong, ed. *Ngoai giao Viet Nam hien dai 1975–2002*. Hanoi: Hoc vien Quan he Quoc te, 2002.

Palmujoki, Eero. *Vietnam and the World: Marxist–Leninist Doctrine and the Changes in International Relations, 1975–93*. London: Macmillan Press, 1997.

Quan doi Nhan dan. "Doan can bo quan su cap cao Viet Nam tiep tuc chuyen tham va lam viec tai An Do", 6 December 2016. Available at <http://www.qdnd.vn/chinh-tri/doi-ngoai-doi-ngoai-quoc-phong/doan-can-bo-quan-su-cap-cao-viet-nam-tiep-tuc-chuyen-tham-va-lam-viec-tai-an-do-494363>.

Thakur, Ramesh C. and Carlyle A. Thayer. *The Soviet Union as an Asian Pacific Power: Implications of Gorbachev's 1986 Vladivostok Initiative*. Boulder: Westview Press, 1987.

Thayer, Carlyle A. "Vietnam's Sixth Party Congress: An Overview". *Contemporary Southeast Asia* 9, no. 1 (1987): 12–22.

———. "Prospects for Peace in Kampuchea: Soviet Initiatives and Indochinese Responses". *The Indonesian Quarterly* 17, no. 2 (1989): 157–72.

———. "Civil Society and the Soviet–Vietnamese Alliance". In *The Transition from Socialism: State and Civil Society in Gorbachev's USSR*, edited by Chandran Kukathas, David W. Lovell and William Maley. Sydney: Longmann Cheshire, 1991, pp. 198–218.

———. "Indochina". In *Reshaping Regional Relations: Asia-Pacific and the Former Soviet Union*, edited by Ramesh Thakur and Carlyle A. Thayer. Boulder, San Francisco and Oxford: Westview Press, 1993, pp. 201–22.

———. "Vietnamese Foreign Policy: Multilateralism and the Threat of Peaceful Evolution". In *Vietnamese Foreign Policy in Transition*, edited by Carlyle A. Thayer and Ramses Amer. Singapore: Institute of Southeast Asia Studies, 1999, pp. 1–24.

———. "Vietnam in 2001: The Ninth Party Congress and After". *Asian Survey* 42, no. 1 (2002): 81–89.

———. "The Prospects for Strategic Dialogue". In *Dialogue on U.S.–Vietnam Relations: Ten Years After Normalization*, edited by Catherin E. Dalpino. San Francisco: The Asia Foundation, 2005, pp. 26–30.

———. "Upholding State Sovereignty Through Global Integration: The Remaking of Vietnamese National Security Policy". Paper presented at the Workshop on Viet Nam, East Asia and Beyond, City University of Hong Kong, Hong Kong, 11–12 December 2008.

———. "The Russia–Vietnam Comprehensive Partnership". *East Asia Forum*, 9 October 2012*a*. Available at <http://www.eastasiaforum.org/2012/10/09/the-russia-vietnam-comprehensive-partnership/> (accessed 19 July 2017).

———. "Vietnam On the Road to Global Integration: Forging Strategic Partnerships Through International Security Cooperation". Paper presented at the The Fourth International Conference on Vietnamese Studies, Hanoi, 2012*b*.

———. "4 Reasons China Removed Oil Rig HYSY-981 Sooner Than Planned". *The Diplomat*, 22 July 2014*a*. Available at <http://thediplomat.com/2014/07/4-reasons-china-removed-oil-rig-hysy-981-sooner-than-planned/>.

———. "Vietnam's Extensive Strategic Partnership with Japan". *The Diplomat*, 14 October 2014*b*. Available at <http://thediplomat.com/2014/10/vietnams-extensive-strategic-partnership-with-japan/> (accessed 21 March 2017).

———. "Vietnam, China and the Oil Rig Crisis: Who Blinked?" *The Diplomat*, 4 August 2014*c*. Available at <http://thediplomat.com/2014/08/vietnam-china-and-the-oil-rig-crisis-who-blinked/>.

———. "Vietnam's Proactive International Integration: Case Studies in Defence Cooperation". *Tap Chi Khoa Hoc 32* (2016): 25–48.

———. "Is a New China–Vietnam Maritime Crisis Brewing in the South China Sea?" *The Diplomat*, 29 June 2017. Available at <http://thediplomat.com/2017/06/is-a-new-china-vietnam-maritime-crisis-brewing-in-the-south-china-sea/>.

The White House. "Joint Statement by President Barack Obama of the United States of America and President Truong Tan Sang of the Socialist Republic of Vietnam", 25 July 2013. Available at <http://www.whitehouse.gov/the-press-office/2013/07/25/joint-statement-president-barack-obama-united-states-america-and-preside> (accessed 29 August 2016).

———. "Joint Statement: Between the United States of America and the Socialist Republic of Vietnam", 23 May 2016. Available at <https://www.whitehouse.gov/the-press-office/2016/05/23/joint-statement-between-united-states-america-and-socialist-republic> (accessed 26 May 2016).

Tung, Nguyen Vu. "Vietnamese Foreign Policy: At a New Crossroad?" Paper presented at the Vietnam Update 2004, Singapore, 2004.

Viet Nam News. "VN, China Agree to Deepen Defence Ties", 31 August 2016*a*. Available at <http://vietnamnews.vn/politics-laws/302032/vn-china-agree-to-deepen-defence-ties.html>.

———. "VN, Russia Agree to Intensify Comprehensive Strategic Ties", 16 May 2016*b*. Available at <http://vietnamnews.vn/politics-laws/296865/vn-russia-agree-to-intensify-comprehensive-strategic-ties.html>.

VnExpress. "Se co nhung lan song dau tu moi den VN sau APEC", 10 November 2006. Available at <http://amp.vnexpress.net/tin-tuc/thoi-su/se-co-nhung-lan-song-dau-tu-moi-den-vn-sau-apec-2072969.html>.

Zing News. "Tuyen bo chung Viet – Phap: Luat bien phai duoc ton trong", 6 September 2016. Available at <http://news.zing.vn/tuyen-bo-chung-viet-phap-luat-bien-phai-duoc-ton-trong-post679516.html>.

Part II
Bilateral Relationships

3

The Evolution of Strategic Trust in Vietnam–U.S. Relations

Phuong Nguyen

The history of Vietnam–U.S. relations since the end of the Vietnam War in 1975 is a long and oftentimes delicate journey of forging mutual trust, where none existed before. The end of the war ushered in a period of renewed hostility between the two countries, and prompted Washington to mobilize extensive international embargoes against Hanoi, especially after the latter sent its troops into Cambodia in late 1978. While some attempts to normalize bilateral relations were made within the first few years after the war ended, it was not until the start of *Doi Moi* in 1986 that Vietnamese leaders became more attuned to the impetus of resuming relations with its former enemy and adapting Vietnam's foreign policy to the new demands of its economic reforms.

In *How Enemies Become Friends: The Sources of Stable Peace*, Charles Kupchan (2010) examines the process and conditions necessary for two states — irrespective of power dynamics — to make peace with one another and forge a relationship that can be considered institutionalized. Accordingly, while strategic necessity is needed to trigger either side to seek out the other, states must come to a point at which they view their bargaining as no longer taking place under "conditions of suspicion and competition". In other words, "mutual confidence and trust" allow two states to "minimize the hindrances of uncertainty". By the same token, states which cannot establish a degree of presumption about the other side's "benign character" do not succeed in reconciling and becoming friends (Kupchan 2010, pp. 389–91).

Given the history of their relations, the creation of the level of mutual trust necessary to rebuild ties was especially challenging, yet critical, for Hanoi and Washington. Despite the cooperation between Ho Chi Minh's revolutionary forces and the United States against the Japanese in the final months of World War II, interactions between the two sides turned precarious at the onset of the Cold War and quickly descended into intense hostility in subsequent decades as they found themselves on opposing sides of the ideological spectrum. As such, building — and reinforcing — trust becomes a prerequisite for not only the normalization but also the strengthening of their relationship.

This chapter examines both the institutional and agency-level factors that helped or impeded bilateral strategic trust, and thus the pace of rapprochement between Vietnam and the United States during four major phases of bilateral ties under *Doi Moi*. These phases are: 1) from the early days of *Doi Moi* in 1987 to 1990; 2) from the seventh national congress of the Communist Party of Vietnam (CPV) in 1991 to normalization of bilateral relations in 1995; 3) from normalization until 2006; and 4) from Vietnam's accession to the World Trade Organization (WTO) in 2007 to the present. The premise is that the two sides were able to move the relationship forward by narrowing down the exhaustive areas of distrust at each stage of the relationship and as strategic calculations by both sides called for.

From the Early Days of *Doi Moi* to 1990

In the early years of *Doi Moi*, the sense of optimism or clear direction was slow to take over, especially regarding the prospect of Vietnam's engagement with the United States. Minister of Foreign Affairs Nguyen Manh Cam later recalled there was simply an "abundance of disagreements" at the time to get the Vietnam–U.S. relationship off to a right start (*Tuoi Tre News* 2015). Earlier efforts by either side to reach a diplomatic thaw had ended in failure. In 1975, not long after the end of the war, Hanoi sent a message to Washington through the Soviet Union to express its willingness to "normalize relations on the basis of bilateral respect", but the administration of President Gerald Ford rejected the overture on the grounds that it was made through an unofficial channel. In 1977, a newly elected Jimmy Carter administration sought to improve relations with Vietnam to obtain its cooperation on U.S. POW/MIAs, but this time, Hanoi's insistence on the U.S. payment of a US$3.25 billion package of so-called war reparations became the main obstacle. Moreover, Washington's decision to normalize relations with China in early 1978, Vietnam's alignment with the Soviet Union through a quasi-alliance treaty later that year, and especially Vietnam's decision to send its troops into Cambodia in early 1979, effectively put an end to early attempts for normalization by both sides.[1] The renewed hostility therefore further added to the mutual scepticism in both capitals about the prospect of normalization.

The distrust between Hanoi and Washington was driven not merely by technical disagreements on war legacy issues, but also by Hanoi's view of U.S. intent toward it, a sentiment that at this stage was systemic and widely institutionalized. At a macro level, although ending the country's international isolation was seen as essential for the success of *Doi Moi*, foreign policy changes toward this end came only slowly because of both the CPV's ideological inertia and the early emphasis of *Doi Moi* on domestic administrative, planning, and personnel changes. As the Resolution issued at the sixth national congress of the CPV in December 1986 indicated, the Party saw its primary challenge for the following five years (1986–91) to be the overhaul of its internal management and organization and the task of engineering what it described as an overdue mindset change among party officials (CPV 1986).

The Resolution of the sixth Party congress, while calling for Vietnam to expand relations with international organizations and all countries on the basis of peaceful coexistence, also reaffirmed solidarity and cooperation with the Soviet Union as the cornerstone of Vietnam's foreign policy. It is notable that while the Resolution indicated Hanoi's readiness to normalize relations with Beijing, it made no mention of the United States beyond general references to the importance of the anti-imperialist cause (CPV 1986). This position reflected the thinking of the majority of leaders in Hanoi, who still divided the outside world into ideological poles, and that, if anything, normalization of ties with Beijing should take precedence over that with Washington. Vietnamese leaders did not necessarily view normalization with Beijing and Washington as being mutually exclusive, but the general consensus was that stable relations with China would be of paramount importance to Vietnam's immediate external environment, and a prerequisite for Hanoi to re-engage Washington and ASEAN countries. In other words, few strategic incentives existed to convince Hanoi to take U.S. demands on POW/MIA cooperation seriously, or to ponder the urgency of normalization with Washington.

In the area of foreign policy, starting from 1979, the issue of Vietnam's military involvement in Cambodia following its overthrow of the Khmer Rouge regime quickly came to the fore of Hanoi's interactions with foreign powers. ASEAN strongly opposed the presence of Vietnamese troops in Cambodia, and, along with the United States and China, pressured Hanoi to withdraw its forces from the country. The Carter administration, which had by then decided to move toward full normalization with China as a means to check the Soviet Union, effectively sidelined efforts to engage Vietnam. As such, Washington tacitly backed Beijing's support for the Cambodian resistance forces and reportedly condoned China's invasion of Vietnam in 1979. This turn of events further heightened the widespread distrust many in Hanoi already felt toward Washington.

By the late 1980s, however, the protracted presence in Cambodia had severely strained Hanoi's resources, and with Soviet aid dwindling, Hanoi announced in 1988 to withdraw all of its troops from Cambodia by the end of 1989 (Erlanger 1989). Ironically, while this development should in theory pave the way for Hanoi and Washington to resume where the two had left off in 1978, the contrary seemed to have happened, driven by the intricacies of personality politics.

At the agency level, then Foreign Minister Nguyen Co Thach was one of the few and strongest proponents of normalizing relations with the United States, despite several false starts and his own frustration with U.S. Indochina policy through the 1980s. He was, however, convinced that Vietnam would be well-placed to establish diplomatic ties with the United States by the time the last Vietnamese troops left Cambodia (Downie 1989). Thach was a believer in the strategic value of a relationship with the United States. He led efforts through 1988 and 1989 to convey Vietnam's willingness to move normalization talks forward with U.S. interlocutors, most notably special envoy of President Ronald Reagan, Gen. John Vessey, by stepping up search for U.S. MIAs (Sutter 1996). Little did Thach know that being the public face of Hanoi on both the Cambodia settlement and U.S. normalization issues sent confusing signals to Americans about his own credibility, pitching him against his own cause.

Thach was uncompromising at the Paris Conference on Cambodia in August 1989, insisting that Vietnam would only accept a political settlement in Cambodia on terms favourable to the Phnom Penh government and thus Hanoi's interests. As a consequence, U.S. officials involved in the talks could not help but doubt Thach's sincerity and Hanoi's seriousness in dealing with Washington. Assistant Secretary of State for East Asia and the Pacific Richard Solomon, upon being requested to meet with Thach at the Paris Conference, later said he had "little confidence in the reliability of the wily Thach". Solomon also admitted that "there was limited enthusiasm in the Bush administration for engaging Hanoi on political issues" at the time of the meeting (Solomon 2000, pp. 82–83). Although lower-level exchanges on POW/MIA picked up pace following a "breakthrough" meeting between Vessey and Gen. Vo Nguyen Giap during the former's visit to Hanoi in 1988 (Becker 2000; Krauss 1990), Solomon's assessment of Thach and Hanoi's intent proved that the deep-rooted distrust was not only systemic but also interpersonal. The breakdown of the Paris peace talks later in 1989 further fuelled the disillusionment of decision-makers in Hanoi and Washington toward each other.

Meanwhile, General Secretary Nguyen Van Linh and the conservative faction in Hanoi, frustrated with Thach's failed overtures to the West, had by the late 1980s begun to explore ways to thaw the hostility with Beijing. Linh was cognizant that Vietnam's strategic dependence on the slowly disintegrating Soviet Union was becoming untenable, and that working directly with China was key to Vietnam's future security as well as the prospect of reaching a final agreement among the Cambodian factions in the Paris peace talks, given China's support for the resistance forces (see, for example, Holley 1990; Zhang 2015, pp. 193–210). Following Linh's successful overture to Beijing and a compromise over the Cambodian issue reached at a secret meeting between Vietnamese and Chinese leaders in Chengdu in September 1990, Thach became increasingly marginalized. Linh was able to deliver normalization with China, whereas the foreign minister worked doggedly and could not achieve the same outcome with the United States.

However, the end of this period witnessed increasingly frequent contacts between Vietnamese officials and U.S. interlocutors on POW/MIA issues that at least helped build a minimal level of understanding about each other's historical sensitivities surrounding the issue.[2]

From the Seventh CPV Congress to Diplomatic Normalization in 1995

Vietnam's complete withdrawal of its troops from Cambodia helped bring interactions between Hanoi and Washington on normalization back to the bilateral context. Nonetheless, a divergence in, and, at times, misunderstanding of each other's strategic intent continued to hinder Vietnam–U.S. engagement.

The administration of George H.W. Bush, which entered office in early 1989, sought contact with Hanoi in 1990 in an effort to reach consensus on a final political agreement on Cambodia. The administration was also motivated by Vietnam's continued collaboration on POW/MIA issues as Hanoi had since 1987 returned hundreds of sets of remains of U.S. servicemen. Yet the still politically charged issue within U.S. society of whether there were remaining Americans held in captivity in Vietnam, and whether Hanoi was warehousing U.S. remains or withholding important information, continued to seize the attention of some members of Congress, veteran organizations, and a slew of non-governmental interest groups (Sutter 1996).

For the Bush administration, this means the ultimate prize in working with Vietnam lied in extracting an expanded cooperation on POW/MIA issues and expedite a Cambodia solution, with the possibility of normalizing U.S.–Vietnam ties being used as a bargaining chip. Many in Hanoi perceived this to be a lack of seriousness about normalization on the part of Washington, while a large swath of senior Vietnamese leaders were sceptical of the strategic benefits to Vietnam, if any, for satisfying U.S. demands on these two issues (Stern 2005, pp. 7–12).

Vietnamese leaders, meanwhile, faced much bigger domestic issues than figuring out a way forward with their former enemy. The implosion of the Soviet Union — with it the end of Soviet largesse — and the collapse of communist regimes across Eastern Europe posed an existential threat to the CPV, which had been struggling to plant the roots of *Doi Moi*, retrain and instil morale in its cadres, clean the party of corrupt elements, and assert power at the same time that it allowed decentralized economic decision-making. The ongoing debate since the end of the sixth Party congress between those who wanted to see *Doi Moi* implemented more rapidly and those who were more cautious about the pace of change peaked in the months leading up to the seventh Party congress. The discourse that resulted would be cast in favour of the cautious reformists (Stern 1993, pp. 91–133).

Hanoi's view of its engagement with Washington was placed against this backdrop. The ultimate prize for Vietnam in dealing with the United States, especially as Hanoi endeavoured to get the fledgling Vietnamese economy to take off, is the lifting of the U.S. trade embargo against Vietnam and Washington's nod for international financial institutions (IFIs) to extend assistance to Hanoi. The leadership calculated that Hanoi's withdrawal from Cambodia would automatically help unlock economic relations with the West and access to loans from IFIs, and attract foreign investment (Stern 1993).

The asymmetry in U.S. and Vietnamese strategic priorities, however, turned out to be a source of disappointment and frustration for both sides. Nonetheless, this period witnessed the most momentous developments in personal trust building between the two former adversaries, culminating in the normalization of diplomatic relations in 1995.

Leadership changes at the seventh CPV congress created a more oriented foreign policymaking apparatus in Hanoi, and clarified for the first time since the launch of *Doi Moi* — at the highest level — the objectives of Vietnam's new foreign policy. Do Muoi was elected to the position of general secretary, replacing Nguyen Van Linh. Linh, an adroit politician but who by 1990 became consumed with walking a fine line to appease both conservatives and reformists, delivered little of substance and took little interest in how foreign policy was conducted. Thach, who commanded outsized influence over foreign policy before falling out with his peers over what they perceived as his hastened approach toward Washington, was removed as foreign minister and from his Politburo seat. The seventh Party congress resulted in an upper hand for the Ministry of National Defence, the People's Army of Vietnam, and the Ministry of Interior in terms of representation on the Central Committee and Politburo, an unmistakable signal that *Doi Moi* would go ahead but only at a pace which the most conservative elements could be comfortable with (Hiebert 1991, pp. 10–11; Stern 1993, pp. 145–55; 2005, pp. 12–14).

At the institutional level, the seventh CPV congress ushered in greater discipline in foreign policy decision-making, giving the Party's External Affairs Commission a stake in formulating and reviewing policy in conjunction with the Ministry of Foreign Affairs. Whereas foreign policy was accorded a rather low priority under the previous leadership, shifting geopolitical circumstances during this period caused top Vietnamese leaders to pay greater attention to the outside world. The election of new Foreign Minister Nguyen Manh Cam to the Politburo in 1994 reflected the growing importance accorded to foreign policy, as Vietnam sought to navigate a post-Cold War world order.

Do Muoi emphasized in a presentation on socio-economic priorities in 1990 the need for Vietnam to "expand relations with foreign countries to develop markets for Vietnamese products, attract increased foreign investment, and obtain access to foreign technology". As party chief, Muoi played an active role in clarifying and managing foreign policy issues, particularly those with regards to full normalization of ties with China, Vietnam–U.S. engagement, and POW/MIA cooperation with Washington (Stern 1993, pp. 121–22).

The end of hostility between China and Vietnam toward the latter half of 1991 provided the new leadership with more room for manoeuvrability. Contacts with Washington became a less risky gamble than during the early years of *Doi Moi*. However, party leaders still held out little hope for any quick normalization with Washington. Meanwhile, even Foreign Ministry officials who were committed to moving Vietnam–U.S. relations forward and willing to accommodate greater assistance in POW/MIA to the United States were careful not to play up the importance of their talks with U.S. counterparts (Stern 2005).

Following three high-level meetings in 1990, including a discussion between Thach and U.S. Secretary of State James Baker, the United States in April 1991 presented the Vietnamese mission to the UN a "road map" for bilateral normalization (Sutter 1996). From the U.S. perspective, the road map showed the Bush administration's willingness to reciprocate Hanoi's helpfulness on POW/MIA and Cambodia issues. Yet, for Vietnam's leadership, the document, which conditioned U.S. actions to reward Vietnam on political progress in Cambodia, put Vietnam at a strategic disadvantage and violated its sacrosanct principles of sovereignty and non-interference. Hand-wringing between the two sides — Hanoi to reconfigure the contours of the road map and Washington to stick to the principles of the document, even if only ostensibly — would play out in the years to follow.

An important force during this period, which Hanoi skilfully deployed in its interactions with Washington, was a growing pressure among U.S. companies and business associations on the U.S. government to lift the trade embargo and business restrictions against Vietnam. Meanwhile, Singaporean Prime Minister Lee Kuan Yew summed up the situation facing

Vietnam in an exchange with Prime Minister Vo Van Kiet in Davos in 1990: "Vietnam's economy could not take off until the United States signalled the World Bank to extend soft loans for its rehabilitation and the big U.S. banks decided that Vietnam was an acceptable risk" (Lee 2000, p. 312).

The interagency working group within the U.S. government in charge of Vietnam policy issues, however, was dominated by the Department of Defence, and showed little appetite for Hanoi's push on lifting the trade embargo. It was regular contacts with U.S. Senators John Kerry and Bob Smith, who were chair and vice-chair of the Senate Select Committee on POW/MIA Affairs, through 1992 and 1993 that brought Hanoi crucial opportunities to make the case that Vietnam was more cooperative on the search for MIAs than it was given credit for, and it was time for Washington to reciprocate Hanoi's efforts. The Senate Select Committee on POW/MIA Affairs, established in October 1991, had a one-year mandate to produce a report on the fate of over 2,265 U.S. servicemen then still unaccounted for from the Vietnam War.

Kerry, who was given access to prisons, military installations, and war museums during his visits to Vietnam and Laos in November 1992, urged Washington to show "reciprocity" as a way of acknowledging expanding Vietnamese cooperation on the POW/MIA issue, hinting at the possibility of easing the trade embargo but stopping short of suggesting normalization (Wallace 1992). Kerry also managed to convince the Bush administration that there are actions Washington can take to show "flexibility" in light of recent overtures from Hanoi. On 1 December 1992, the Bush administration allowed U.S. companies to open representative offices in Vietnam and sign contracts that could only be executed following the lifting of the embargo (Stern 2005, pp. 19–22). While some in Hanoi saw the announcement as a positive development, Vietnamese leaders could not help but feel that nothing would put the issue of POW/MIA to rest with Americans, at a time when Hanoi was hoping to extract more substantive economic deliverables from Washington to help *Doi Moi* take off.[3]

Kerry continued to play a pivotal role in trust building and channelling high-level communications between the two sides, especially as a sense of cynicism about the payoffs of engaging Washington threatened to set in in Hanoi, even among those in favour of normalization. The Senate Select Committee submitted its final report on 13 January 1993, affirming that "there is, at this time, no compelling evidence that proves that any American remains alive in captivity in Southeast Asia" (U.S. Senate 1993). Kerry returned to Vietnam again in 1993 to convey his commitment to deliver the lifting of the trade embargo in exchange for Hanoi to hand over *specific* POW/MIA information, a message his Vietnamese interlocutors did not count much on (Stern 2005, pp. 26–27).

The new U.S. President, Bill Clinton, refused during his first months in office to commit to a forward-leaning approach toward Hanoi on POW/MIA issues. But he soon dispatched Gen. Vessey to Hanoi in April 1993, and decided in July 1993 not to oppose efforts by Japan, France, and others to settle Vietnam's arrears with the International Monetary Fund and the World Bank (Wallace 1993). As business pressure to lift the trade embargo grew louder, congressional delegations and senior administration officials paid visits to Vietnam through 1993 to evaluate progress in POW/MIA issues and ways to advance "American interests" and "influence" in Vietnam, marking a change in Washington's tone (Day 1993; Sutter 1996). The two countries also broadened cooperation in areas such as consular and humanitarian issues — a signal not lost on Hanoi that the Clinton administration was open to widening the space for dialogue.

Yet, the White House's decision to renew the Trading with the Enemy Act against Vietnam later in 1993 dealt a blow to the fragile trust built over the previous two years, and prompted the majority of leaders in Hanoi to conclude that Washington was not serious in its intent toward Vietnam.[4] High-level meetings — between Secretary of State Warren Christopher and Deputy Prime Minister Phan Van Khai in New York in October 1993, and between Assistant Secretary of State for Asia and the Pacific Winston Lord and senior Vietnamese officials in Hanoi in December 1993 — were touted as productive but seemed unable to produce any major breakthroughs.

In the end, it was the palpable pressure from businesses and a concerted show of support from the Senate that led the administration to consider lifting the trade embargo more seriously. For example, Senator John Kerry, Senator John McCain, and other members of Congress involved in veteran and POW/MIA affairs voted on a non-binding resolution in January 1994 urging Clinton to lift the embargo (Greenhouse 1994).

Against this backdrop, on 3 February 1994, Clinton ordered the removal of provisions imposed on Vietnam under the Trading with the Enemy Act, effectively lifting the trade embargo. The importance of this decision cannot be overstated. It injected confidence into the stalemate of

U.S.–Vietnam relations and helped convince Vietnamese officials in the Party Central Committee, the Defence Ministry, the People's Army, and the Ministry of Interior that the United States was not out to humiliate Vietnam after all. Following the lifting of the embargo, even the most orthodox elements in Hanoi became less ardent about their past narrative that Washington would never give anything strategic in return for Hanoi's efforts.[5] A more open atmosphere on POW/MIA cooperation led the Veterans of Foreign Wars of the United States to throw its support behind the normalization of ties with Vietnam in June 1995. One month later, President Clinton announced the restoration of diplomatic ties with the unified Vietnam on 11 July, thereby opening a new, promising, but just as challenging era in bilateral relations.

From Normalization until 2006

While the normalization of diplomatic relations was historically significant, a climate of uncertainty about where the nascent relationship was headed still prevailed on both sides. During the immediate years after normalization, the United States was careful to portray that POW/MIA issues should still remain at the centre stage of the relationship even as the two sides expanded talks to other areas unrelated to war legacy.[6] Vietnamese leaders, meanwhile, viewed diplomatic normalization as a necessary condition for normalization of economic relations and to set a new stage in engagement with Washington that would be conducive to Hanoi's own reform and international integration agenda.

The drawn-out process of normalization unmistakably left a legacy of mistrust between the two sides. Many in Hanoi were still under the impression that Washington was more interested in exacting concessions from Hanoi on issues of U.S. interest than in building a relationship based on mutual respect and understanding.[7] In the words of a senior U.S. official when explaining Washington's demand that Hanoi settle past debts incurred by the Saigon regime, "the Vietnamese leaders have a clear economic agenda [...] and they knew that resolving this debt issue was one of the hurdles they had to get past before they get the trading rights they want" (Sanger 1997).

In contrast, Vietnam's normalization of relations with China was more straightforward, with both sides agreeing to shelve difficult issues for the future and focus on immediate areas of cooperation. For Hanoi, which was searching for a new equilibrium for its post-Cold War open-door foreign policy, building diversified and balanced relationships with all foreign powers was seen to be of paramount importance.

For most of this period, U.S. officials paid little attention to the strategic role Vietnam could play in the region, reflecting the view of many in Washington that Southeast Asia was an auxiliary to U.S.–China relations in the post-Cold War years. When Secretary of State Warren Christopher visited Hanoi in August 1995, he had two key messages: Vietnam would need to negotiate a bilateral trade agreement with the United States before being granted the Most Favoured Nation (MFN) status by Washington; and it was important for the two countries to have a dialogue on human rights issues as a means of deepening ties (Ahearn and Sutter 1996). In the absence of larger shared strategic interests, the two governments worked together during the decade after normalization to advance economic and trade cooperation, which fortuitously fit with Vietnam's reform objectives and came to be the driving force of bilateral relations.

Those in Hanoi who were always ambivalent about the United States saw normalization as a precursor for Washington to pressure Hanoi on democracy and human rights issues, and more dangerously, spurring the process of "peaceful evolution" in Vietnam. Yet, so great was the impetus of *Doi Moi* that Vietnam's leadership had little hesitation about going through what turned out to be a long and difficult process with Washington to conclude the Bilateral Trade Agreement (BTA), which was required before the Clinton administration could request the U.S. Congress to grant Vietnam with the Permanent Normal Trade Relations (PNTR) status. U.S. negotiators also made clear they would need to reach a BTA with Vietnam first before supporting its accession to the WTO. With economic growth and foreign investment inflows beginning to slow in the aftermath of the 1997 Asian Financial Crisis, Vietnam's leadership concluded that increased U.S. investment and access to U.S. market would be crucial for Vietnam's growth (Manyin 2002).

Talks on the BTA thus began in 1996. Frequent contacts during this period, both at the senior and working levels, played a major role in helping institutionalize government-to-government engagement. In particular, the U.S.–Vietnam Trade Council, a body formed in 1989, was crucial in helping socialize Vietnamese officials to new ideas of standards and mechanisms of a market economy. The Council did this by conducting countless study missions in both countries for Vietnamese officials, and working alongside U.S. government agencies to boost technical and legal assistance for Vietnam.[8] The BTA was signed in 2000, and Vietnam's National Assembly ratified the deal in November 2001, a delay that U.S. officials attributed primarily to internal tension between reformists and more conservative elements in Hanoi about the pace of economic integration (Manyin 2002).

Nonetheless, the completion of the BTA gave faith to Vietnamese leaders and provided at least a foundation for the U.S. support for Vietnam's accession to the WTO. The two sides reached a bilateral agreement on Vietnam's WTO accession package in May 2006, taking much longer than initially anticipated. Vietnam's accession to the WTO in January 2007, and the United States' granting of PNTR status to Vietnam in December 2006 — after a few false starts and stumbling blocks — helped improve mutual trust and add initial depth to the relationship (Manyin, Cooper, and Gelb 2006; *Thanh Nien News* 2006).

But while the trade and economic component of the relationship became gradually institutionalized, the first serious military-to-military contacts during this period showed that strategic trust between Hanoi and Washington was still dismal. Normalization of relations encouraged the Ministry of Defence and the People's Army to adopt a more forward-leaning stance on POW/MIA cooperation. But by the same token, Hanoi did not take kindly to the fact that Washington continued to put war legacy issues at the forefront of bilateral engagement. Vietnamese defence leaders were even more puzzled by U.S. suggestions not long after normalization to explore the potential for defence exchanges and engagement in a broader security context (Stern 2005, pp. 105–10). From Hanoi's perspective, this approach was getting ahead of what circumstances would have allowed. There was, for Vietnam's military leadership, little common ground at the time to warrant higher levels of investment into the security component of the relationship, while, in principle, there could be no normal military-to-military cooperation so long as Washington still imposed a lethal arms sales ban on Vietnam.

As the Political Report presented at the eighth CPV congress in late June of 1996 made clear, Vietnam's foremost foreign policy orientation for the period 1996–2000 was to help sustain the momentum of *Doi Moi* by creating favourable international conditions for domestic socio-economic development, and to diversify foreign relations in bilateral and multilateral settings. More specifically, the Political Report called for improving relations with ASEAN member countries, committing to a peaceful and stable Southeast Asia region, and expanding Vietnam's relations with traditional partners, including developing and non-aligned countries in Asia, Africa, Latin America, and elsewhere (CPV 1996). As Hanoi's focus was on sustaining the momentum of *Doi Moi*, and as the Vietnam People's Army continued to adjust to the demands of operating in a more fluid external environment, Vietnam's collective leadership was careful about agreeing to any initiatives — particularly with the United States — without deriving from it clear, serious strategic benefits. Guiding Vietnamese leaders' decision-making was a perennial concern of not allowing Vietnam to be used as a pawn among the major powers, especially in the context of China's rise in the Asia Pacific.

Following intense deliberations among Vietnamese officials and government ministries, Hanoi agreed to an inter-agency visit in October 1996 led by Deputy Assistant Secretary of Defence Kurt Campbell to test the waters and serve as an occasion for each side to put forth its own parameters of the future defence relationship. Campbell's visit turned out to be a valuable opportunity for Vietnamese leaders to hear and understand U.S. thinking on key regional security issues and for senior Vietnamese officials to communicate their own priorities and positions. The two sides shared views on, among other things, cross-strait relations, the then-simmering South China Sea dispute, and POW/MIA issues (Stern 2005, pp. 117–21). Campbell's visit became an example of a classic trust-building exercise between the two countries.

Campbell's visit, aided by more frequent working-level channels of communication, significantly helped to re-conceptualize U.S.–Vietnam security cooperation in a peacetime setting and against the backdrop of a fast-changing Asia-Pacific region. Secretary of Defence William Cohen visited Vietnam in March 2000, becoming the first U.S. Defence Secretary to do so since the end of the Vietnam War. In 2003, a week after Defence Minister Pham Van Tra's visit to the Pentagon, the USS *Vandegrift* became the first U.S. Navy ship to return to Vietnam since the end of the war, docking at a port in Ho Chi Minh City. In 2005, the U.S. government established an International Military Education Training programme for Vietnam's military officers, with a focus on humanitarian assistance/ disaster relief capacity building. Two presidential visits, one by President Clinton in November 2000 and the other by President George W. Bush in November 2006, were critical milestones in the process of fully normalizing all aspects of U.S.–Vietnam relations. In 2007, the Bush administration amended the International Traffic in Arms Regulations to enable exports of non-lethal weapons to Vietnam (U.S. Embassy in Hanoi, undated).

While marking the start of more institutionalized trust building, this period also witnessed the elevation of human rights into one of the top priorities of bilateral relations, a matter taken seriously by those in Hanoi worried about the threats of "peaceful evolution" and Washington's overall intent toward Vietnam. The U.S. House of Representatives indeed passed the Vietnam Human Rights Act H.R. 2833 by a vote of 410–1 on the same day it ratified the BTA, in none too subtle a message that Washington possesses the means to link trade with human rights issues when dealing with Hanoi (Manyin 2002, p. 8).

The early 2000s saw the most difficulties for bilateral engagement on human rights issues. The Vietnam Human Rights Act would be reintroduced in the Congress in 2003 and passed the year after over concerns about religious freedom in Vietnam's Central Highlands, and Vietnam was designated a Country of Particular Concern under the U.S. Religious Freedom Act in September 2004. Continuing U.S. pressure and criticisms, even as it sought to work with Vietnam on trade and security issues, reportedly antagonize conservatives in Hanoi. They were infuriated that Washington had done little to address the war legacy in Vietnam (e.g., Vietnam's own MIA issue, unexploded ordnance, Agent Orange) while heaping excessive demands upon Hanoi to help it locate missing American servicemen and adopt changes that might shake the very foundation of Vietnam's political system.[9] During these years, tension dominated in any discussions on human rights issues, with the Vietnamese government viewing U.S. actions as an interference in its internal affairs.

However, the end of this period witnessed a turnaround, even if tactically, in human rights engagement, whereby Hanoi and Washington signed an accord on religious freedom a month before Prime Minister Phan Van Khai's visit to the White House in June 2005 (*NBC News* 2006). The two sides resumed annual bilateral talks on human rights in early 2006, following a three-year hiatus due to what the U.S. side termed as "insufficient progress" on key issues by Vietnam (*Sai Gon Giai Phong* 2006).

From 2006 to Present

The familiarity built through BTA and WTO negotiations, as well as the initial comfort level attained through the establishment of military-to-military contacts, provided a foundation for the United States and Vietnam to enter an era of fast changing geopolitical developments in Asia. For Vietnamese leaders, the core of the relationship should ideally lie in deepening economic ties through trade and investment, hence contributing to Vietnam's development and reform agenda.[10] Vietnam has partly achieved this goal as its exports to the United States have grown exponentially since its WTO accession, reaching more than US$38.5 billion in 2016 from a low base of US$12.5 billion in 2007. Yet a major shift in Vietnam–U.S. relations began in the mid-2000s due to both sides' concerns about a rising China and its activities in the South China Sea.

While China and the South China Sea situation were covered in the very first bilateral engagements after normalization, the China question has only become pronounced recently. From the perspective of Vietnamese leaders, understanding Washington's views regarding its strategic interests in Asia and its relations with Beijing was vital for the formulation of Hanoi's strategy toward Washington. Hanoi also prefers not to let its emerging partnership with Washington be seen as an attempt to target any third parties, one of the key tenets of Vietnam's defence policy.[11] From the perspective of Washington during the early 2000s, although ties had begun to take on more depth, Vietnam was seen to be of little strategic importance to the United States as long as security and geopolitical threats posed by China to U.S. predominance in the Western Pacific remained dormant.

But with China's expansionist drive in the South China Sea becoming more visible since 2009, and as the Obama administration looked to rebalance U.S. foreign policy to the Asia Pacific soon after taking office, the United States and Vietnam have come to quickly share a common strategic interest in preserving regional stability and the maritime security in the South China Sea. This regional context became the backdrop against which Hanoi and Washington began to deepen their strategic engagements.

Secretary of State Hillary Clinton, who was in charge of implementing the rebalance during Obama's first term, raised with Vietnamese officials the possibility of upgrading bilateral relations to a "strategic partnership" early on in the rebalance (*Vietnam Plus* 2011). U.S. officials have now come to see a strong Vietnam that can exercise its strategic autonomy as being crucial to U.S. strategy in the region. In the aftermath of the *Haiyang Shiyou* 981 oil rig crisis in mid-2014, more and more Vietnamese leaders long ambivalent about relations with the United States have recognized the necessity of boosting Hanoi's strategic manoeuvrability and making overtures to Washington where appropriate (see, for example, Nguyen 2015*a*).

However, the factors that strained the relationship during previous periods — the still mighty narrative on "peaceful evolution" in Hanoi and the conundrum over human rights issues — remain a sticking point in bilateral ties. Ironically, while it was China's growing assertiveness in the region that gave a new impetus to U.S.–Vietnam relations, Vietnamese leaders have also become more uneasy than ever before about the possibility of getting caught between the two major powers — a by-product of the legacy of mistrust toward U.S. grand strategy and great power politics (Nguyen 2015b).

These sometimes contradictory systemic forces form the background of current U.S.–Vietnam engagement. It is no coincidence that Vietnam's leadership continuously stresses the need for the United States to take actions designed to foster greater mutual trust and prove that it sees Vietnam as a serious, long-term partner before the two sides can agree on expanded cooperation in specific areas. In the Vietnamese psyche, China's seizure of the Paracel Islands from then U.S.-backed South Vietnam was a consequence of Washington's rapprochement with Beijing two years earlier. Likewise, China's bloody incursion against Vietnam on Johnson South Reef in 1988 could not have been carried out without U.S. acquiescence, even if tacitly (Nguyen 2015b). In other words, while the areas of mistrust have shrunken, the strategic stakes for Vietnam have grown higher, causing the imperative for greater confidence building to become even more pressing than in the past.

In February 2009, two years after Vietnam became a WTO member, it joined talks on the Trans-Pacific Partnership (TPP) trade agreement as an associate member. It was a vital decision that helped push U.S.–Vietnam cooperation further along. A number within Vietnam's leadership understood that the country would need to undertake drastic reforms to turn the broad-based economic growth delivered by *Doi Moi* thus far into high-quality growth, further expand market access for Vietnam's exports, integrate Vietnam deeper into the global economy, and ultimately, reduce its economic dependence on China (Bland and Donnan 2015). The TPP is seen as a structural and strategic tool to achieve these objectives; and Washington has strongly backed Hanoi's interest in being part of the agreement from the start.

But within Hanoi, the decision to embrace the TPP wholeheartedly was not without controversy. The long-established U.S. policy of linking trade to human rights in its dealings with Vietnam left a legacy of suspicion that required significant consensus building domestically and trust building between the two governments to overcome. For Vietnam, joining the TPP means it will have to comply with international labour standards, grant workers the freedom to associate, and loosen the Party's grip on and the state-sanctioned labour union's monopoly over the Vietnamese workforce. As recent as 2015, as negotiations were nearing conclusion, some Vietnamese leaders were still wary of the TPP's impacts on Vietnam.[12] In this context, the visit to the United States by CPV General Secretary Nguyen Phu Trong in July 2015 was seen by Hanoi as a historic milestone in establishing mutual strategic trust. For the CPV, the visit was needed to prove Washington's pledge that both sides respect "each other's political systems, independence, sovereignty, and territorial integrity" (The White House 2013). Receiving Vietnam's party chief in the White House in accordance with diplomatic protocol reserved for a head of state — not a small concession on the part of Washington — sent the signal that Washington recognizes the CPV as a legitimate force and does not seek to dislodge it. Obama himself later emphasized the significance of his meeting with Trong in the Oval Office in July 2015, saying that "We just moved the Vietnamese Communist Party to recognize labour rights in a way that we could never do by bullying them or scaring them" (Goldberg 2016).

Following this meeting, U.S. and Vietnamese negotiators reached an agreement on concrete steps for Vietnam to legalize independent labour unions under the TPP. Most notably, Trong's decision to highlight the TPP's importance and throw his support behind it on the eve of the twelfth CPV congress in February 2016 was evidence that joint trust-building efforts helped affect the thinking of even the most conservative elements in Hanoi. The current regional geopolitical environment seems to have caused liberal reformists and conservatives to converge on the need to move more closely to the United States; where they differ is over the pace at which to proceed and how to do so without alarming China unnecessarily. Yet there is little doubt that the decision of President Donald Trump in early 2017 to withdraw the United States from the TPP dealt a blow to those in Hanoi who had long argued for it, and would again serve for many others as another example of the risks that excessive reliance on Washington, in whatever respect, may bring Vietnam.

Meanwhile, although remaining a source of friction in the relationship, human rights issues have also witnessed progress. Bilateral talks on human rights have become regularized and institutionalized with the tone turning from confrontational to frank and constructive. This is due primarily to Hanoi's recognition that the promotion of human rights is part and parcel of U.S. foreign policy, even if its leadership may never be able to entirely shake off its suspicion of U.S. intent. As for Washington, U.S. officials have found ways to widen the scope of human rights talks with Hanoi to include areas such as legal reform, rule of law, and disability rights, in lieu of past practices of focusing exclusively on treatment of political dissidents, freedom of expression, and religious freedom, in an effort to find more common ground.[13]

A crucial area in which the two sides have significantly stepped up cooperation during this period is military-to-military cooperation. Following initial efforts to expand military-to-military engagement beyond POW/MIA issues and to include military medicine, humanitarian assistance/disaster relief, and demining cooperation in the early 2000s, the two sides made great strides in incorporating cooperation at the defence policy level into the relationship, and laying the foundation for regularized exchanges and joint operational activities in the areas of maritime security and maritime law enforcement.

Simultaneously, from the perspective of Vietnamese military officials, recent progress made does not mean Vietnam–U.S. military ties have been fully normalized until Washington fully removes its embargo on lethal arms sale to Vietnam. Although the Obama administration partially lifted the ban in October 2014, Vietnamese leaders were convinced to varying degrees that the remaining ban was, once again, an issue of lack of strategic trust (Hiebert and Nguyen 2016). This last barrier was removed when President Barack Obama visited Vietnam in May 2016 and announced the full lifting of the ban.

As in previous periods, high-level visits continue to be the hallmark of bilateral relations. They act both as trust-building exercises and action-forcing events. For instance, Chairman of the Joint Chiefs of Staff Gen. Martin Dempsey paid a prominent visit to Hanoi, Danang, and Ho Chi Minh City in the weeks leading up to Washington's announcement of the partial lifting of the arms ban. Prior to Dempsey's visit, senior leaders of the U.S. Pacific Command — including from the Pacific Fleet, the Pacific Air Forces, and the Army Pacific — had all passed through Hanoi. Two other eminent congressional delegations — led by Sen. McCain and Sen. Bob Corker — also stopped in Vietnam shortly before Dempsey's visit. McCain subsequently played a leading role in orchestrating congressional support behind the executive decision to remove the arms sale ban (McCain 2016).

Meanwhile, the visit of President Sang to the United States in July 2013, during which he and Obama elevated bilateral ties to a "comprehensive partnership", paved the way for more regular channels of exchange between the two governments at all levels, and notably, between the CPV and U.S. political parties and civil society. Whatever the Party's misgivings about U.S. intent are, the fact that its leaders agreed to expose rising party cadres to U.S. society, political system, and institutions on a regularized basis reflects the increasing strategic trust between the two former enemies.

An increasingly potent force that has helped strengthen bilateral relations is public opinion inside Vietnam about the United States and the direction of the partnership. According to the 2015 Pew Global Attitudes survey, a whopping 78 per cent of Vietnamese surveyed said they have a favourable view of the United States, while 69 per cent prefer strong economic ties with the United States, and 71 per cent welcome increased U.S. military presence in Asia (Pew Research Center 2015a, 2015c). In contrast, only 19 per cent of those surveyed hold a favourable view toward China and 18 per cent prefer strong economic ties with China, while 74 per cent of Vietnamese respondents believe it is important to be tough with China on territorial disputes (Pew Research Center 2015a, 2015b). A study by the Vietnam Academy of Social Sciences conducted in 2015 produced even more striking results: nearly 92 per cent of Vietnamese surveyed expressed a favourable view of the United States, and interestingly, 30 per cent of respondents believe that progress in Vietnam–U.S. relations has been slower than expected (Loi 2015).

This trend has not been lost on U.S. officials, and there is across-the-board consensus in Washington that investing in Vietnam's youth and education system will pay strategic dividends for U.S. standing in Vietnam in the long run. There have been simmering concerns within the CPV leadership that growing U.S. soft power might be utilized as a tool for "peaceful evolution". It is unclear how Hanoi will take into account the currents of public opinion in its future foreign policymaking, or at what point conservative elements within the leadership might grow more apprehensive of this trend.

Conclusion

In the words of a senior Vietnamese official, the United States and Vietnam have transformed the nature, scope, and depth of their relationship. The two countries went from being enemies to being partners, and from engaging exclusively on issues related to war legacy to charting a forward-leaning path of deeper cooperation, both bilaterally and regionally.

This journey was made possible by consistent efforts to narrow the areas of mistrust — which were overwhelming at the start of *Doi Moi* — and replace them with shared interests and mutually built trust. The concept of strategic trust has been and will continue to be central to the trajectory of Vietnam–U.S. relations. It is clear that without the dynamics ushered in by *Doi Moi*, it would have been impossible for Hanoi and Washington to begin such a search for common ground and strategic trust.

Today, the areas of divergence between the two have shrunken significantly, but remaining areas of mistrust, especially over the human rights issue, are fundamental and structural, making them perhaps more intractable to address. At the same time, given the increasingly uncertain regional geostrategic landscape, the incentives for the United States and Vietnam to build further mutual trust and strengthen their partnership will likely continue to stay strong.

NOTES

1. For more information on bilateral normalization, see Manyin (2005).
2. Interviews with former U.S. government officials and individuals outside the U.S. government involved in the normalization process.
3. Interviews with individuals in the United States familiar with the normalization process.
4. Although the Clinton administration still maintained the trade embargo on Vietnam in late 1993, it moved to allow U.S. companies to bid for Vietnamese projects funded by international financial institutions.
5. Interviews with individuals familiar with the normalization process and U.S.–Vietnam bilateral relations.
6. For the debate on U.S. interests and policy approaches toward Vietnam following normalization, see Sutter (1996).
7. For the internal debate on Vietnam's new open-door foreign policy and post-Cold War relations with the United States, see Thayer (1999, pp. 10–17).
8. Interviews with individuals closely involved in U.S.–Vietnam bilateral relations.
9. Interviews with Vietnamese analysts and former U.S. officials.
10. Interviews with Vietnamese officials and analysts.
11. Vietnam's contemporary defense policy emphasizes three no's — no military alliances, no foreign bases on Vietnamese territory, and no use of relations with one country to oppose another.

12. Off-the-record discussions with U.S. officials.
13. Exchanges with U.S. officials.

REFERENCES

Ahearn, Raymond J. and Robert G. Sutter. "Vietnam: Economic/Political Developments and U.S. Relations". *CRS Report 96-898*, 22 November 1996.

Becker, Elizabeth. "Vietnam Circles Slightly Closer to Military Ties to U.S." *New York Times*, 27 April 2000. Available at <http://www.nytimes.com/2000/4/27/world/vietnam-circles-slightly-closer-to-military-ties-to-us.html> (accessed 19 June 2016).

Bland, Ben and Shawn Donnan. "Vietnam Looks for Reform and Investment Boost from TPP Deal". *Financial Times*, 6 October 2015. Available at <https://www.ft.com/content/e104d4b8-6c11-11e5-aca9-d87542bf8673> (accessed 19 June 2016).

Communist Party of Vietnam (CPV). "Nghị quyết Đại hội đại biểu toàn quốc lần thứ VI Đảng Cộng sản Việt Nam (Ngày 18 tháng 12 năm 1986)", 1986. Available at <http://dangcongsan.vn/tu-lieu-van-kien/van-kien-dang/van-kien-dai-hoi/khoa-vi/doc-592420154022856.html> (accessed 12 July 2017).

———. "Báo cáo Chính trị của Ban Chấp hành Trung ương Đảng khóa VII tại Đại hội đại biểu toàn quốc lần thứ VIII của Đảng", 1996. Available at <http://dangcongsan.vn/tu-lieu-van-kien/van-kien-dang/van-kien-dai-hoi/khoa-viii/doc-292420154134156.html> (accessed 12 July 2017).

Day, J.S. "Muskie Urges Normalization Toward Vietnam, Administration Holding Out for POW Disclosure". *The Bangor Daily News*, 23 June 1993. Available at <http://archive.bangordailynews.com/1993/06/23/muskie-urges-normalization-toward-vietnam-administration-holding-out-for-pow-disclosure/> (accessed 19 June 2016).

Downie, Sue. "Vietnam, U.S. Ties Possible". *The Sun-Sentinel*, 13 April 1989. Available at <http://articles.sun-sentinel.com/1989-04-13/news/8901190536_1_vietnam-war-health-clinics-vietnamese> (accessed 19 June 2016).

Erlanger, Steven. "Vietnam Promises Troops Will Leave Cambodia by Fall". *New York Times*, 6 April 1989. Available at <http://www.nytimes.com/1989/04/06/world/vietnam-promises-troops-will-leave-cambodia-by-fall.html> (accessed 19 June 2016).

Goldberg, Jeffrey. "The Obama Doctrine". *The Atlantic*, April 2016. Available at <http://www.theatlantic.com/magazine/archive/2016/04/the-obama-doctrine/471525/> (accessed 19 June 2016).

Greenhouse, Steven. "Senate Urges End to U.S. Embargo Against Vietnam". *New York Times*, 28 January 1994. Available at <http://www.nytimes.com/1994/01/28/world/senate-urges-end-to-us-embargo-against-vietnam.html> (accessed 19 June 2016).

Hiebert, Murray. "Party Congress Switches Leaders but Skirts Policy Issues: More of the Same". *Far Eastern Economic Review* (11 July 1991).

Hiebert, Murray and Phuong Nguyen. "Fully Lifting the U.S. Lethal Arms Ban Will Add Momentum to U.S.–Vietnam Relations". *CSIS Commentary*, 12 May 2016. Available at <https://www.csis.org/analysis/fully-lifting-us-lethal-arms-ban-will-add-momentum-us-vietnam-relations> (accessed 12 July 2017).

Holley, David. "Vietnam, China Reveal Meeting of Top Leaders". *Los Angeles Times*, 18 September 1990. Available at <http://articles.latimes.com/1990-09-18/news/mn-614_1_vietnam-war> (accessed 19 June 2016).

Krauss, Clifford. "Vietnam Agrees to Expand Efforts on U.S. Missing". *New York Times*, 18 October 1990. Available at <http://www.nytimes.com/1990/10/18/world/vietnam-agrees-to-expand-efforts-on-us-missing.html> (accessed 19 June 2016).

Kupchan, Charles A. *How Enemies Become Friends: The Sources of Stable Peace*. Princeton: Princeton University Press, 2010.

Lee Kuan Yew. *From Third World to First: The Singapore Story (1965–2000)*. New York: HarperCollins, 2000.

Loi, Cu Chi. "Public Opinion is Strong Foundation for Future U.S.–Vietnam Relations". *CSIS CogitAsia*, 22 July 2015. Available at <http://cogitasia.com/public-opinion-is-strong-foundation-for-future-u-s-vietnam-relations/> (accessed 12 July 2017).

Manyin, Mark E. "The Vietnam–.S. Bilateral Trade Agreement". *CRS Report RL30416* (9 September 2002).

———. "The Vietnam–U.S. Normalization Process". *CRS Report IB98033* (17 June 2005). Available at <https://www.fas.org/sgp/crs/row/IB98033.pdf>.

Manyin, Mark E., William H. Cooper, and Bernard A. Gelb. "Vietnam PNTR Status and WTO Accession: Issues and Implications for the United States". *CRS Report RL33490* (2 August 2006). Available at <https://www.fas.org/sgp/crs/row/RL33490.pdf> (accessed 19 June 2016).

McCain, John. "Statement by Senator John McCain Regarding Vietnam", 18 May 2016. Available at <http://www.mccain.senate.gov/public/index.cfm/2016/5/statement-by-senator-john-mccain-on-president-obama-s-visit-to-vietnam> (accessed 12 July 2017).

NBC News. "Bush, Vietnam Leader Sign Religious Accord", 21 June 2006. Available at <http://www.nbcnews.com/id/8294202/ns/world_news-asia_pacific/t/bush-vietnam-leader-sign-religious-accord/> (accessed 19 June 2016).

Nguyen, Phuong. "Vietnam Eyes Greater International Integration — & That's Good News for the United States". *CSIS CogitAsia*, 15 October 2015a. Available at <http://cogitasia.com/vietnam-eyes-greater-international-integration-thats-good-news-for-the-united-states/> (accessed 19 June 2016).

———. "Vietnam's Careful Dance with the Superpowers". *East Asia Forum*, 21 January 2015b. Available at <http://www.eastasiaforum.org/2015/01/21/vietnams-careful-dance-with-the-superpowers/> (accessed 18 June 2016).

Pew Research Center. "Global Attitudes & Trends: Asia in Focus", 2015*a*. Available at <http://www.pewglobal.org/2015/06/23/3-asia-in-focus/>.

———. "Global Attitudes & Trends: Global Indicators Database—Opinion of China", 2015*b*. Available at <http://www.pewglobal.org/database/indicator/24/country/239/>.

———. "Global Attitudes & Trends: Global Indicators Database — Opinion of the United States", 2015*c*. Available at <http://www.pewglobal.org/database/indicator/1/country/239/>.

Sai Gon Giai Phong. "Vietnam, US Resume Human Rights Dialog to Strengthen Mutual Understanding", 24 February 2006. Available at <https://www.vietnambreakingnews.com/2006/02/viet-nam-us-resume-human-rights-dialog-to-strengthen-mutual-understanding/> (accessed 19 June 2016).

Sanger, David E. "Hanoi Agrees to Pay Saigon's Debts to U.S." *New York Times*, 11 March 1997. Available at <http://www.nytimes.com/1997/03/11/world/hanoi-agrees-to-pay-saigon-s-debts-to-us.html> (accessed 19 June 2016).

Solomon, Richard H. *Exiting Indochina: U.S. Leadership of the Cambodia Settlement & Normalization of Relations with Vietnam.* Washington: United States Institute of Peace Press, 2000.

Stern, Lewis M. *Renovating the Vietnamese Communist Party: Nguyen Van Linh and the Programme for Organizational Reform, 1987–91.* Singapore: Institute of Southeast Asian Studies, 1993.

———. *Defense Relations Between the United States and Vietnam: The Process of Normalization, 1977–2003.* Jefferson: McFarland & Company, 2005.

Sutter, Robert G. *Vietnam–U.S. Relations: The Debate Over Normalization.* California: University of California Libraries, 1996.

Thanh Nien News. "US Casts Doubt on Vietnam WTO Entry by Bush Visit", 2 October 2006. Available at <https://www.vietnambreakingnews.com/2006/10/us-casts-doubt-on-vietnam-wto-entry-by-bush-visit/> (accessed 19 June 2016).

Thayer, Carlyle A. "Vietnamese Foreign Policy: Multilateralism and the Threat of Peaceful Evolution". In *Vietnamese Foreign Policy in Transition*, edited by Carlyle A. Thayer and Ramses Amer. Singapore: Institute of Southeast Asia Studies, 1999, pp. 1–24.

The White House. "Joint Statement by President Barack Obama of the United States of America and President Truong Tan Sang of the Socialist Republic of Vietnam", 25 July 2013. Available at <http://www.whitehouse.gov/the-press-office/2013/07/25/joint-statement-president-barack-obama-united-states-america-and-preside> (accessed 29 August 2016).

Tuoi Tre News. "20 Years of Vietnam–U.S. Diplomatic Ties — P1: Untold Stories behind Normalization", 8 July 2015. Available at <http://tuoitrenews.vn/features/29106/untold-stories-behind-the-normalization-of-vietnamus-ties> (accessed 19 June 2016).

U.S. Embassy in Hanoi. "Defense Cooperation in Vietnam", undated. Available at <http://photos.state.gov/libraries/vietnam/8621/pdf-forms/15anniv-DAO-Factsheet.pdf> (accessed 12 July 2017).

U.S. Senate. "POW/MIA's Report of the Select Committee on POW/MIA Affairs: Executive Summary". *Senate Report 103–1* (13 January 1993). Available at <http://fas.org/irp/congress/1993_rpt/pow-exec.html> (accessed 19 June 2016).

Vietnam Plus. "US Ambassador Prioritises Economic Ties with Vietnam", 9 September 2011. Available at <http://en.vietnamplus.vn/us-ambassador-prioritises-economic-ties-with-vietnam/31073.vnp> (accessed 19 June 2016).

Wallace, Charles P. "Senators Cite Vietnam's MIA Aid, Ask Eased Embargo". *Los Angeles Times*, 22 November 1992. Available at <http://articles.latimes.com/1992-11-22/news/mn-2341_1_vietnam-war> (accessed 19 June 2016).

———. "Clinton Urged to Lift Vietnam Business Ban". *Los Angeles Times*, 6 July 1993. Available at <http://articles.latimes.com/1993-07-06/business/fi-10402_1_trade-embargo> (accessed 19 June 2016).

Zhang Xiaoming. *Deng Xiaoping's Long War: The Military Conflict between China and Vietnam, 1979–1991*. Chapel Hill: University of North Carolina Press, 2015.

4

The 2014 Oil Rig Crisis and its Implications for Vietnam–China Relations

Nguyen Thanh Trung and Truong-Minh Vu

In early May 2014, Chinese deep-water oil rig *Haiyang Shiyou* 981 (HYSY-981), accompanied by around eighty ships, started oil exploration activities at an area off Vietnam's central coast. Vietnam sent naval vessels to the area to prevent the stationing of the rig. Vietnamese authorities also said they would do everything they could to protect the country's sovereign rights and jurisdiction since the HYSY-981 was positioned well within the 200-nautical-mile exclusive economic zone (EEZ) measured from Vietnam's baseline. China responded by claiming that the rig was still inside China's waters measured from the Paracel Islands and within Beijing's maritime claims based on the nine-dash line.

The subsequent standoff, which lasted until July, witnessed a cat and mouse game between maritime law enforcement forces of the two countries, with naval vessels of both sides looming in the background. Chinese ships aggressively rammed and fired water cannons at Vietnamese vessels that were trying to obstruct the rig's operation. The crisis led to two deadly anti-China riots in Vietnam, and created a sense of brinksmanship in the country for weeks. Following the incident, strategic trust between the two countries fell to its lowest point since bilateral normalization in 1991.

The incident further reinforces Vietnam's perception of the China threat in the South China Sea where China has since the late 2000s become increasingly assertive. Over the years, Vietnam has taken various measures to counter China's pressures and to improve its strategic position vis-à-vis China in the South China Sea. In the wake of the crisis, Vietnam has even stronger motivations to step up these efforts and to adjust its domestic as well as foreign policies in anticipation of higher levels of coercion from China in the future.

This chapter analyses the impact of the 2014 oil rig crisis on Vietnam–China relations, focusing on Vietnam's responses to counter the growing threat from China after the crisis. The chapter first reviews the significance of territorial and maritime disputes as a sticking point in bilateral relations. It then details how the 2014 oil rig crisis evolved and discusses mechanisms and diplomatic efforts that Vietnam and China made to mend their relations during and after the crisis. Finally, the chapter investigates Vietnam's domestic and foreign policy responses after the incident to counter the China threat in the South China Sea.

We argue that the incident is a watershed in bilateral relations, causing Vietnam to step up its efforts to counter China's mounting pressures through four key measures: strengthening its relations with the United States and other major powers; reducing its economic vulnerabilities vis-à-vis China; stepping up the modernization of its navy and maritime law enforcement forces; and relaxing control over anti-China nationalism. These initiatives by Vietnam, as well as corresponding reactions by China and other regional powers, may further complicate the future trajectory of bilateral ties and add new dynamics to the shifting geopolitical landscape of the region.

Territorial and Maritime Disputes in Vietnam–China Relations

Vietnam was occupied by China for more than one thousand years until AD 938, and thereafter was in a constant struggle against repeated invasions from the northern juggernaut. Maintaining Vietnam's independence and autonomy against the China threat is therefore a recurring theme in Vietnam's history. The modern China and Vietnam established their diplomatic ties in January 1950 as communist allies, but their relations have not always been smooth since then.

In January 1974, China used force to capture the western part of the Paracel Islands from South Vietnam. In 1979, the two countries fought a brief yet bloody war, and nine years later, they engaged in a bloody naval clash in the Spratlys, which claimed the lives of sixty-four Vietnamese sailors. In 1991, Beijing and Hanoi restored diplomatic relations and took measures to remove obstacles to bilateral ties. The two countries signed multiple cooperation agreements and made significant efforts to resolve both land border and maritime disputes. They have also institutionalized a set of mechanisms of cooperation, including frequent exchanges of visits by state and party leaders, inter-governmental committees, as well as working groups at expert level.

In the post-normalization period, Hanoi managed to maintain a generally stable and peaceful relationship with Beijing. Bilateral economic cooperation also flourished and contributed significantly to Vietnam's domestic economic reforms. In particular, bilateral trade grew exponentially and China has been Vietnam's largest trade partner since 2004. In 2008, the two countries established a "comprehensive strategic cooperative partnership". At the same time, the two communist parties maintain regular dialogues and close cooperation.

In order to stabilize the relationship, soon after bilateral normalization, Vietnam and China took measures to solve their long-standing territorial and maritime disputes. On 19 October 1993, the two sides signed an agreement on the principles for settling disputes regarding their land border and the Tonkin Gulf. This agreement was the first successful attempt to resolve territorial and maritime disputes between the two countries. In December 1999, Hanoi and Beijing signed a treaty on land border demarcation after sixteen rounds of talks. One year later, in December 2000, the two countries signed an agreement on the delimitation of the Gulf of Tonkin, and another agreement on fishing cooperation in the Gulf. These agreements brought the optimism that bilateral territorial and maritime disputes in the South China Sea could eventually be resolved.

However, Vietnam and China still maintain conflicting claims over the Paracels and the Spratlys, as well as the surrounding waters. While the dispute over the Paracels is essentially bilateral, the Spratlys dispute is much more complicated with the involvement of four other claimants, namely the Philippines, Malaysia, Brunei, and Taiwan, which occupy various features in the archipelago.

Although the ideological affinity between the two countries has buffered their maritime tensions to a certain degree, the South China Sea disputes remain the most serious sticking point in bilateral ties that has the potential to develop into an armed conflict if incidents at sea are not well managed. Both sides have shown their strong determination in asserting their claims, and such incidents have happened more frequently in recent years. For example, before the 2014 oil rig crisis, Vietnamese authorities in 2011 twice accused Chinese boats of cutting cables of PetroVietnam's seismic surveying ships within Vietnam's claimed EEZ.

Against this backdrop, there is a lingering resentment in Vietnam against China's increasing maritime assertiveness in the South China Sea. Vietnam has repeatedly accused China of violating Vietnam's EEZ by such activities as imposing a unilateral fishing ban, chasing and ramming Vietnam's fishing boats, detaining Vietnamese fishermen, and harassing Vietnam's oil and gas exploration activities. To strengthen the legal grounds for Vietnam's claims in the South China Sea and guard against such encroachments by China, in June 2012, the Vietnamese National Assembly passed the Law of the Sea of Vietnam, which applies to the Paracels, the Spratlys as well as surrounding waters. Such efforts, however, tend to create even more tensions between the two countries as China also takes legal and administrative measures to substantiate its claims, and deploy its forces on the ground to challenge Vietnam's. The 2014 oil rig crisis can therefore be seen as the culmination of the rising maritime tensions between the two countries over the past decade.

The May 2014 Oil Rig Crisis

The standoff in May 2014 was an evidence of the two countries' increasing rivalry over not only competing sovereignty claims but also their race to exploit maritime resources in the South China Sea. The US$1 billion deep-water oil rig was believed to enhance China's ability to drill for oil and natural gas in the South China Sea where international oil firms have been rather hesitant to operate due to competing claims from regional states. In the first week of May 2014, the oil platform was spotted in an area around 17 nautical miles off the Paracels' Triton island and approximately 120 nautical miles off the coast of central Vietnam. The location of the oil rig is well within Vietnam's claimed EEZ. Hanoi therefore interpreted the stationing of the platform as a serious provocation and an obvious violation of its sovereign rights over the area. Meanwhile, China claimed that the oil rig was operating within the waters of the Paracels, hinting that certain features in the archipelago are qualified as islands and entitled to an EEZ of 200 nautical miles.[1]

A war of words between the two countries ensued over the status of the waters where the rig was stationed. The incident soon escalated to a new level when both countries sent coast guard vessels to the site. Vietnam sought to disrupt the rig's operations and China wanted to protect its maritime claims by chasing Vietnam's vessels away. Vietnam, whose flotilla was outnumbered and outgunned by China's fleet, accused China of ramming and firing water cannons at its vessels. China, in turn, accused Vietnam of provocations.

In an effort to "shame" China and rally international support, Vietnam allowed international journalists to board its vessels to the crisis location. Footages and news reports of the confrontation between the two countries' law enforcement forces were soon broadcast worldwide. Unlike other bilateral maritime incidents that had normally been covered up, the image of Chinese ships ramming and firing water cannons at Vietnamese vessels were broadcast widely to the Vietnamese public through mass media channels. A sense of brinksmanship was spread across the country for weeks and led to two serious anti-China riots in the provinces of Binh Duong and Ha Tinh. Angry Vietnamese protesters torched and looted many Taiwanese and South Korean factories that they mistook for Chinese ones.

During the crisis, the United States, Japan, the Philippines, India and Australia issued statements which either condemned China's actions or asked both parties to peacefully resolve the dispute in accord with international law. For example, the U.S. Senate passed a resolution (S. RES.412) on 10 July calling on China to withdraw the oil rig and accompanying ships (Thayer 2014a). Meanwhile, the U.S. State Department issued a statement describing China's deployment of the oil rig as a "provocative … unilateral action" that "appears to be part of a broader pattern of Chinese behaviour to advance its claims over disputed territory in a manner that undermines peace and stability in the region" (U.S. State Department 2014).

On 15 July, China announced that the oil rig was being withdrawn as its commercial exploration operations had been completed. The withdrawal came a full month before its original deadline of 15 August (Thayer 2014a). After China withdrew the rig, although bilateral ties gradually improved, the crisis has left serious dents in bilateral relations and worsened Vietnam's perception of China as well as Beijing's long-term intentions in the South China Sea.

Bilateral Mechanisms and Diplomatic Efforts to Mend Relations

Regional institutions in East Asia have not been efficient in mediating past standoffs or conflicts between regional states.[2] China and Vietnam therefore had to resort to bilateral channels to manage and resolve their disputes, which tends to favour China due to its greater power and leverage. Nevertheless, these bilateral mechanisms have produced certain successes, such as the 1999 land border treaty and the 2000 Tonkin Gulf delimitation agreement. In October 2011, the two sides also reached an Agreement on Basic Principles Guiding the Resolution of Maritime Issues (Wu and Hong 2014, p. 32). In 2012, Hanoi and Beijing initiated talks at the working level on the "demarcation of areas outside the mouth of the Gulf of Tonkin" (Amer 2015, p. 85). At the end of 2013, some preliminary cooperation in marine environment management was conducted near the gulf (Hai and Zhang 2014). Since then, however, there has been no further progress beyond these areas of cooperation.

Another notable institutional framework for China–Vietnam cooperation is the party-to-party mechanism. The ideological affinity between the two parties has facilitated the convergence of their interests in other spheres. In case state-to-state mechanisms cannot resolve tensions in a given bilateral crisis, the party-to-party channel is an avenue that the two sides can resort to. In bilateral settings, Vietnam is often supposed to be the first to make the conciliatory gestures due to its junior status in the dyad. However, deference might not work immediately since the stronger party may want to maintain its pressure on the junior partner to extract concessions.

After the oil rig incident started, Vietnamese Deputy Minister of Foreign Affairs Ho Xuan Son went to Beijing in an effort to defuse tensions, but no concrete results were achieved. One month later, State Councillor Yang Jiechi paid a visit to Vietnam to discuss the dispute, but, again, the two sides could not reach a settlement. After the oil rig had been withdrawn, Vietnamese Politburo member Le Hong Anh, in his capacity as a special envoy of Communist Party of Vietnam (CPV) General Secretary Nguyen Phu Trong, visited Beijing in late August. Anh's trip could be seen as a conciliatory gesture from Vietnam and a diplomatic success for Beijing as it signalled that Vietnam still complied with the bilateral mechanism of dispute management. During his talks with President Xi Jinping, Anh said that Vietnam would do its utmost to enhance mutual understanding and trust, and consolidate the comprehensive strategic partnership with China (*Global Times* 2014).

In October 2014, during a meeting between Chinese State Councillor Yang Jiechi and Vietnamese Minister of Foreign Affairs Pham Binh Minh, China and Vietnam agreed to use existing border dispute management mechanisms, such as the Steering Committee on Bilateral Cooperation and the Vietnam–China governmental-level negotiations on border and territorial issues, to find a solution to the South China Sea disputes. According to the joint statement issued after the meeting, "Vietnam–China relations developing healthily and stably is suitable with the desire and fundamental interests of the two countries, benefitting peace, stability and development. Both sides will together make an effort to seriously implement the agreements" (Nguyen and Blanchard 2014). Also in the same month, at the invitation of his

Chinese counterpart, Vietnamese Defence Minister, General Phung Quang Thanh, led a delegation of eleven senior generals and one admiral to visit Beijing. According to a Vietnamese account, the trip was to "strengthen friendly relations and comprehensive cooperation between the two armed forces and discuss measures to promote bilateral defence relations to maintain an environment of peace, stability, friendship and cooperation between the peoples and armies of the two countries" (Thayer 2014c).

In November 2014, Vietnamese President Truong Tan Sang met with President Xi Jinping on the sidelines of the 22nd Asia-Pacific Economic Cooperation (APEC) Meeting in Beijing in another effort to repair ties between the two countries. The next month, Chinese Communist Party Politburo Standing Committee member Yu Zhengsheng paid a visit to Vietnam. A series of high-level talks and visits within a short span of time following the crisis suggest that the two sides were interested in restoring their relations and preventing further deterioration of mutual trust.

However, the complex interplay of historical, economic, nationalist and geostrategic aspects of the South China Sea issue makes it extremely difficult for claimant states to find an effective mechanism for dispute resolution. With China and Vietnam holding firmly to their positions, the root cause of bilateral frictions in the South China Sea remains unaddressed, with open avenues for future incidents at sea.

From Vietnam's perspective, the country needs to maintain a stable relationship with China to facilitate its domestic development. But the 2014 oil rig crisis shows that the South China Sea issue is now Hanoi's s biggest security and foreign policy challenge. As the weaker nation in the dyad, Vietnam feels the larger impact whenever the relationship enters a state of disarray, which is likely to become more frequent with China's increasing maritime assertiveness. Therefore, following the 2014 oil rig crisis, Vietnam has gradually retuned its domestic and foreign policy to deal with the increasing maritime pressures from China. These responses can be grouped into four major categories: strengthening relations with the United States and other major powers; reducing economic vulnerabilities vis-à-vis China; stepping up the modernization of naval and maritime law enforcement forces; and relaxing control over anti-China nationalist sentiments.

Vietnam's Responses after the Crisis

Enhancing Relations with the United States and Other Regional Powers

The 2014 oil rig crisis created significant ramifications for both the Vietnam–China relationship and the overall geopolitical dynamics in Southeast Asia. As protecting national sovereignty has always been a source of legitimacy for the CPV and given the rising anti-China nationalist sentiments in the country, Vietnamese leaders faced domestic pressures to adopt a more assertive stance with regards to the South China Sea disputes. China's "bullying" behaviours during the crisis encouraged Hanoi to pursue stronger relationships with the great powers to balance against China's pressures.

As some Vietnamese strategists have suggested (see, for example, Cuong 2015; *VietTimes* 2016), only the United States is powerful enough to alter China's strategic designs towards the South China Sea and deter Beijing from using military force or coercion to settle the disputes. The 2014 oil rig incident was a catalyst that strengthened this perception and provided Hanoi with a strong rationale to justify its further rapprochement with Washington. Before the incident, Vietnamese leaders were divided on how fast Vietnam should develop its relations with the United States, but such divisions seemed to significantly diminish after May 2014. Vietnamese strategists realized that it is too difficult for Vietnam to resolve the South China Sea disputes on a bilateral basis with China. Without enhancing defence and security cooperation with the United States and other major powers, Vietnam will be at a significant disadvantage in dealing with China's maritime ambitions. A slow but steady move to strengthen military cooperation with the United States and other powers therefore became a strategic imperative for Hanoi.

In August 2014, just one month after the oil rig crisis ended, General Martin Dempsey became the first chairman of the Joint Chiefs of Staff of the United States to visit Vietnam since 1971. The visit helped to build trust and boost military-to-military relations between the two former foes. In October 2014, during the course of a visit by Vietnamese Minister of Foreign Affairs Pham Binh Minh to Washington, the United States announced the partial lifting of the longstanding U.S. embargo on lethal weapons sales to Vietnam. While the ban did not bring changes in Vietnam's arms procurement structure immediately, it indicates a move towards the full normalization of bilateral ties and paves the way for further military cooperation in the future. In February 2016, commander of the U.S. Pacific Command, Admiral Harry Harris Jr., suggested that the United States should lift all the remaining restrictions on weapons sales to Vietnam (Taylor 2016).

In July 2015, CPV General Secretary Nguyen Phu Trong paid a historic visit to the United States to further promote bilateral cooperation. As analysed by Phuong Nguyen in Chapter 3, the visit was a landmark in bilateral ties and a testimony of the growing political trust between the two former Cold War enemies. It was not a coincidence that growing tensions in the South China Sea were high on the agenda of the visit. Addressing the issue, Trong said that he hoped the "U.S. will continue to have appropriate voice and actions to contribute to peaceful settlement of disputes in the [South China Sea] in accordance with international law in order to ensure peace and stability in the Asia-Pacific and the world" (Neuman 2015). These words revealed Vietnam's view of the United States as a strategic balancer and a stabilizing force in Southeast Asia. Meanwhile, for Washington, deepening relations with Vietnam creates an opportunity for the Obama administration to strengthen its strategic rebalance to the Asia Pacific.

In early March 2016, Vietnam inaugurated a US$90-million international port facility in Cam Ranh Bay. This harbour was used by the United States during the Vietnam War and by the Soviet Union/ Russia from the late 1970s until 2002. The facility provides maintenance, refuelling and logistics service for foreign warships. Three U.S. naval ships visited the port as part of the bilateral Naval Engagement Activity (NEA) programme in 2016. Even though the port calls were publicized by both sides as technical visits, they can also be seen as a symbol of the deepening military ties between the two countries.

During his visit to Hanoi in May 2016, U.S. President Barack Obama announced the full lifting of the U.S. ban on sales of lethal arms to Vietnam. The move goes beyond symbolism as it does open up new avenues for bilateral defence cooperation and contributes to the strengthening of Vietnam's maritime capabilities. Although so far

Vietnam has not acquired any U.S. weapon system, Hanoi is reportedly interested in U.S. equipment that can help strengthen its maritime domain awareness, such as patrol boats and surveillance aircraft. In May 2017, Hanoi received six Metal Shark fast patrol boats worth US$18 million for its Coast Guard. The purchase was funded by U.S. aid. In the same month, a decommissioned U.S. Coast Guard cutter was also transferred to Vietnam to help enhance its maritime law enforcement capacity (LaGrone 2017).

China's quest for greater regional influence has alerted the other major powers and led to more intense power competition in the Asia-Pacific region. Against this backdrop, China's rise might be both a boon and a bane for Vietnam. Vietnam may benefit from exploiting the rivalry between China and other powers, but it might also backfire if Vietnam misses the chance to do so or gets entangled too deeply in the great power game.

For example, Vietnam has also capitalized on the growing rivalry between Japan and China to strengthen its strategic posture vis-à-vis China. As argued by Do and Dinh in Chapter 5 of this volume, Japan's defence and foreign policy under the Abe administration is becoming more assertive as Tokyo seeks to become less dependent on Washington in terms of defence and to have more options in dealing with China's increasing regional influence. Japan's initiatives, such as providing Hanoi with maritime capacity building assistance, have served the strategic objectives of both Tokyo and Hanoi. By the same token, as demonstrated by Chaturvedi in Chapter 6, Vietnam has been able to promote its defence ties with India thanks to New Delhi's Act East Policy under the Modi administration as well as India's intensifying strategic rivalry with China. Vietnam's "alliance politics", which seeks to "forge close security and defence ties short of formal, treaty-bound alliances with key partners who have highly convergent perceptions of interests and threats in the South China Sea" (Hiep 2015b), therefore enjoyed favourable conditions to thrive. Following the oil rig crisis, Vietnam had even greater motivation to pursue "alliance politics" to counter China's pressures. In addition to the United States and Japan, Vietnam has also tried to leverage its relations with Russia as part of its "alliance politics", although Hanoi's engagement with Moscow is rather shallow due to Moscow's lack of interest in the South China Sea issue as well as its warm relations with Beijing. Table 4.1 summarizes the exchange of high-level visits

TABLE 4.1
Exchange of High-level Visits between Vietnam and the United States, Japan, India and Russia, May 2014–May 2017

Date	Visits by Vietnamese Leaders to the Major Powers	Visits by Leaders of the Major Powers to Vietnam
September 2014		Indian President Pranab Mukherjee
October 2014	PM Nguyen Tan Dung to India	
November 2014	CPV General Secretary Nguyen Phu Trong to Russia	
April 2015		Russian PM Dmitry Medvedev
May 2015	President Truong Tan Sang to Russia	
July 2015	PM Nguyen Tan Dung to Japan[1]	
July 2015	CPV General Secretary Nguyen Phu Trong to the United States	
September 2015	CPV General Secretary Nguyen Phu Trong to Japan	
February 2016	PM Nguyen Tan Dung to the United States[2]	
May 2016	PM Nguyen Xuan Phuc to Russia and Japan	U.S. President Barack Obama
September 2016		Indian PM Narendra Modi
January 2017		Japanese PM Shinzo Abe
February 2017		Japanese Emperor Akihito
May 2017	PM Nguyen Xuan Phuc to the United States	

[1] To attend the Mekong–Japan Summit in Tokyo, met with Japanese Prime Minister Shinzo Abe.
[2] To attend the U.S.–ASEAN Summit in Sunnylands, California, met with President Barrack Obama.
Source: Authors' own compilation.

between Vietnam and the United States, Japan, India, and Russia as an indication of Vietnam's efforts to promote its "alliance politics" following the 2014 oil rig crisis.

Reducing Economic Vulnerabilities vis-à-vis China

As Keohane and Nye (1997, p. 125) argue, "It is asymmetries in dependence that are most likely to provide sources of influence for actors in their dealings with one another. Less dependent actors can often use the interdependent relationship as a source of power in bargaining over an issue and perhaps to affect other issues." While the growing economic interdependence between Vietnam and China has served, to some extent, as a buffer against bilateral maritime tensions in the South China Sea, the interdependence is asymmetric and Vietnam's greater dependence on China as its largest trading partner and biggest source of imports has constrained Vietnam's options in dealing with China.

In 2016, for example, Vietnam's imports from China reached US$49.9 billion, accounting for 28.68 per cent of its total imports. Meanwhile, Vietnam's exports to China in the same year amounted to US$22 billion, accounting for 12.44 per cent of its total exports (MOIT 2017, pp. 203, 213). As a consequence, Vietnam's trade deficit with China reached a staggering amount of US$27.9 billion in 2016, which was equal to 14 per cent of its GDP in the same year. Many Vietnamese enterprises, including export-oriented ones, are becoming increasingly reliant on China for input materials, components, machinery and equipment. In the textile industry, for example, nearly 50 per cent of Vietnam's imported yarn and fabrics is from China. If China disrupted yarn supply, it would greatly damage Vietnam's garment industry, leading to loss of exports as well as mass unemployment. Vietnam's heavy dependence on China, especially in terms of imports, therefore subjects Vietnam to vulnerabilities in case China resorts to trade sanctions to coerce Vietnam into concessions in the South China Sea.

Against this backdrop, the economic overdependence on China has become a source of concern for Vietnam. High tensions with China over the oil rig incident further reminded Vietnamese leaders of this vulnerability. To mitigate this risk, Vietnam needs to diversify its trade partners, especially import sources, to reduce its dependence on China. Although the problem could not be solved overnight,

Vietnam has made some visible adjustments in its foreign trade policy. During meetings, Vietnamese leaders have frequently asked their Chinese counterparts to import more from Vietnam. At the same time, Vietnam has pursued a wide range of free trade agreements (FTAs) with various partners. Among these, the Trans-Pacific Partnership (TPP) Agreement is of particular importance. On the one hand, TPP membership will contribute to Hanoi's balancing act against Beijing in the South China Sea by further strengthening Vietnam's ties with the United States and Japan. On the other hand, the TPP will also help reduce Vietnam's dependence on China for material imports by encouraging imports from TPP member countries (Hiep 2015a, p. 11). As such, the TPP may enhance Vietnam's strategic position vis-à-vis China in the South China Sea.

After the oil rig incident, Vietnam became more vulnerable to China's economic clout when the latter froze the funding for its projects in Vietnam (Bowring 2014) and discouraged its citizens to travel to the country (Deng and Geng 2014). In August 2014, Chinese tourist arrivals fell by 29 per cent compared to a year earlier. After the oil rig incident, Vietnam's tourism industry also witnessed consecutive months of decline until early 2015, mainly due to the fall in tourist arrivals from China (World Travel and Tourism Council 2015). Vietnamese farmers were also affected when they had difficulties in exporting their produces to China.

These factors contributed to the decision by the Vietnamese leadership to speed up their participation in FTAs. With regards to the TPP, certain Vietnamese politicians and policymakers were initially concerned about the political implications of some TPP obligations, such Vietnam's commitment to allow the establishment of independent trade unions that might undermine the CPV's monopoly of power in the long run. However, given Vietnam's increasing vulnerabilities towards China's pressures following the oil rig crisis, and the prospect that the TPP would help gravitate Vietnam "economically closer to the United States, and thus reduce Chinese economic preponderance" (Naughton, Kroeber, Jonquières, and Webster 2015), Vietnamese leaders started to express stronger endorsement for the agreement. During his historic visit to the United States in July 2015, CPV General Secretary Nguyen Phu Trong discussed the TPP with President Obama and announced that the two countries would conclude the TPP negotiations soon (*VOV World* 2015). In late 2015, the Central Committee of the

CPV voted to endorse Vietnam's participation in the TPP, thereby paving the way for the National Assembly to ratify the agreement. Even though President Donald Trump's decision to withdraw the United States from the TPP in early 2017 has dealt a major blow to Vietnam as greater access to the U.S. market was Vietnam's biggest expected gain, Vietnam and the remaining ten signatory nations were still working to revive the deal as of August 2017.

In addition to the TPP, as pointed out by Thu in Chapter 11, Vietnam has also pursued a number of other high profile FTAs, especially the Vietnam–EU FTA and the Regional Comprehensive Economic Partnership (RCEP). Apart from seeking greater impetus for economic growth and domestic reforms, Hanoi's efforts to diversify international economic relations and reduce its vulnerabilities vis-à-vis Beijing, which have become more acute following the oil rig crisis, provide yet another important driver behind Vietnam's pursuit of these FTAs.

Modernizing Defence and Maritime Law Enforcement Forces

Another visible feature in Vietnam's strategy after the oil rig crisis is its efforts to step up the modernization of its naval and maritime law enforcement forces. The crisis showed the large gap between the two country's maritime capabilities. During the crisis, while China deployed from 80 to more than 100 ships of various types (Vietnam Television 2014; *VnExpress* 2014), Vietnam reportedly dispatched only 29 ships to the crisis zone (Brummitt 2014). Damages caused by Chinese ships' ramming to Vietnamese vessels even generated concerns among some Vietnamese analysts that Vietnam might not have enough vessels to confront China if the crisis was prolonged (Thayer 2014*b*). Moreover, China's recent construction and militarization of seven artificial islands in the Spratlys, which further testify to China's strategic ambitions of establishing *de facto* control over the South China Sea, have further unnerved Vietnamese leaders.

Against this backdrop, Vietnam could not solely rely on other powers to protect its interests in the South China Sea. Developing its own military and maritime law enforcement capabilities to at least establish a credible deterrence against China's intimidation has therefore become another strategic imperative for the country. Although this effort started long before the 2014 oil rig crisis, the incident further stressed the importance of the process to Vietnam's national defence and provided a rationale for Vietnam to pursue the military modernization programme despite budgetary constraints. Apart from acquiring more hardware by its own money, Vietnam has also sought maritime capacity building assistance from its security partners, especially Japan and the United States. This source of assistance has increased remarkably in the wake of the 2014 oil rig crisis.

As summarized in Table 4.2, from mid-2014 to early 2017, major additions to Vietnam's naval capabilities include four Kilo-class submarines; six missile corvettes, two gunboats and one naval sailing ship used for training purpose. Vietnam also received a Pohang-class Flight III corvette transferred from South Korea (*Sputnik News* 2017). Vietnam's coastal defence capabilities have also improved with the purchase of Israel's EXTRA missile systems. Vietnam also secured a Russian license to produce 3,000 KCT-15 anti-ship missiles (Hoa 2016). In the coming years, Vietnam plans to acquire more frigates, anti-submarine warfare (ASW) helicopters, radar systems, and possibly a dock landing ship (Rogoway 2017; *VietnamNet* 2016).

TABLE 4.2
Major Additions to Vietnam's Naval Capabilities, mid-2014 to mid-2017

Class	Origin	Type	Quantity	Note
Kilo-class	Russia	Submarine	4	Two others had been delivered earlier.
Molnya-class	Vietnam (under Russian license)	Missile corvette	6	12 ordered, first 2 built in Russia and delivered in 2007 and 2008, 4 more to be built in Vietnam
Pohang-class	South Korea	Corvette	1	Transferred from South Korea
TT-400TP	Vietnam	Gunboats	2	2 finished in 2014 during and after the crisis
N/A	Poland	Training vessel	1	Vietnam's first naval sailing ship

Source: Authors' own compilation from various media sources.

At the same time, the Vietnam Coast Guard (VCG) has also received significant investments between mid-2014 and mid-2017 with twenty-five new vessels commissioned, leading to a 30 per cent increase in the total number of vessels and a 50 per cent increase in the total tonnage. As shown in Table 4.3, assistance from the United States, Japan and South Korea has played an important role in helping Vietnam strengthen its maritime capacity with the VCG receiving fifteen vessels and patrol boats from these three partners. In the coming years, Vietnam is likely to invest more in the VCG as well as the newly-established Vietnam Fishery Resources Surveillance Force. As seen in the 2014 oil rig crisis, China is deploying its large fleet of white-hulked vessels to impose its control over the South China Sea waters. Vietnam therefore needs to apply the same strategy and strengthen its maritime law enforcement forces in order to deal with China's increasing pressures and better protect its maritime interest in the South China Sea.

TABLE 4.3
Vietnam Coast Guard's Major Acquisitions, mid-2014 to mid-2017

Class	Origin	Type	Quantity	Note
DN-2000	Vietnam–Netherlands	2,500 tons	3	4 in total
Hamilton-class	U.S.	3,250 tons	1	Transferred from the U.S. Coast Guard; VCG's biggest vessel so far
Metal-shark 45 Defiant	U.S.	High-speed patrol boat	6	Aid from the U.S.
Teshio-class	Japan	600 tons	5	Transferred from Japan
Unknown class	South Korea	1,500 tons	1	Transferred from South Korea
Unknown class	South Korea	280 tons	2	Transferred from South Korea
TT-400	Vietnam	400 tons	7	
H-222	Vietnam	Transport	1	

Source: Authors' own compilation from various media sources.

Relaxing Control on Popular Anti-China Sentiments

Anti-China nationalism has long been a powerful undercurrent in Vietnam's domestic politics. Popular protests are rather rare and strictly controlled in the country as the government does not allow any mass mobilization without its consent for fear of social instability. Prior to 2014, Vietnam had tried to suppress any large-scale protests against China as it did not want to create a public sphere for political expressions which may be exploited by anti-government groups under the guise of anti-China mass demonstrations.

In the past, anti-China protests were often dealt with heavy-handedly by Vietnamese authorities in order not to irritate China. In 2007, widespread anti-China protests in big cities erupted when the National People's Congress of China passed a law establishing a county-level city to administer the Paracels and the Spratlys. In May 2011, when Vietnam accused China of cutting the cables of a Vietnamese seismic surveying vessel operating in the Vietnamese EEZ, anti-China rallies were also staged in Hanoi and Ho Chi Minh City. These anti-China demonstrations occurred almost every Sunday until November and assembled a few hundred people each time. However, in both cases, the demonstrations were eventually dispersed violently by the police. Hanoi leaders said these protests were damaging Vietnam's relations with China and causing social disturbance. Some protesters were also arrested by the police (*BBC Vietnamese* 2011). As a consequence, the Vietnamese government faced growing domestic criticism for being too soft on China's maritime expansionism.

The 2014 oil rig crisis was a remarkable case in which the Vietnamese government initially allowed anti-China protests to be organized across the country. While there is no clear evidence that the Vietnamese government played a direct role in organizing these protests, it seems the government tolerated these protests as they helped rally popular support for the government's South China Sea policy and sent a warning message to Beijing over the oil rig standoff. However, after two anti-China protests turned into devastating riots in Binh Duong and Ha Tinh, the government moved to stop these protests and prevented new ones from being staged.

The outburst of violence during the riots confirmed the fear of the government that anti-China sentiments, if not properly controlled, could backfire and wreak havoc on the country. As a consequence, after the oil rig crisis ended, the government appeared to be more careful in managing anti-China public protests, and sporadic anti-China demonstrations continued to be suppressed.

However, as Chinese pressures in the South China Sea continues to build up after the crisis with China starting to construct and militarize seven artificial islands in the Spratlys, Hanoi, while trying to prevent anti-China nationalism from causing social disorder and instability, has also allowed a certain level of anti-Chinese nationalist sentiments to be vented through both the social media as well as state-sanctioned media networks.

In the past, events such as the 1974 Chinese invasion of the Paracels, the 1979 Sino–Vietnamese border war, or the 1988 Sino–Vietnamese naval clash in the Spratlys, were treated as "sensitive" issues. They were hardly mentioned in Vietnamese history textbooks and their commemoration was restricted. However, in recent years, especially after the oil rig crisis, the commemoration of these events has been openly endorsed by the state, with various media reports in official outlets covering these events and detailing their brutality. In March 2015, Vietnamese authorities also started the construction of a monument complex in Cam Ranh to commemorate the 1988 naval clash in the Spratlys. In August 2017, the Vietnam Academy of Social Sciences published a new volume of Vietnamese history, in which the 1979 Sino–Vietnamese border war was covered in a much greater level of detail than any other official history books ever published in Vietnam. The volume also describes the war as a "war of aggression", and China was labelled explicitly as the "aggressor" (*VnExpress* 2017). Both terms were hitherto censored in sections dealing with the event in other history books of Vietnam.

These are examples of how the anti-China rhetoric has been quietly promoted by the Vietnamese party-state after the oil rig crisis as a response to China's increasing maritime assertiveness as well as a measure to buttress the CPV's image as the ultimate protector of national sovereignty and territorial integrity.

Conclusion

This chapter has examined the foreign policy strategies that Vietnam has been implementing in response to the May 2014 oil rig crisis with China, the worst bilateral stand-off since the two countries normalized their relations in 1991. Facing mounting pressures in the South China

Sea from a more powerful and increasingly assertive neighbour, Vietnam has sought to deepen its relations with the major powers, especially the United States, Japan and India; reduce economic vulnerabilities vis-à-vis China; modernize its naval and maritime enforcement capabilities; and leverage anti-China nationalism.

One possible scenario for future bilateral ties is that incidents similar to the 2014 crisis might happen again. As China's power gap with Vietnam keeps widening, it is likely that China will continue to flex its muscles in the South China Sea. In response, Vietnam may lean further towards other regional powers, especially the United States. Hanoi may also seek to rally support from other Southeast Asian nations and make use of ASEAN channels to counter China's pressures. In a more extreme scenario, Vietnam may initiate legal proceedings against China's claims in the South China Sea. In all these cases, China is likely to be upset and bilateral relations will be constrained.

Another possible scenario is that Vietnamese leaders may return to their traditional mechanisms, including party-to-party and government-to-government channels, to manage bilateral ties. They will also try to compartmentalize the South China Sea disputes from the overall relations. Since China is Vietnam's largest trading partner and main source of imports, as well as its ideological ally, Vietnam may want to prevent the South China Sea issues from excessively harming bilateral relations. This option is even more appealing given Hanoi's wish to maintain a peaceful environment to support its domestic economic growth. Yet, this conciliatory approach is difficult to sustain due to rising nationalism in Vietnam as well as China's maritime assertiveness. Although Vietnam appreciates its friendly relations with China, it is unlikely that Hanoi will sacrifice its national interests in the South China Sea just to please Beijing.

In any case, it is in the national interest of both countries to keep their relationship peaceful and stable, and to prevent new incidents like the 2014 oil rig crisis from reoccurring. Toward this end, both Hanoi and Beijing may need to adopt a more compromising stance. While China should refrain from coercive measures in the South China Sea and try to be more sensitive to Vietnam's security concerns, Vietnam should also pay due attention to China's unease about external powers' strategic manoeuvres in its near-broad, and try to assure Beijing that its improved ties with other major powers will not harm China.

At the same time, bilateral political engagement, economic cooperation and people-to-people contacts should also be further promoted to enhance mutual trust and nurture the habit of cooperation.

NOTES

1. In light of the 2016 arbitral tribunal ruling in the *Philippines vs. China* case, it is highly likely that these features do not qualify as islands. However, the ruling was applied to the Spratlys features noted in the ruling only, and Vietnam may need to file a similar case against China if it wants to press the claim that none of the features in the Paracels qualify as island.
2. Recent examples include the Thailand–Cambodia border skirmish (2008–11) and the standoff between China and the Philippines over the Scarborough Shoal in 2012.

REFERENCES

Amer, Ramses. "China–Vietnam Bilateral Overhang or Legacy". In *Bilateral Legacies in East and Southeast Asia*, edited by N. Ganesan. Singapore: Institute of Southeast Asian Studies, 2015.

BBC Vietnamese. "Bieu tinh chong TQ nhanh chong bi giai tan", 17 July 2011. Available at <http://www.bbc.com/vietnamese/vietnam/2011/07/110717_new_protest.shtml> (accessed 24 August 2017).

Bowring, Gavin. "Vietnam Yields Cautionary Tale Over Chinese Investment". *Financial Times*, 27 November 2014. Available at <https://www.ft.com/content/6ea71dd6-ccea-3779-87be-d4654fc9379b> (accessed 15 September 2017).

Brummitt, Chris. "Vietnam Tries to Stop China Oil Rig Deployment". *Associated Press*, 7 May 2014. Available at <http://news.yahoo.com/vietnam-tries-stop-china-oil-rig-deployment-083726984.html> (accessed 12 December 2014).

Cuong, T. Nguyen. "The Dramatic Transformation in US–Vietnam Relations". *The Diplomat*, 2 July 2015. Available at <http://thediplomat.com/2015/07/the-dramatic-transformation-in-us-vietnam-relations/> (accessed 1 5 September 2017).

Deng, Chao and Olivia Geng. "Chinese Travel to Vietnam Plummets Amid South China Sea Standoff". *Wall Street Journal*, 21 May 2014. Available at <https://blogs.wsj.com/chinarealtime/2014/05/21/chinese-travel-to-vietnam-plummets-amid-south-china-sea-standoff/> (accessed 15 August 2017).

Global Times. "Xi Calls for Mended China–Vietnam Ties", 28 August 2014. Available at <http://www.globaltimes.cn/content/878643.shtml> (accessed 15 September 2017).

Hai Min and Zhang Aizhu. "Cooperation in the South China Sea Under International Law". *China Institute of International Studies*, 19 March 2014. Available at <http://www.ciis.org.cn/english/2014-03/19/content_6756309. htm> (accessed 15 August 2017).

Hiep, Le Hong. "The TPP's Impact on Vietnam: A Preliminary Assessment". *ISEAS Perspective* 63 (2015*a*).

———. *Vietnam's Alliance Politics in the South China Sea* (Vol. 6). Singapore: Institute of Southeast Asian Studies, 2015*b*.

Hoa, Ngoc. "Viet Nam se san xuat 3.000 qua ten lua chong ham KCT-15?" *Dat Viet*, 11 June 2016. Available at <http://baodatviet.vn/quoc-phong/ quoc-phong-viet-nam/viet-nam-se-san-xuat-3000-qua-ten-lua-chong-ham-kct-15-3310845/> (accessed 23 August 2017).

Keohane, Robert and Joseph S. Nye. "Interdependence in World Politics". In *The Theoretical Evolution of International Political Economy: A Reader*, edited by George T. Crane and Abla Amawi. Oxford: Oxford University Press, 1997.

LaGrone, Sam. "Former U.S. Cutter Morgenthau Transferred to Vietnamese Coast Guard". *USNI News*, 26 May 2017. Available at <https://news.usni. org/2017/05/26/former-u-s-cutter-morgenthau-transferred-vietnamese-coast-guard> (accessed 16 August 2017).

Ministry of Industry and Trade (MOIT), Vietnam. *Bao cao xuat nhap khau Viet Nam 2016*. Ha Noi: Cuc Xuat nhap khau and Bao Cong thuong, 2017.

Naughton, Barry, Arthur Kroeber, Guy De Jonquières, and Graham Webster. "What Will the TPP Mean for China?" *Foreign Policy*, 7 October 2015. Available at <https://foreignpolicy.com/2015/10/07/china-tpp-trans-pacific-partnership-obama-us-trade-xi/> (accessed 22 August 2017).

Neuman, Scott. "Obama To Meet With Vietnam's Communist Party Chief Amid Concern Over China". *NPR*, 6 July 2015. Available at <http://www.npr.org/ sections/thetwo-way/2015/07/06/420295261/obama-to-meet-with-vietnams-communist-party-chief-amid-concern-over-china> (accessed 16 August 2017).

Nguyen, Mai and Ben Blanchard. "China, Vietnam Say Want Lasting Solution to Sea Dispute". *Reuters*, 27 October 2014. Available at <http://www. reuters.com/article/2014/10/27/us-china-vietnam-idUSKBN0IG0Y220141027> (accessed 15 August 2017).

Rogoway, Tyler. "Vietnam Eyes Israel's Delilah Standoff Missile, and F-16s Could Be Next". *The Drive*, 10 March 2017. Available at <http://www. thedrive.com/the-war-zone/8219/vietnam-eyes-israels-delilah-standoff-missile-and-f-16s-could-be-next> (accessed 15 August 2017).

Sputnik News. "Viet Nam duoc Hàn Quoc tang chien ham có suc manh không ngo?", 8 June 2017. Available at <https://vn.sputniknews.com/ military/201706083444662-han-quoc-tang-chiem-ham-cho-viet-nam-anh/> (accessed 23 August 2017).

Taylor, Guy. "U.S. Mulls Selling Weapons to Vietnam to Stave Off China Military Buildup in Region". *The Washington Times*, 23 February 2016. Available at <www.washingtontimes.com/news/2016/feb/23/us-mulls-selling-weapons-vietnam-stave-china-milit/>.

Thayer, Carlyle A. "4 Reasons China Removed Oil Rig HYSY-981 Sooner Than Planned". *The Diplomat*, 22 July 2014*a*. Available at <http://thediplomat.com/2014/07/4-reasons-china-removed-oil-rig-hysy-981-sooner-than-planned/>.

———. "Vietnam Mulling New Strategies to Deter China". *The Diplomat*, 28 May 2014*b*. Available at <http://thediplomat.com/2014/05/vietnam-mulling-new-strategies-to-deter-china/> (accessed 2 February 2015).

———. "Why the Upcoming China–Vietnam Defense Ministers Meeting is Immensely Important". *The Diplomat*, 17 October 2014*c*. Available at <http://thediplomat.com/2014/10/why-the-upcoming-china-vietnam-defense-ministers-meeting-is-immensely-important/> (accessed 15 August 2017).

U.S. State Department. "Vietnam/China: Chinese Oil Rig Operations Near the Paracel Islands", 7 May 2014. Available at <https://vn.usembassy.gov/vietnamchina-chinese-oil-rig-operations-near-the-paracel-islands/> (accessed 15 August 2017).

Vietnam Television. "Tron 2 thang Trung Quoc ha dat trai phep gian khoan Hai Duong 981 o Bien Dong" [Two Months Since China Placed Oil Rig HYSY 981 in the East Sea], 2 July 2014. Available at <http://vtv.vn/trong-nuoc/tron-2-thang-trung-quoc-ha-dat-trai-phep-gian-khoan-hai-duong-981-o-bien-dong-148275.htm> (accessed 11 December 2014).

VietnamNet.. "Vietnam to Buy More Russian Gepard-Class Warships", 30 May 2016. Available at <http://english.vietnamnet.vn/fms/government/157201/vietnam-to-buy-more-russian-gepard-class-warships.html> (accessed 15 August 2017).

VietTimes. "Cuu dai su Le Van Bang: My co the giup can bang luc luong Bien Dong", 14 May 2016. Available at <http://viettimes.vn/content/MjczNjI=.html> (accessed 15 September 2017).

VnExpress. "Trung Quoc tang luc luong bao ve gian khoan 981" [China Expands Forces for Protecting Oil Rig HYSY 981], 15 May 2014. Available at <http://vnexpress.net/tin-tuc/thoi-su/trung-quoc-tang-luc-luong-bao-ve-gian-khoan-981-2991181.html> (accessed 12 December 2014).

———. "Chien tranh xam luoc cua Trung Quoc duoc dua trong sach Lich su Viet Nam", 19 August 2017. Available at <http://vnexpress.net/tin-tuc/thoi-su/chien-tranh-xam-luoc-cua-trung-quoc-duoc-dua-trong-sach-lich-su-viet-nam-3629609.html> (accessed 24 August 2017).

VOV World. "Vietnam, US Will Soon Finalize TPP Negotiation", 17 July 2015. Available at <http://vovworld.vn/en-US/current-affairs/vietnam-us-will-soon-finalize-tpp-negotiation-351909.vov> (accessed 23 August 2017).

World Travel & Tourism Council. "Travel & Tourism: Vietnam's Economic Impact 2015", 2015. Available at <http://www.wttc.org/-/media/files/reports/economic%20impact%20research/countries%202015/vietnam2015.pdf> (accessed 22 August 2017).

Wu Shicun and Nong Hong, eds. *Recent Developments in the South China Sea Dispute: The Prospect of a Joint Development Regime*. London: Routledge, 2014.

5

Vietnam–Japan Relations: Moving Beyond Economic Cooperation?

Thuy T. Do and Julia Luong Dinh

Unlike most other major bilateral relationships in East Asia, the Vietnam–Japan ties are generally "problem-free". Although their official relationship was only established in 1973, Vietnam and Japan have a long history of people-to-people connections which date back to the eighth century, when a Vietnamese Buddhist monk named Phat Triet carried out his missionary works in Japan. In the sixteenth century, Japanese merchants set up "Japanese towns" in Hoi An and Pho Hien in central and northern Vietnam, where bilateral trade flourished. As the first Asian country to successfully transform itself into a major power and avoid Western colonization, Japan served as a source of inspiration and a regional hub where Vietnamese patriots would come to learn how to liberate their country from French colonization and to revive their nation. A primary example was the *Dong Du Movement* led by Phan Boi Chau.[1] Although the movement was short-lived due to the adverse historical context at the time, Phan Boi Chau's famous quote that "Vietnamese and Japanese peoples share the same culture, same racial roots, and same continent" [*đồng văn, đồng chủng, đồng châu*] still rightly describe the closeness between the two peoples and societies to date. Despite Japan's military occupation of Indochina during World War II, Vietnam–Japan relations do not carry a historical baggage. Instead, the reconciliation and rapprochement between Hanoi and Tokyo since the restoration of their ties in 1992 have resulted in one of the most fruitful relationships in East Asia.

In 2009, Vietnam and Japan established their "strategic partnership" framework. Due to domestic and external constraints, this strategic partnership has until recently been confined to the economic domain. However, the changing regional geopolitical landscape due to China's rise and its increasing assertiveness in territorial and maritime disputes, the ambiguity of U.S. commitment to Asia, and the lack of effective multilateral frameworks for conflict prevention and management in the region, has made it necessary for Vietnam and Japan to strengthen their strategic partnership as a hedge against economic, security, and strategic challenges of mutual concern. Cooperation in security and strategic realms has been strengthened since 2011, and in March 2014, Hanoi and Tokyo decided to elevate their ties to the level of an "Extensive Strategic Partnership for Peace and Prosperity in Asia".

This chapter reviews recent developments in Vietnam–Japan relations and analyses the rationales for the two countries to lift their bilateral ties from mainly economic cooperation to a partnership of greater strategic focus. It argues that Vietnam–Japan relations bear great significance for the two countries at bilateral as well as regional levels. While the bilateral relationship has been based mainly on strong mutual trust and convergent economic interests, recent shifts in the regional strategic landscape also prompted Hanoi and Tokyo to increasingly acknowledge the role that they can play in maintaining East Asian security.

The chapter also attempts to analyse the existing and emerging challenges that the two countries are facing in materializing their "Extensive Strategic Partnership". Towards this end, the chapter examines the impact of Japan's "ambivalent" strategy towards Asia, Vietnam's delicate balancing strategy, as well as other potential setbacks of the bilateral relations. The authors posit that despite its certain shortcomings, the Vietnam–Japan relationship presents a case for how middle powers in East Asia can help shape the ongoing regional power shift.

The chapter proceeds in three sections. First, it analyses the importance of Vietnam and Japan in each other's foreign policy, particularly in the context of Asia's shifting geopolitical landscape. The chapter then reviews major developments in bilateral ties since 1992. Finally, the chapter discusses the existing shortcomings of bilateral ties, offers suggestions for improvement, and analyses the implications of the relationship for East Asian security.

The Significance of Vietnam–Japan Ties to Each Country

After the establishment of diplomatic ties in 1973, Japan started providing Official Development Assistance (ODA) for Vietnam as a form of "war reparations" (Do 2014, p. 15). Bilateral relations were soon interrupted as Japan joined Western countries to sanction Vietnam following Hanoi's military intervention in Cambodia between 1979 and 1991. Nonetheless, Japan quickly became a key economic partner of Vietnam after diplomatic relations were restored in 1992 following the conclusion of the Paris Peace Accords on Cambodia. Indeed, Japan was among the first foreign investors in Vietnam after the country opened up its economy, and burgeoning economic ties with Japan have been contributing to Vietnam's robust economic growth ever since. As the Communist Party of Vietnam (CPV) is increasingly deriving its political legitimacy from socio-economic performance (Hiep 2012), which is heavily reliant on foreign trade and investment, economic ties with Japan have become all the more important for Vietnam.

In recent years, Vietnamese leaders have repeatedly referred to Japan as their "first-ranking economic partner" or "the most important development partner" (*Nhan Dan* 2014; *Tuoi Tre* 2015). By 2016, Japan had become the biggest source of ODA, the second largest foreign investor, the third largest source of tourist arrivals, and the fourth largest trade partner of Vietnam (see the next section for more details). Japan was also the only foreign partner that Hanoi selected to support its long-term industrialization blueprint as showcased in the

"Vietnam's Industrialization Strategy in the Framework of Vietnam–Japan Cooperation toward 2020, Vision to 2030".

Vietnam–Japan interaction is inextricably linked to Vietnam's international economic integration process. Bilateral economic cooperation is considered as an important instrument for Vietnam to enhance the effectiveness of its participation in multilateral economic arrangements of which the two countries are members (Dang 2015, pp. 6–7). To accelerate its industrialization and modernization, Vietnam must rely on capital and technology sourced from Japan not only within the bilateral framework but also through regional multilateral economic arrangements such as the Mekong–Japan Cooperation mechanism, the ASEAN–Japan Comprehensive Economic Partnership, and the Asia-Pacific Economic Cooperation (APEC) forum. For example, as Tokyo plays an increasingly active role in promoting economic cooperation and sustainable development in the Mekong subregion, Vietnam–Japan relations are now also framed within the broader context of Mekong–Japan cooperation. Emphasizing Japan's importance to Vietnam's development, former Vietnamese Prime Minister Nguyen Tan Dung told his Japanese counterpart Shinzo Abe that "intensifying and consolidating the friendly and cooperative relationship with Japan is not only the consistent guideline and top priority of our foreign policy, but also the strategic choice of the Party and the Government of Vietnam" (*Voice of Vietnam* 2013).

In portraying its relationship with Japan as a "top priority" and a "strategic choice", Vietnam was taking into consideration not only Japan's economic significance, but also its enhanced role in helping Vietnam to manage rising tensions in the South China Sea. Hanoi's foreign policy attaches great importance to its relations with neighbouring countries and ASEAN, and seeks to promote regional integration with the hope that "institutional membership will constrain potential Chinese aggression by tying China down, and by binding regional states together" (Goh 2008, p. 129). This dovetails with Japan's and other ASEAN countries' desire to "socialize" China and to hedge against great power rivalry through multilateral cooperative mechanisms. Boosting relations with Japan can therefore be seen as a means to increase Hanoi's leverage while reducing its over-reliance on China in security and economic terms.[2]

From a broader perspective, Vietnam's strategy towards Japan and other major powers largely remains a delicate balancing act which aims to forge a network of equidistant and mutually dependent relations with all the major powers without leaning too much on any single partner. Hanoi therefore seeks to create multiple interdependent relationships with the major powers both in bilateral and multilateral formats in order to involve these powers in defending their common interests with Vietnam (Goh 2008; Thayer 1994, p. 528). As such, strengthening strategic relations with Japan can be seen as an important component of Vietnam's enmeshment strategy to counter China's increasing assertiveness in the South China Sea.

Meanwhile, for decades, pursuing post-war pacifism and strengthening the security alliance with the United States have served as the cornerstones of Japan's foreign policy. However, since the end of the Vietnam War, Japan has sought to expand its influence in Asia, starting with the 1977 Fukuda Doctrine aimed at Southeast Asia. Recently, the region has once again gained enhanced prominence in Japanese foreign policy under the Abe administration, which is based on three pillars: strengthening the Japan–U.S. alliance, deepening cooperative relations with neighbouring countries, and strengthening economic diplomacy as a means to revitalize the Japanese economy (Kishida 2014). As an emerging economy and an increasingly important strategic player in the region, Vietnam is becoming an important gateway for Japan to undertake its "pivot to ASEAN".

Japan's Asia policy is challenged by constitutional constraints and the changing power dynamics in East Asia. China is resurging as a great power while U.S. long-term commitment to Asia has been ambivalent. Moreover, this power transition is taking place in a region that lacks effective multilateral frameworks that could mitigate the vicious circles of security dilemma and prevent potential conflicts. Experiencing geopolitical pressure in Northeast Asia, Japan is increasingly "looking South" and has established strategic partnerships with Australia (2006), India (2007), and ASEAN (five bilateral strategic partnerships with ASEAN members and one with ASEAN itself). This represents Japan's "dual hedge" against strained relations with its Northeast Asian neighbours as well as concerns over Washington's long-term engagement with Asia in general and its commitment to defend Japan in particular (Wallace 2013). This hedging strategy also serves the key objectives of Abe's foreign policy, such as supporting economic revitalization, strengthening maritime security, and expanding Japan's sphere of influence. In all of these areas, Japan sees Vietnam as "a strategic partner that shares common interests" (*Japan Times* 2013).

The importance of Vietnam to Japan is therefore threefold. *First,* as economic diplomacy constitutes a key component of Japanese foreign policy under Abe, Tokyo is interested in engaging Southeast Asia in general and Vietnam in particular. Prime Minister Abe has stated that ASEAN's aspiration to form a single market with a combined GDP of US$2,000 billion and a population of 600 million by 2015 may help revitalize Japan's economy (*Tuoi Tre News* 2013).[3] Japanese companies are also increasingly interested in Southeast Asia as a new destination for investment under their so-called "China plus One" investment strategy.[4] Vietnam has attracted a good number of investors from Japan thanks to its large population, young and skilled workforce, as well as its political stability and the government's commitment to further reform and deepen international economic integration. Japan's expansion of investment and exports to Vietnam may eventually contribute to the implementation of Prime Minister Abe's economic reforms under his trademark *Abenomics* blueprint (Dang 2015, p. 6).

Moreover, Vietnam and Japan share concerns over "the strategic implications of economic overreliance on China's future economic growth and the potential for intersecting economic and military coercion" (Wallace 2013, p. 499). China is the largest trade partner of both Japan and Vietnam, and also their largest source of trade deficit. Some Japanese scholars (see, for example, Ogasawara 2011) have argued that the two countries should promote bilateral economic cooperation to avoid economic dependence on China which could constrain both countries' freedom of action. For example, in an effort to bypass China's near-monopoly in the supply of rare-earth elements, the two countries have opened a joint research centre in Hanoi to improve the extraction and processing of such materials from Vietnam's large and untapped rare earth reserves (*BBC* 2012).

Second, Japan considers Southeast Asia as an important ground for expanding its sphere of influence. This is well manifested in Japan's campaign to win regional countries' support in its bid for a permanent seat at the United Nations Security Council (UNSC). Vietnam was one of the few ASEAN countries (together with Singapore) that endorsed Japan's bid from the very beginning despite

China's diplomatic pressure (Yoshimatsu 2010). Japan also recognized the role that Vietnam could play in managing Tokyo's relations with North Korea given Vietnam's rather sound diplomatic ties with Pyongyang. Prime Minister Abe used to ask Vietnam to help with resolving the issue of Japanese citizens abducted by Pyongyang (*Kyodo News* 2013). In addition, the two countries have frequently held consultations and effectively coordinated their positions at international forums and regional mechanisms such as the East Asia Summit (EAS) and the ASEAN+3 Summit.

Third, for the first time, Japan's Southeast Asia policy under the Abe administration contains explicit security and defence dimensions. Although Japan has always been "an important economic player that enjoys positive public sentiment in most Southeast Asian countries", its policy toward Southeast Asia never went beyond the 1977 Fukuda Doctrine, which stressed mutual trust-building with Southeast Asian states and whereby Japan pledged to forever renounce its military power (Nguyen 2014). Under the Abe administration, however, Japan has expressed its desire to pursue both enhanced economic relations and broader security cooperation with the region. In the security sphere, Tokyo pledges to "actively promote joint training, exercises and capacity building assistance in addition to its cooperation in the field of disaster management" (Government of Japan 2013). Vietnam, with its rich military history and war-fighting experience, "is being admiringly portrayed by some as a kindred spirit, and by a few as a military role model to be emulated" for Japan (*Japan Times* 2014).

In addition to bolstering the military alliance with the United States, Abe's regional policy also places emphasis on maritime security and Japan's identity as "a sea-faring nation" in maritime Asia. The proposed "security diamond strategy", whereby Australia, India, Japan and the U.S. state of Hawaii form a diamond to safeguard the maritime commons stretching from the Indian Ocean to the western Pacific, may be seen as a counterbalance to China's "String of Pearls" Strategy (Hayashi 2013). In this connection, Japan sees Vietnam, along with the Philippines and Indonesia, as driving forces behind ASEAN regionalism as well as key actors that help to maintain the regional balance of power. Prime Minister Abe has indeed called for Vietnam and Japan to "play a more active role" in maintaining regional peace and security, particularly in the face of growing maritime tensions with China (*VCCI News* 2013). In the near future, concerns over China's ambitions, the lack of trust in U.S. commitments, and a desire to reassert national pride and autonomy may generate stronger momentums for a more independent Japanese regional posture. The re-emergence of Japan as a major regional security stakeholder under Abe has been viewed by Vietnam as a positive factor in the shaping of a multi-polar East Asian security order. Given that the gap between Japan and other major regional powers in terms of "comprehensive national power" is not substantial, the support of small and medium powers like Vietnam is important for Japan's re-emergence as a "normal power" and a pillar of the regional security order.

In sum, Hanoi and Tokyo have found growing incentives for cooperation in not only economic but also security and strategic realms. With Japan's resurgence under the Abe administration, Hanoi has increasingly viewed Japan as an important strategic player in regional security as well as a key partner in its balancing strategy to deal with rising tensions in the South China Sea. For Japan, relations with Southeast Asia in general and Vietnam in particular are crucial to Tokyo's hedge against the volatile relations with its Northeast Asian neighbours, as well as the ambivalent U.S. commitment to defend Japan's core interests. These convergent interests have served as the foundations for the continuous growth of Vietnam–Japan relations in recent years.

Vietnam–Japan Relations: Key Developments since 1992

Vietnam–Japan relations have been on a steady rise since they were officially restored in 1992. The Japanese government renewed aid to Vietnam in the same year and played a key role in lobbying for the restoration of Vietnam's ties with the International Monetary Fund (IMF) and the World Bank (WB), as well as the broader international community, including the Organisation for Economic Co-operation and Development (OECD) countries. Vietnam and Japan exchanged most favoured nation (MFN) status in 1999. Later on, Japan supported Vietnam's accession to the World Trade Organization (WTO) and was one of the first developed countries to recognize Vietnam's full market economy status in 2011.

Over the past two decades, the regular exchange of high-ranking visits has helped strengthen mutual trust and overall relations. For example, when Japanese Minister of Foreign Affairs Yoriko Kawaguchi visited Vietnam in July 2004, Hanoi and Tokyo signed a joint statement titled "Toward a Higher Sphere of Enduring Partnership". In October 2006, during an official visit to Japan by Vietnamese Prime Minister Nguyen Tan Dung, the two countries announced their plan to move the relationship toward a "Strategic Partnership for Peace and Prosperity in Asia". Three years later, the visit by CPV General Secretary Nong Duc Manh to Tokyo resulted in the official establishment of such a partnership. In March 2014, during a visit to Japan by Vietnamese President Truong Tan Sang, the two countries upgraded their relationship to the level of an "Extensive Strategic Partnership". In February 2017, Emperor Akihito became the first Japanese monarch to ever visit Vietnam. The visit marked yet another historical milestone in bilateral relations, contributing to the strengthening of not only economic and political but also social and cultural connections between the two countries (Hiep 2017).

Alongside official cooperation channels, the Vietnam–Japan strategic partnership is also strengthened through people-to-people contacts. Vietnam received 671,379 Japanese tourists in 2015, accounting for about 10 per cent of tourist arrivals in the country. In 2016, the number increased to almost 700,000. Meanwhile, 200,000 Vietnamese tourists visited Japan in 2016, a 217 per cent increase from 2014.[5] As an educational hub, Japan is among the most generous providers of grants for Vietnam in human resources development (Tran 2016). Examples include the recent launch of the Japan–Vietnam University in Hanoi and Tokyo's pledge to help train 1,000 Vietnamese doctoral students in a thirteen-year-long project worth JPY20 billion funded through Japanese ODA (*Hanoi Times* 2008). As a result, the number of Vietnamese students in Japan has been growing steadily. In 2015, 38,882 Vietnamese were studying in Japan, a 47.1 per cent increase from 2014, turning Vietnam into the second largest source of foreign students in Japan after China (Japan Student Services Organization 2016).

Labour exports also witnessed positive developments. From 1992 to 2013, Vietnam sent about 31,000 workers and interns to Japan. As of 2015, there were 146,956 Vietnamese people studying and working in Japan, which was a 47.2 per cent jump from the previous year (*Nippon* 2016). Japan has also started to receive and train nurses and care-workers from Vietnam within the framework of the 2009

Economic Partnership Agreement. Mirroring the Dong Du Movement in the early twentieth century, these Japanese-trained human resources (including students, workers, and interns) may help transfer technologies and know-hows from Japan to Vietnam, thereby facilitating socio-economic transformations in the country.

Extensive political and people-to-people exchanges create additional impetus for economic relations. Japan is currently one of the most important economic partners of Vietnam. Since 2006, Japan has been the biggest ODA supplier to Vietnam, accounting for about 30 per cent of the total ODA committed to the country by international donors. Specifically, Tokyo committed nearly US$20 billion in ODA to Vietnam between 1992 and 2011. In the 2011 financial year, Japan's ODA to Vietnam reached the record of approximately US$2.8 billion even when Japan was hit by the 2011 Tōhoku earthquake and tsunami disasters (*Nhan Dan* 2015). These ODA funds have been useful for the development of Vietnam's infrastructure and human resources, as well as the modernization of financial and administrative institutions. At the same time, as pointed out by Motonori Tsuno, Chief Representative of Japan International Cooperation Agency (JICA) in Vietnam, they also facilitate Japanese investment in Vietnam and contribute to the deepening of the relations between the two governments and the two peoples (*VnExpress* 2013).

Japan is also Vietnam's second largest source of foreign direct investment (FDI), both in terms of registered and disbursed capital. By the end of 2016, Japanese companies had invested US$42.05 billion in 3,280 projects in Vietnam (Vietrade 2017), mostly in the processing and manufacturing industries. More importantly, Japan has been investing in large-scale industrial and infrastructure projects such as Nghi Son Oil Refinery, or Lach Huyen Port. In July 2013, the two countries approved "Vietnam's industrialization strategy within the framework of Vietnam–Japan cooperation by 2020 and vision toward 2030". Within this framework, Japan has pledged to invest in six key industrial sectors in Vietnam, namely consumer electrics/electronics, food processing, shipbuilding, agricultural machinery, environment and energy conservation, and automobile/spare part manufacturing. The programme, focusing on industries of strategic significance to Vietnam's future economic development, is tailored to enhance the competitiveness of Vietnamese enterprises in the context of Vietnam's deeper international economic integration (*Tuoi Tre News* 2013).

The goal of raising bilateral trade turnover to US$15 billion by 2010 was achieved two years ahead of the schedule. In 2015, Japan was Vietnam's third largest trading partner, and two-way trade turnover hit US$28.28 billion. In the same year, Japan accounted for 8.7 per cent and 8.55 per cent of Vietnam's total exports and imports, respectively (World Bank 2015). In 2016, two-way trade turnover reached US$29.68 billion, with Japan being Vietnam's fourth largest trading partner after China (US$71.91 billion), the United States (US$46.17 billion), and South Korea (US$43.46 billion) (General Department of Customs 2017).

Vietnam's major exports to Japan include crude oil, garments and textiles, transport vehicles and spare parts, and timber products, while its main imports from Japan are machinery, equipment, computers, electronic products and components, as well as iron and steel. Japanese businesses are also interested in importing Vietnamese agricultural products, especially seafood, rice, coffee and vegetables. If Vietnamese farms manage to improve the quality of these products, exports may increase sharply (*Tuoi Tre News* 2013). Cooperation in the field of agriculture will therefore likely rank high on the agenda of bilateral cooperation in the near future.

A new but increasingly important aspect of bilateral ties is security and defence cooperation. For years, cooperation in this area was considered a "sensitive issue" given Japan's low profile in regional security and Hanoi's consideration of Beijing's reactions. However, bilateral security ties started to pick up since 2009 when China made a series of assertive moves in its territorial and maritime disputes with neighbouring countries. Recent examples include Beijing's establishment of an Air Defence Identification Zone in the East China Sea in November 2013, the placement of a giant oil rig in Vietnam's exclusive economic zone (EEZ) in May 2014, and the construction and militarization of seven artificial islands in the Spratly Islands between 2014 and 2016. Tokyo and Hanoi share common interests in maintaining the regional *status quo* and the peaceful resolution of their respective territorial disputes with China, as well as the freedom of navigation and aviation in the region.

In July 2010, Japan and Vietnam agreed to conduct, on a regular basis, subcabinet-level "two-plus-two" dialogues involving the two sides' Ministry of Foreign Affairs and Ministry of Defence, a security arrangement that Japan has only with the United States, Australia,

India and Russia. In 2011, defence ministers of the two countries signed a Memorandum of Understanding on Japan–Vietnam Defence Cooperation and Exchange, which provides for, among other things, regular vice-ministerial talks, regular mutual working-level visits, and cooperation on humanitarian assistance and disaster relief. In 2013, during the Japanese defence minister's visits to Vietnam, the two parties agreed to cooperate in human resource training, bomb disposal and mine clearance, Vietnam Coast Guard modernization, and other military-technical areas. In terms of multilateral cooperation, during his visit to Japan in 2013, then Vietnamese Chief of the General Staff Do Ba Ty proposed deeper coordination at multilateral forums, especially regional ones such as the ASEAN Regional Forum (ARF) and ASEAN Defence Ministers' Meeting Plus (ADMM+) (*Vietnam News* 2013)

Vietnam is showing particular interest in learning from Japanese naval and maritime security expertise (*Japan Times* 2014). Each year, a cohort of Vietnamese students is sent to study at the National Defence Academy of Japan (*Japan Times* 2014). In July 2013, Hanoi dispatched a team of officers to Japan to learn how to enhance its maritime patrol activities, and Vietnam Coast Guard officers have called for closer cooperation with their Japanese counterparts. During the first bilateral talk on maritime security between senior officials of the two countries' foreign and defence ministries in Hanoi in May 2013, Japan announced the provision of six used 1,000-ton patrol vessels to Vietnam to help Hanoi strengthen its maritime capacity. The agreement was finalized during the visit to Hanoi by Japanese Foreign Minister Fumio Kishida in July 2014, and by 2017, these boats had been delivered. During his visit to Vietnam in January 2017, Prime Minister Abe pledged to provide concessional loans for Vietnam to purchase six additional newly-built vessels worth US$338 million to enhance the capacity of the Vietnam Coast Guard and the newly established Vietnam Fisheries Resources Surveillance Force (Hiep 2017). Before that, in another sign of enhanced maritime security cooperation between the two countries, two Japanese Maritime Self-Defence Force destroyers were among the first foreign warships to visit Vietnam's newly launched Cam Ranh International Port in April 2016.

As a result of the robust cooperation between the two countries, the Vietnamese public's perception of Japan is generally favourable. According to a survey in 2004 by Asia Barometer, Japan is the second most favoured foreign country (after Russia) as perceived by the surveyed (Yamamoto 2007, p. 320). In another survey conducted by the Japanese Ministry of Foreign Affairs in six ASEAN countries in 2008, Vietnamese respondents were the most positive about Japan. Ninety-eight per cent of the interviewees believed that Japan was a trustworthy friend to Vietnam and all of them welcomed Japanese companies to establish manufacturing facilities in their localities. Vietnamese people also chose Japan as the most important partner for their country in both the present and immediate future. In the same survey, 87 per cent of the Vietnamese respondents considered Japanese acts during World War II no longer to be a problem (Ministry of Foreign Affairs of Japan 2008).[6] In a more recent survey conducted by the Pew Research Centre in 2014, 77 per cent of the Vietnamese surveyed held favourable views of Japan and 65 per cent of them had confidence in the Japanese leadership under Prime Minister Shinzo Abe (Pew Research Center 2014).

In sum, the Vietnam–Japan partnership is both broad and deep, and has contributed to the advancement of both countries' national interests. The continuous expansion of the partnership since 1992 also provides Hanoi and Tokyo with more leverage and strategic confidence in their foreign relations against the backdrop of the evolving security architecture in East Asia. Nevertheless, there are still certain challenges that the two countries need to overcome to further strengthen their partnership. The next section will analyse these challenges as well as the future prospects of the relationship and its implications for East Asian security.

Challenges and Prospects of Bilateral Relations

First, economic cooperation has long been considered as the key pillar of Vietnam–Japan relations, but so far the outcomes have not been commensurate with the strategic significance of the relationship as well as its potentials. Despite the Vietnam–Japan Economic Partnership Agreement that came into force in 2009, Vietnam still lags far behind more developed ASEAN peers in terms of trade, investment and tourism ties with Japan. For example, in 2012, there were only 579,617 Japanese tourist arrivals in Vietnam compared to 1,373,716 in Thailand.[7] By the same token, as shown in Figure 5.1, Japan's annual FDI in Vietnam generally remains lower than in Indonesia, Singapore and Thailand.

FIGURE 5.1
Japanese FDI into Key ASEAN Economies

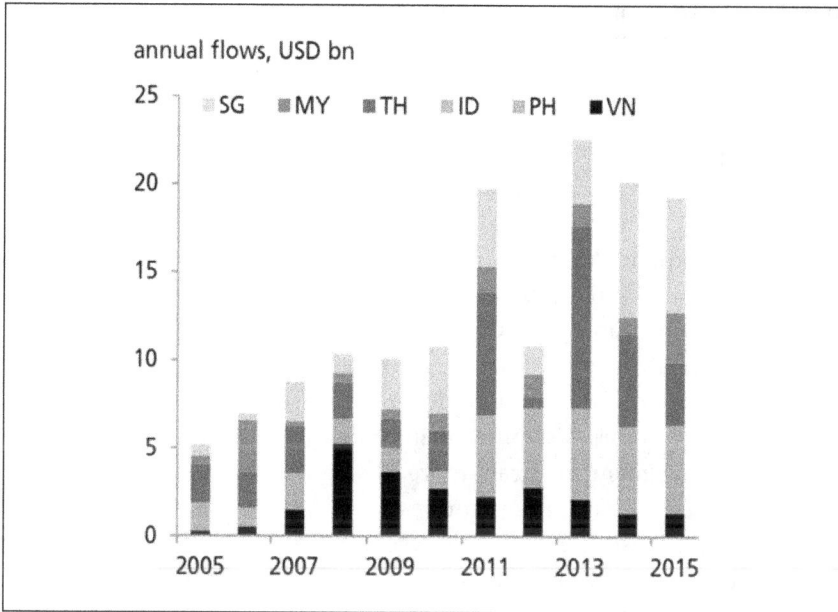

annual flows, USD bn

SG MY TH ID PH VN

Source: DBS Group Research (2016).

Japan's economic protectionism is yet another impediment to economic cooperation between the two countries. A key example is the agricultural sector where lowering trade barriers remains a difficult challenge for Japan in both bilateral and multilateral trade arrangements. However, an encouraging sign is that although the opening-up of the agricultural market to each other's exporters have been rather slow, certain progress has been made. For example, during Prime Minister Shinzo Abe's visit to Hanoi in January 2017, the two sides announced that Japan would allow the import of red-fleshed dragon fruits from Vietnam, and Vietnam would do the same to Japanese pears.

On the part of Vietnam, due to certain limitations of its economy, such as the low development base, corruption, poor infrastructure and lack of supporting industries, Vietnam has been unable to make full use of Japanese resources to accelerate its economic modernization. On the one hand, Japan's transfer of new, environmentally friendly and energy-saving technologies to Vietnam has been limited, and Vietnam is hardly ready to be a reliable partner of Japan in large-scale manufacturing projects for hi-tech or highly value-added products. On the other hand, along with the establishment of the ASEAN Economic Community (AEC), lower tariff barriers within ASEAN and the declining returns from labour-intensive industries could steer Japanese companies away from Vietnam in the near future if Hanoi cannot further improve its investment environment with legal reforms, policy incentives, and infrastructure and human resource upgrades. In a survey in 2013, about 70 per cent of Japanese investors in Vietnam said they planned to expand their business in the country if the government created a more favourable environment for their investment (*Voice of Vietnam* 2013). Since the CPV's twelfth national congress in early 2016, the Vietnamese government under Prime Minister Nguyen Xuan Phuc has conducted various reforms towards this end. However, whether such reforms would bring lasting improvements to the business environment to attract more investment from Japan as well as other countries remains an open question.

Meanwhile, despite recent progress, security and strategic cooperation remains modest due to some visible gaps in the two states' perception of their national interests as well as their expectation of the relationship. While Japan needs stronger political and security ties with Vietnam to support Japan's proactive role in the region and at the United Nations, Vietnam's biggest interest is to tap into Japan's economic resources to facilitate its domestic economic reforms and national development. The perception of Japan as a country without an independent security policy due to constitutional restraints and its dependence on the United States remains strong among certain Vietnamese policymakers. Moreover, Japan itself is facing domestic public opinion divisions between a pacifist orientation supported by the majority of the Japanese public and the "remilitarization" promoted by the Abe administration. Given Japan's complicated domestic politics and its militarist historical record, Japan's "Look South" policy has so far been limited to "indirect balancing", i.e. strengthening economic ties and capacity building assistance in maritime security for Vietnam and some ASEAN countries (Wallace 2013) rather than a full-fledged "Go South" strategy. As for Vietnam, despite recent heightened tensions with China in the South China Sea, Hanoi has not changed its long-standing non-alignment policy towards a hard balancing strategy against China (Do 2016). Rather, Hanoi has been carefully building strategic partnerships with Japan and other powers "so that it can be seen as acting independently while keeping options open with China" (Hoang 2012).

Therefore, it can be argued that the extent to which Hanoi may further enhance its security and defence cooperation with Tokyo largely depends on two factors: future shifts in great power relations, especially those within the China–Japan–U.S. triangle, and the degree of China's assertiveness in the South China Sea. In this context, Vietnam and Japan may want to be cautious in strengthening bilateral security and defence cooperation so as not to aggravate the security dilemma in the region. Despite the fact that both Japan and Vietnam have clearly stated that their cooperation will not target any third countries, Beijing may misinterpret Vietnam's support for Japan's "proactive pacifism in Asia" as an attempt to contain China's rise and undermine its regional influence. Moreover, as China remains an important partner of Vietnam in various aspects, should China adopt a more moderate stance on the South China Sea disputes, Vietnam may be discouraged from pursuing deepened securities ties with Japan for fear of unsettling its relations with Beijing.

In sum, although Hanoi and Tokyo have tried to strengthen their security and defence ties, their divergent views and positions vis-à-vis China and the ongoing power shifts in East Asia may constrain their strategic cooperation. With Japan's support, Vietnam is now in a better strategic position to deal with China's pressures. Hanoi, however, will not go as far as to form an alliance with Tokyo to openly counterbalance Beijing in the near future. As China's neighbours, Vietnam and Japan share interests in maintaining healthy economic relations and peaceful co-existence with China.[8] As such, although defence and security ties between Vietnam and Japan have been strengthened in recent times, economic cooperation will likely remain the top priority for bilateral agenda in the foreseeable future.

Conclusion

The Vietnam–Japan relationship is driven by the two countries' shared economic and strategic interests, ranging from trade and investment to maritime cooperation. Based on strong political trust and well-developed people-to-people connections, Vietnam–Japan relations have been continuously upgraded to better serve their expanding national interests and to respond to the shifting geopolitical landscape of the region. So far, the greatest successes in bilateral cooperation have been in the economic domain, but the partnership also bears significance in strategic terms. Japan aims to strengthen Vietnam's and ASEAN's resilience against the backdrop of China's rise and its uncertain consequences. Meanwhile, Vietnam also wishes to strengthen its strategic ties with Japan to improve its posture in the South China Sea. However, future prospects of the bilateral relationship are also facing certain challenges, most notably the mismatch between the two countries' expectations in strategic terms. While Japan's strategic rapprochement with Vietnam is hindered by its constitutional constraints, Vietnam is also cautious not to firm up its securities ties with Japan too quickly at the expense of its relationship with China.

Despite such shortcomings and challenges, Vietnam–Japan cooperation is not only important for the security and economic well-being of both countries, but also bears significant implications for the evolving power shift in Asia. A resurgent Japan and an empowered Vietnam will contribute to the maintenance of the regional balance of power. While the U.S.–China relationship remains central to East Asian security, other regional players like Japan and Vietnam may still play a role in shaping the network of bilateral ties that may prove useful to regional security and stability, especially if U.S.–China strategic rivalry intensifies, or the U.S. disengages itself from the region. Japan and Vietnam share a common interest in ensuring that the changing strategic balance in East Asia will not become detrimental to the stability, security, and prosperity of themselves and the region, and that any unilateral attempts to change the *status quo* through force and coercion will be deterred. As such, the enhanced strategic partnership between Japan and Vietnam may contribute to the shaping of a balanced multi-polar regional order that is not solely dependent on the turbulent dynamics of U.S.–China relations.

NOTES

1. The Dong Du Movement (*Toyu Undo* or *Donzu Undo* in Japanese, *Phong trào Đông Du* in Vietnamese) was a patriotic movement of Vietnamese intellectuals in the early twentieth century. Led by Phan Boi Chau, it was

aimed at encouraging talented Vietnamese youths to go to Japan to learn from Japan's experience of modernization, thereby helping to liberate Vietnam from French colonialism. At its peak in 1907, about 200 Vietnamese students were sent to Japan.

2. While this is more evident in economic terms, Vietnam's reliance on China in the security realm should not be disregarded, at least in three dimensions: regime security (ideology), land border security, and maritime security.

3. For a broader understanding of the importance of ASEAN and Vietnam to Japan's overall economic diplomacy, see Section 3 "Economic Diplomacy" in Japan's 2016 Bluebook, *Japan's Foreign Policy to Promote National and Worldwide Interests*, available at <http://www.mofa.go.jp/files/000106463.pdf>.

4. For an analysis of the strategy, see Dinh (2009), p. 127.

5. Data compiled from the Vietnam National Administration of Tourism and Japan National Tourism Organization.

6. This is the highest rate among ASEAN nations.

7. Data of Japanese overseas travellers was retrieved and compiled from the website of Japan National Tourism Organization (JNTO), JETRO (available at <https://www.jetro.go.jp/en/reports/statistics/>), and Vienam National Administration of Tourism (available at <http://www.vietnamtourism.com/en/index.php/news/items/4764>).

8. For a detailed discussion of Vietnam's position in ongoing Sino–Japanese rivalry, see Vuving and Do (2017).

REFERENCES

BBC. "Asian Countries Challenge China on Rare Earth Minerals", 20 June 2012. Available at <http://www.bbc.com/news/science-environment-18508692> (accessed 2 May 2017).

Dang, Cam Tu. "Promoting Extensive Strategic Partnership Vietnam–Japan: From a Vietnamese Perspective". Paper presented at the Nexus between Japan's Path of Postwar 70 Years and Vietnam's International Integration, 2015.

DBS Group Research. "Japan: Rising Direct Investment in Southeast Asia", 18 March 2016. Available at <https://www.dbs.com/aics/pdfController.page?pdfpath=/content/article/pdf/AIO/160318_insights_japan_looks_to_southeast_asia_for_growth.pdf> (accessed 11 May 2017).

Dinh, Thi Hien Luong. "Vietnam–Japan Relations in the Context of Building an East Asian Community". *Asia-Pacific Review* 16, no. 1 (2009): 100–30.

Do, Thuy Thi. "Locating Vietnam–Japan Strategic Partnership in the Changing East Asian Security Landscape". *JIIA Working Paper* (11 July 2014).

————. "'Firm in Principles, Flexible in Strategy and Tactics': Understanding the Logic of Vietnam's China Policy". *Asian Journal of Comparative Politics* 2, no. 1 (2016): 24–39.

General Department of Customs. "Preliminary Assessment of Vietnam International Merchandise Trade Performance in December and the Whole Year 2016", 6 February 2017. Available at <https://www.customs.gov.vn/Lists/EnglishStatistics/ViewDetails.aspx?ID=627&Category=Express%20news&Group=Trade%20news%20%26%20Analysis&language=en-US> (accessed 18 March 2017).

Goh, Evelyn. "Great Powers and Hierarchical Order in Southeast Asia: Analyzing Regional Security Strategies". *International Security* 32, no. 3 (2008): 113–57.

Government of Japan. "National Defense Program Guidelines for FY 2014 and Beyond", 2013. Available at <http://www.kantei.go.jp/foreign/96_abe/documents/2013/__icsFiles/afieldfile/2013/12/17/NDPG(Summary).pdf> (accessed 25 April 2017).

Hanoi Times. "Japan to Help Train 1,000 Vietnamese Doctoral Students", 4 March 2008. Available at <http://www.hanoitimes.com.vn/my-hanoi/lifestyle/2008/03/81E20DF5/japan-to-help-train-1-000-vietnamese-doctoral-students> (accessed 17 April 2017).

Hayashi, Yuka. "Abe's Diamond Defense Diplomacy". *Wall Street Journal*, 17 January 2013. Available at <https://blogs.wsj.com/japanrealtime/2013/01/17/abes-diamond-defense-diplomacy/> (accessed 12 April 2017).

Hiep, Le Hong. "Performance-based Legitimacy: The Case of the Communist Party of Vietnam and *Doi Moi*". *Contemporary Southeast Asia* 34, no. 2 (2012): 145–72.

————. "The Strategic Significance of Vietnam–Japan Ties". *ISEAS Perspective* 23 (2017).

Hoang, Lien. "Vietnam Floats between China and US". *Asia Times*, 12 May 2012. Available at <http://www.atimes.com/atimes/Southeast_Asia/NE12Ae01.html> (accessed 17 April 2017).

Japan Student Services Organization. "International Students in Japan 2015", 2016. Available at <http://www.jasso.go.jp/en/about/statistics/intl_student/data2015.html> (accessed 2 May 2017).

Japan Times. "Japan, Vietnam to Hold Maritime Security Talks in May", 15 April 2013. Available at <http://www.japantimes.co.jp/news/2013/04/15/national/politics-diplomacy/japan-vietnam-to-hold-maritime-security-talks-in-may/> (accessed 12 April 2017).

————. "Vietnam Seen as a Potential Role Model for Japan", 14 June 2014. Available at <http://www.japantimes.co.jp/news/2014/06/14/national/media-national/vietnam-seen-potential-role-model-japan/> (accessed 9 May 2017).

Kishida, Fumio. "Foreign Policy Speech by Minister for Foreign Affairs Fumio Kishida to the 186th Session of the Diet", 24 January 2014. Available at <http:// www.mofa.go.jp/fp/pp/page18e_000037.html> (accessed 22 April 2017).

Kyodo News. "Japan, Vietnam to Tighten Maritime Relations amid China Threat", 7 October 2013.

Ministry of Foreign Affairs of Japan. "Opinion Poll on Japan in Six ASEAN Countries", 2008. Available at <http://www.mofa.go.jp/region/asia-paci/ asean/survey/qa0803.pdf> (accessed 10 May 2017).

Nguyen, Phuong. "Japan's Pivot Should Be Sustained: View from Southeast Asia". *Cogitasia,* 8 October 2014. Available at <https://www.cogitasia.com/ japans-pivot-should-be-sustained-view-from-southeast-asia/> (accessed 12 April 2017).

Nhan Dan. "Thuc day quan he huu nghi, doi tac chien luoc Viet Nam — Nhat Ban ngay cang phat trien", 15 March 2014. Available at <http://www. nhandan.com.vn/chinhtri/xa-luan/item/22609702-thuc-day-quan-he-huu-nghi-doi-tac-chien-luoc-viet-nam-nhat-ban-ngay-cang-phat-trien.html> (accessed 7 May 2017).

———. "Promoting and Deepening the Vietnam–Japan Strategic Partnership", 15 September 2015. Available at <http://en.nhandan.com.vn/indepth/ item/3624802-developing-and-deepening-vietnam-japan-strategic-partnership. html> (accessed 9 May 2017).

Nippon. "Japan's Foreign Population Climbs to All-Time High", 29 March 2016. Available at <http://www.nippon.com/en/features/h00137/> (accessed 10 May 2017).

Ogasawara, Takayuki. "The Prospects for a Strategic Partnership between Japan and Vietnam". *AJISS-Commentary* 124 (16 June 2011).

Pew Research Center. "Chapter 4: How Asians View Each Other". *Spring 2014 Global Attitudes Survey,* 14 July 2014. Available at <http://www.pewglobal. org/2014/07/14/chapter-4-how-asians-view-each-other> (accessed 10 May 2017).

Thayer, Carlyle A. "Sino–Vietnamese Relations: The Interplay of Ideology and National Interest". *Asian Survey* 34, no. 6 (1994): 513–28.

Tran, My Hoa. "Quan he Viet Nam — Nhat Ban trong linh vuc giao duc nhung nam gan day" [Vietnam–Japan Relations in the Field of Education in Recent Years]. *Center for Japanese Studies* (2016). Available at <http://cjs. inas.gov.vn/index.php?newsid=1085> (accessed 7 May 2017).

Tuoi Tre. "Nhat Ban la doi tac quan trong hang dau", 6 September 2015. Available at <http://tuoitre.vn/tin/the-gioi/20150916/nhat-ban-la-doi-tac-quan-trong-hang-dau/969723.html> (accessed 2 May 2017).

Tuoi Tre News. "Japanese Govn't to Back 6 Key Industries in VN", 5 December 2013. Available at <http://tuoitrenews.vn/business/9519/japanese-govnt-to-back-6-key-industries-in-vn> (accessed 5 April 2017).

VCCI News. "Japanese Prime Minister Shinzo Abe's Visit to Vietnam: Deepening Strategic Partnership", 25 February 2013. Available at <http://vccinews. com/news_detail.asp?news_id=27977> (accessed 9 May 2017).

Vietnam News. "Vietnam, Japan Boost Defence Cooperation", 16 April 2013. Available at <http://vietnamnews.vn/politics-laws/238284/vietnam-japan-boost-defence-cooperation.html> (accessed 8 August 2017).

Vietrade. "Thuong mai Viet Nam – Nhat Ban: Ky vong dat 60 ty vao nam 2020", 10 February 2017. Available at <http://www.vietrade.gov.vn/tin-tc/6118-thuong-mai-viet-nam-nhat-ban-ky-vong-dat-60-ty-usd-vao-nam-2020.html> (accessed 10 May 2017).

VnExpress. "Viet Nam la doi tac ODA quan trong nhat cua Nhat" [Vietnam is the Most Important ODA Partner of Japan]", 31 January 2013. Available at <http://kinhdoanh.vnexpress.net/tin-tuc/vi-mo/viet-nam-la-doi-tac-oda-quan-trong-nhat-cua-nhat-2726083.html> (accessed 3 May 2017).

Voice of Vietnam. "Viet Nam – Nhat Ban: Doi tac chien luoc tin cay, ben vung", 12 December 2013. Available at <http://vov.vn/vov-binh-luan/viet-namnhat-ban-doi-tac-chien-luoc-tin-cay-ben-vung-296521.vov> (accessed 10 May 2017).

Vuving, Alexander L. and Thuy T. Do. "Vietnam between China and Japan in the Asian Security Complex". In *Chinese–Japanese Competition and the East Asian Security Complex*, edited by Jeffrey Reeves, Jeffrey Hornung and Kerry L. Nankivell. New York: Routledge, 2017, pp. 159–77.

Wallace, Corey J. "Japan's Strategic Pivot South: Diversifying the Dual Hedge". *International Relations of the Asia-Pacific* 13, no. 3 (2013): 479–517.

World Bank. "Vietnam Product Exports and Imports from Japan 2015", 2015. Available at <http://wits.worldbank.org/CountryProfile/en/Country/VNM/Year/2015/TradeFlow/EXPIMP/Partner/JPN/Product/All-Groups> (accessed 9 May 2017).

Yamamoto, Kazuya. "Vietnam from the Perspective of the Asia Barometer Survey: Identity, Images of Foreign Nations, and Global Concerns". *Memoirs of the Institute of Oriental Culture* 150 (2007).

Yoshimatsu, Hidetaka. "The Mekong Region, Regional Integration, and Political Rivalry Among ASEAN, China and Japan". *Asian Perspective* 34 (2010): 71–111.

6

The Reinvigoration of India–Vietnam Partnership under Prime Minister Modi

Rajeev Ranjan Chaturvedy

Bilateral ties between Hanoi and Delhi have been on the upswing in recent years with a focus on strategic cooperation and trade. While Vietnam sees India as a natural ally, India also treats Vietnam as one of its trusted and privileged partners. The strengthening of bilateral ties mainly results from changes in the two countries' foreign policy agenda that aim to respond to shifts in the geostrategic landscape of the Indo-Pacific region.

The current chapter examines the drivers of the deepening partnership between India and Vietnam. It posits that the elevation of the India–Vietnam Strategic Partnership to a Comprehensive Strategic Partnership in September 2016 is a natural outcome of the increasing convergence of the two countries' strategic interests and can contribute positively to the regional stability and prosperity.

The chapter starts with an introduction of India's foreign policy under the government of Prime Minister Narendra Modi, followed by a brief background of India–Vietnam relations. The chapter then analyses drivers of recent developments in bilateral ties and the various measures that both sides have taken to improve their relationship. Finally, the chapter concludes by assessing the implications of the deepening bilateral ties for the broader region.

India's Foreign Policy under Modi

As one of the fastest growing economies in an increasingly interdependent world, India has been pursuing an active international economic integration agenda, which has enabled the country to benefit from a wide range of economic engagements. At the same time, India's rising economic clout and diplomatic dynamism have uplifted its global status, bringing about remarkable transformations in the country's foreign policy. India now stands at a critical juncture, preparing itself to become a responsible stakeholder in the emerging global and regional economic and security architectures. The direction and key elements of Indian foreign policy are driven by both India's national interests and the political ideology of the party in power.

In order to understand India's foreign policy in general and its policy towards Vietnam in particular, it would be pertinent to begin with understanding what India's key national interests are. These interests can be grouped into three major categories:[1] *first*, securing the country against external and internal threats to its territory, population, and vital economic interests; *second*, obtaining the external inputs necessary to achieve economic prosperity and inclusive growth; and *third*, playing an active role in international forums and global governance structures to secure a fair and equitable share of global public goods, ensuring their compatibility with India's national interests, and contributing to their development (Kumar and Kumar 2010). Under the government of Prime Minister Narendra Modi, these guiding principles have been shaping India's external engagements and its relationships with countries in the world, including Vietnam.

The Bharatiya Janata Party (BJP) came to power in a landslide victory in May 2014 under the leadership of Narendra Modi. At the time, little was known about Modi's approach to foreign policy. Since his inauguration as prime minister on 26 May 2014, however, Modi has "surprised many by investing considerable political capital in high-powered diplomacy so early in his term" (Chellaney 2014). He has been active in engaging India's bilateral partners as well as regional and global multilateral institutions. Indeed, by "gaining the attention of different international power groups and having them compete for India's friendship" (Desouza 2015), Modi has demonstrated remarkable performance on the foreign policy front. Although he is being criticized by opposition leaders for his frequent foreign trips, the broader consensus among India watchers is that Modi has pursued India's foreign policy with exceptional dynamism. To a certain extent, Modi is "globalising and revolutionising" (Chaulia 2016, p. 5) India's foreign policy in an unprecedented way.

While there is no articulation of a foreign policy grand strategy by New Delhi, it is easy to identify the key elements of India's engagements with the world. The major powers want India to succeed economically and to become a responsible stakeholder at the global stage. As such, the performance of the Indian economy, together with its democratic vibrancy, will shape the global views of a rising India in the years ahead. The Modi government understands that the real challenges for India's international stature lie in how to achieve sustained economic and inclusive growth for the country. Hence, Modi has demonstrated his keenness to put economics first, and has made national economic development the focus of India's global relations. Modi's emphasis on the five Ts — trade, tourism, talent, technology and tradition (Modi 2014) — reflects this mindset behind his foreign policy. The challenge for Indian diplomacy would therefore be how to align India's national interests with these aspects and project India as a reliable and responsible stakeholder in global affairs.

To achieve sustained economic growth, India needs a peaceful periphery. India's ability to manage its neighbourhood, both continental and maritime, is also critical to its efforts to become a responsible stakeholder in regional and global affairs. Therefore, the Modi government has attached great importance to the building of stronger ties with India's neighbours (Chaturvedy 2015a).

Engaging the Extended Neighbourhood

Deeper engagement with countries in the Indo-Pacific region has become an "integral, inseparable and irreversible plank" (Ram 2015, p. 19) of India's foreign policy. India has long been expected to play a bigger role in the Indo-Pacific region, but it is still addressing the consequences of years of relative neglect of the region. Over the years, there has been steady and substantial progress in India's overall engagement with ASEAN countries and its East Asian neighbours under the rubric of the "Look East Policy". Designed to help India reposition itself further towards its eastern neighbours, the Look East Policy has indeed shaped New Delhi's engagement with the Indo-Pacific for over two decades, substantially deepening its economic, institutional, and security relations with the region (Das and Thomas 2016). For example, India's trade turnover with ASEAN has increased from about US$10 billion in 2000 to US$76.53 billion in 2014–15, turning ASEAN into India's fourth largest trade partner (Ministry of External Affairs 2017a). India's trade with other East Asian and Asia-Pacific countries, such as China, South Korea, Japan and Australia, has also increased significantly over the same period. Apart from trade, India–ASEAN bilateral investment has also increased substantially. ASEAN's foreign direct investment (FDI) into India between April 2000 and May 2016 was about US$49.40 billion, while FDI outflow from India to ASEAN countries from April 2007 to March 2015 was about US$38.672 billion (Ministry of External Affairs 2017a). Initially designed to develop India's economic ties with Southeast Asia, India's engagement with its eastern neighbours under the Look East Policy has since been expanded to include Northeast Asia, Australia and New Zealand as well. In recent years, the policy has acquired a strategic dimension with a significant emphasis on naval cooperation (Ram 2012, 2015).

While India's deeper engagement with its extended neighbourhood promises to enhance India's economic and strategic space, how much India will benefit from such a policy will hinge upon the implementation of announcements made in the past and by the current government. The Modi government is shifting the discourse from "Look East" to "Act East".[2] The "Act East" term reflects a more dynamic and action-oriented engagement. The challenge for India in pursuing this policy, however, would arise from the changing regional balance of power due to China's increasing strategic and economic influence and its assertiveness in regional territorial and maritime disputes, including those in the South and East China Seas. Nevertheless, with its growing economic and strategic interests and capabilities, India still seeks to play a greater role in the Indo-Pacific region through its Act East Policy.

Engaging the Maritime Neighbourhood

Over 90 per cent by volume and 70 per cent by value of India's external trade is shipped by sea. Maritime resources also play a central part in India's strategy to develop its blue economy, which is expected to help bolster the country's rising economic power. Articulating his vision of the blue economy at the International Fleet Review in Vishakhapatnam on 7 February 2016, Prime Minister Modi remarked:

> An important part of India's transformation is my vision of "Blue Economy". The Blue Chakra — or the wheel — in our National Flag, represents the potential of the Blue Economy. An essential part of this pursuit is the development of India's coastal and island territories: but, not just for tourism. We want to build new pillars of economic activity in the coastal areas and in linked hinterlands through sustainable tapping of oceanic resources. Strengthening our marine research, development of eco-friendly, marine industrial and technology base, and fisheries are other elements of our goal (Ministry of External Affairs 2016c).

To take Modi's visions forward, the National Institution for Transforming India (NITI Aayog) has started a consultation process which highlights India's status as a major maritime nation with a long coastline and the potential to become a significant blue economy (Mahendra Singh 2016). The importance of the maritime domain to India's well-being is also well reflected in former Chief of Naval Staff Admiral R.K. Dhowan's statement that the twenty-first century is the "century of the seas" for India, and that "the seas will remain a key enabler in her (India's) global resurgence" (Ministry of Defence 2015, p. i). The maritime domain has therefore emerged as a crucial element in India's internal development as well as external engagement strategies. Against this backdrop, India's revised maritime security strategy titled "Ensuring Secure Seas: Indian Maritime Security Strategy" released in October 2015 has taken a holistic approach towards maritime security and underlined the great importance India attaches to securing its maritime interests.

In recent years, New Delhi has intensified its efforts to engage with states in the Indo-Pacific region (Chaturvedy 2014, pp. 47–48). The Modi government has laid out a comprehensive framework for India's maritime engagement which includes deepening security cooperation with India's maritime neighbours; building multilateral cooperative maritime security in the Indian Ocean; focusing on sustainable economic development for all through expanding cooperation on the blue economy; cooperating with extra-regional powers; and defending India's maritime interests (Mohan 2015*b*). As such, the Modi government appears pragmatic and decisive in pursuing a larger role in the promotion of regional mechanisms for collective security and economic prosperity.

As the protection of sea lines of communication (SLOCs) has emerged as a fundamental feature of India's foreign policy, the Indian navy is playing an increasingly central role in India's overall strategy towards its maritime neighbours. Indeed, Modi's first visit outside Delhi after his inauguration was to go aboard the Indian aircraft carrier *Vikramaditya* in June 2014 and induct the warship into the Indian navy (Chaudhury 2015). The Indian navy and other defence forces hold regular training, exercises and visits with almost all the countries in East Asia, including China. India has also started supplying defence equipment, parts, and technologies to some Southeast Asian countries, including Malaysia, Indonesia, Laos and Vietnam (Jha 2011; Muni 2012, pp. 216–17). In addition, Delhi has made arrangements with most countries in the Indian Ocean region to allow Indian naval ships, submarines and aircraft to avail refuelling and turnaround facilities at very short notice (Prakash 2013).

Against this backdrop, the maritime dimension of the Act East Policy will likely become a major focus of India's future regional policy, especially when the notion of the security and development interlinkage between the Pacific Ocean and the Indian Ocean has been increasingly accepted in recent years. Known collectively as the Indo-Pacific,[3] the term has gained salience in India as Delhi begins to appreciate the importance of its economic and strategic interests (see, for example, Medcalf 2015; Ministry of External Affairs 2017*b*; Mohan 2015*a*; Townshend and Medcalf 2016). At the same time, given India's rise and its expanding military capabilities, there is a growing regional interest in India's larger contribution to peace and stability in Southeast Asia (Mohan 2013, p. 134). Indeed, India has engaged in joint naval exercises and exchanged port calls with some Southeast Asian states, including Singapore, Malaysia, Indonesia and Vietnam. The Indian Navy has also been involved in several high-profile humanitarian assistance and disaster relief operations in the region.[4]

Moreover, India's policy initiatives and announcements also denote its pursuit of a stable, rules-based Asian security architecture. Towards this end, India has established or co-established its own multilateral regional institutions, including the Mekong-Ganga Cooperation (MGC), the Bay of Bengal Initiative for Multi-Sectoral Scientific, Technological and Economic Cooperation (BIMSTEC), and the Indian Ocean Rim Association (IORA) (Mukherjee and O'Donnell 2013). Through these policy initiatives, India seeks to strengthen regional physical connectivity and create a connected Asia that must be governed by commonly agreed international norms, rules and practices.

At the same time, India has also stressed that nations should be committed to upholding freedom of navigation (FON) and solving disputes through peaceful measures. Speaking at the Second Raisina Dialogue in January 2017 in New Delhi, Prime Minister Modi remarked that "respecting Freedom of Navigation and adhering to international norms *is essential* for peace and economic growth in the larger and *inter-linked marine geography of the Indo-Pacific*" (emphasis added) (Ministry of External Affairs 2017*b*). India's position regarding the FON has been consistent. For example, "India–Germany Joint Statement during the visit of Prime Minister Modi to Germany" underlines the importance of FON in international waters, the right of passage and other maritime rights and obligations in accordance with the 1982 UNCLOS and other principles of international law. Similarly, the "US–India Joint Strategic Vision for the Asia-Pacific and Indian Ocean Region" adopted in 2015 affirms the importance of safeguarding maritime security and ensuring freedom of navigation and aviation throughout the region, especially in the South China Sea. It notes: "We call on all parties to avoid the threat or use of force and pursue resolution of territorial and maritime disputes through all peaceful means, in accordance with universally recognized principles of international law, including the United Nations Convention on the Law of the Sea" (The White House 2015).

Key Drivers of India–Vietnam Strategic Relations

The foundation of the modern India–Vietnam relationship can be traced back to their shared history of decolonization and early nationalism, especially their mutual support for each other's national independence (Duong 2008, p. 339). India was considered by the Democratic Republic of Vietnam's leadership as one of the most trusted friends, and Delhi was also where one of the republic's first foreign missions was established in 1948. In October 1954, Indian Prime Minister Jawaharlal Nehru was the first foreign leader to visit North Vietnam after the country was temporarily divided following the conclusion of the Geneva Accords. From India's perspective, its main policy goal in Vietnam during this early era of bilateral relations was "to extend the area of peace and of non-alignment in Southeast Asia" (Sardesai 1968, p. 248). Since then, India has remained a trusted friend of Vietnam, providing Hanoi with consistent diplomatic support throughout the Vietnam War as well as during its international isolation in the 1980s.

While bilateral ties have flourished comprehensively since Vietnam launched its economic reforms in 1986, Delhi and Hanoi have particularly strengthened their strategic cooperation in recent years. Indeed, as India pursues its Act East Policy, Vietnam has become a valuable partner in India's political and security engagements in the Indo-Pacific region. The two countries are working together to address shared strategic concerns, such as energy security and open and secure SLOCs, and to ensure that their extended neighbourhood is free to make policy choices without undue external meddling (Prasad and Mullen 2013). Given India's broadening economic and strategic interests in the region and Vietnam's desire for strategic autonomy, both countries will benefit from a stronger bilateral relationship.

Despite their dissimilar models of governance, India and Vietnam continue to be bound by shared interests. As observed by strategic analyst David Brewster, "India is at least partly motivated by a desire to balance against China through strengthening Vietnam's military power and to challenge the perceived growth in China's naval capabilities" (Brewster 2009, p. 24). From India's perspective, the uncertainty surrounding Beijing's long-term ambitions in the Indo-Pacific means that India is likely to benefit from a comprehensive strategic partnership with Vietnam, given the latter's geostrategic location as one of China's gateways to Southeast Asia, as well as its long history of resistance against China's expansionism. Meanwhile, Vietnam also views its deepening ties with India as consistent with its overall foreign policy of "diversification and multilateralization", and a helpful means to improve its strategic position vis-à-vis China (Hiep 2013*a*, 2013*b*).

More importantly, India has a vital interest in the South China Sea of which Vietnam is a littoral state. Recent tensions over territorial and maritime disputes there due to China's increasing assertiveness have jeopardized regional peace and stability, and alarmed not only Vietnam but also India. In particular, two incidents have deepened Delhi's awareness of its strategic and economic interests in the South China Sea as well as its desire to strengthen its engagement with Vietnam. In the first incident on 22 July 2011, India's warship *INS Airavat* reportedly received a warning from China when it was about 45 nautical miles off the Vietnamese coast after paying a friendship visit. The second occurred in September 2011, when oil exploration by India's state-owned Oil and Natural Gas Corporation Videsh (ONGC Videsh) in Vietnam's territorial waters was objected by China (Muni 2011).

At the broader level, India's renewed interest in Southeast Asia's maritime domain in general and the South China Sea in particular can be attributed to five major reasons (Mohan 2012, pp. 184–86). *First*, due to India's increasing trade with East Asia, it has begun to recognize the importance of SLOCs beyond India's geographical proximity, including in the Western Pacific. *Second*, India seeks to be less dependent on major powers for its maritime needs in the Western Pacific. *Third*, India is apprehensive about China's "new assertiveness" (Yahuda 2013) that could turn the South China Sea into a "Chinese lake" at its discretion, including by force. *Fourth*, to enhance its maritime intelligence, India desires to maintain a presence in the region to track potential developments that could harm its national interests. *Fifth*, the Indian navy underlines the critical importance of a forward maritime presence and naval partnerships to deter potential adversaries. Indian policymakers are acutely aware of expectations of Southeast Asian littoral states and Delhi is willing to take a principled stand on territorial disputes in a hope to contribute to the stabilization of the Indo-Pacific (Abhijit Singh 2016, p. 17).

India's interests and its approach towards the South China Sea have been clearly articulated on several platforms by Indian policymakers. For example, speaking at the Raisina Dialogue in New Delhi, Indian Foreign Secretary Subrahmanyam Jaishankar said, "Respect for the global commons should not be diluted under any circumstances. Much depends on the commitment of nations to uphold freedom of navigation and peaceful resolution of disputes. *There should be no place for use or threat of use of force*" (emphasis added) (Ministry of External Affairs 2016*d*).

The statement underlines three key features of India's approach to maritime issues, including the South China Sea disputes. Specifically, India has a strong interest in maintaining the freedom of navigation in the South China Sea, which India considers to be essential for peace and prosperity in the Indo-Pacific region. India also emphasizes the preservation of regional peace and stability, and therefore opposes the use or threat of force to resolve competing claims. Finally, India insists that the resolution of disputes must be in accordance with international law, including the 1982 United Nations Convention on the Law of the Sea (UNCLOS). Such positions align closely with Vietnam's stance on the management of the South China Sea disputes.

To a certain extent, India's increasing maritime presence in the South China Sea could be seen as an indicator of India's desire to play a more active role in the region's emerging security architecture. India believes that its strategic interests, both in handling its external threats and in meeting its aspirations to be a global power, demand a close partnership with ASEAN (Mansingh 2012, pp. 188–89). While India has been mindful of the China factor in expanding its footprint in Southeast Asia, ASEAN countries, including Vietnam, also want to engage India in the region more effectively to counterbalance China's presence (Sibal 2012, p. 193). Such a congruence of strategic interests between India and Vietnam has contributed to the strengthening of bilateral ties.

Strengthening Delhi–Hanoi Ties under Modi

During Prime Minister Narendra Modi's visit to Vietnam in September 2016, the two sides officially upgraded their "strategic partnership" to a "comprehensive strategic partnership".[5] The move was remarkable as it is an example of how the Modi government put its Act East Policy into action. In his press statement, Modi remarked, "Our decision to upgrade our strategic partnership to a Comprehensive Strategic Partnership captures the intent and path of our future cooperation. It will provide a new direction, momentum and substance to our bilateral cooperation. Our common efforts will also contribute to stability, security and prosperity in this region" (Ministry of External Affairs 2016*b*).

Modi has made it very clear why India and Vietnam upgraded their relationship. *First*, Modi has shown his zeal and vigour in engaging

India's partners at the highest political level, which could be seen as an effort to build political connectivity. The previous Indian government under the leadership of Dr Manmohan Singh was unable to put forward an overarching political framework to engage important partners. Modi's visit is the first bilateral visit by an Indian Prime Minister to Hanoi since Atal Bihari Vajpayee's in 2001, and he understands that political relations are as important as economic initiatives. The Indian government under his leadership is consciously making efforts to improve political connectivity along with economic and cultural cooperation. Towards this end, New Delhi is also actively engaging state governments in foreign policy manoeuvres and encouraging them to engage Vietnamese counterparts in a meaningful way. For example, Modi emphasized the need for "intensifying the exchanges among states of India and provinces of Vietnam" (Ministry of External Affairs 2016b). As India's centralized foreign policymaking is facing resistance from various state governments, Modi's approach may help develop a more diverse political framework that better promotes India's foreign policy agenda in general and India–Vietnam ties in particular.

Second, as discussed earlier, Modi had announced the intention to step up India's engagement with eastern neighbours by replacing the "Look East Policy" with the "Act East Policy". His visit to Hanoi in September 2016 reaffirms Modi's sincerity in pursuing this policy initiative. To add substance to the upgraded partnership, the two governments have also assigned their foreign ministries, in collaboration with other ministries and agencies, to coordinate the formulation of an action plan to implement the Comprehensive Strategic Partnership.

Third, as a resurgent global force, India is willing to assume greater global responsibilities and Modi wants to see India transform "from being a balancer to becoming a leader, from following rules to making rules and setting agendas" (Jaitley 2016, p. xi). Hence, elevating India–Vietnam ties can be seen as a move by the Modi government towards that end, which India expects to contribute to the region's stability, security and prosperity.

Vietnam and the Panchamrit (Five Elements) of Modi's Foreign Policy

At party level, Modi's 2016 visit to Vietnam also reflected important features of the BJP's foreign policy framework. In its resolution on foreign policy, the BJP underlined the *Panchamrit*, or the five new pillars of Indian foreign policy, namely, *Samman* (dignity and honour), *Samvad* (greater engagement and dialogue), *Samriddhi* (shared prosperity), *Suraksha* (regional and global security) and *Sanskriti evam Sabhyata* (cultural and civilizational linkages) (BJP 2015).

First, India's partnership with Vietnam is based on strong existing trust which was forged through decades of friendship and solidarity. As the two countries offered each other mutual support and did not experience any conflict in the past, their leaders "feel totally at ease and completely trust each other" (Loc 2016). Promoting relations with a traditional, longstanding friend like Vietnam can therefore be seen as a commitment to "dignity and honour" in India's foreign policy, a value that the BJP under Modi has emphasized.

Second, in terms of engagement and dialogue, several two-way high profile visits have taken place between the two countries since Modi took office, which facilitated the increasing convergence of views on various bilateral and international issues between Delhi and Hanoi. At the same time, both sides have agreed to "increase the exchange of high-level and other visits, step up relations between political parties and legislative institutions of both sides, establish relations between provincial/state governments on both sides, uphold established bilateral cooperation mechanisms, and effectively implement the agreements signed between two countries" (Ministry of External Affairs 2016*b*). Shortly after Modi's visit to Hanoi, for example, a Vietnamese parliamentary delegation led by Vietnam National Assembly Chairwoman Nguyen Thi Kim Ngan visited India in December 2016 and signed agreements on aviation, energy, and parliamentary cooperation (*Times of India* 2016).

Third, to enhance shared prosperity, Modi and his Vietnamese counterpart Nguyen Xuan Phuc emphasized that "enhancing bilateral economic engagement is a strategic objective". In January 2015, the India–Vietnam Joint Sub-Commission on Trade identified five key sectors as thrust areas for bilateral trade, including garment and textile, pharmaceuticals, agro-commodities, leather and footwear, and engineering. Currently, India is among the top ten trade partners of Vietnam, with bilateral trade turnover in 2016 reaching US$5.5 billion, a tenfold increase from 2006. Both sides have set a new bilateral trade target of US$15 billion by 2020. Major exports from India are machinery and equipment, seafood, pharmaceuticals, cotton, automobile, textile and leather accessories, cattle feed ingredients, chemicals, plastic resins, fibres, steel, fabrics, metals, jewellery and precious stones. Meanwhile, the top ten items that India imports from Vietnam include mobile phones and accessories, computers and electronics hardware, machinery and equipment, chemicals, rubber, ordinary metals, wood and wooden products, fibres, pepper, and means of transport. In terms of investment, there is ample room for improvement given the rather limited bilateral investment ties. By March 2017, Indian companies had invested in only 131 projects in Vietnam, with the total registered capital of about US$707.95 million. Major sectors of investment were energy, mineral exploration, agro-processing, sugar manufacturing, agro-chemicals, IT, and auto components. Accordingly, India ranked 25th among 110 countries and territories investing in Vietnam. Given this low base, Indian investment in Vietnam is expected to rise in the coming years (Binh 2016, pp. 115–16; Embassy of India in Vietnam 2017; Hoang 2014, pp. 212–15, 221; Kumar 2014).

Fourth, promoting regional and global security through defence cooperation has become one of the top priorities of India–Vietnam relations in recent years. Modi said in a press statement during the course of a visit to India by Vietnamese Prime Minister Nguyen Tan Dung in October 2014 that "our defence cooperation with Vietnam is among our most important ones" (Press Information Bureau 2014). To further promote defence ties, the two countries signed a Joint Vision Statement on Defence Cooperation for 2015–2020 in New Delhi in May 2015. During his visit to Vietnam in 2016, Modi reaffirmed India's significant interests in promoting bilateral defence industry cooperation and announced a new defence line of credit of US$500 million for Vietnam to facilitate its defence procurement from India (Ministry of External Affairs 2016b). Although the two sides did not elaborate on what Vietnam would use the loan for, Vietnam was reportedly interested in acquiring patrol vessels and BrahMos missiles from India to enhance its maritime defence capabilities.

During the same visit, Modi also announced a grant of US$5 million for the construction of an Army Software Park at the Telecommunication University in Nha Trang. In addition, the two countries signed a Memorandum of Understanding on cyber security and agreements on cooperation to explore the outer space for peaceful purposes, and to establish a Tracking and Data Reception Station and a Data Processing Facility near Ho Chi Minh City.

Defence cooperation between the two countries has brought about some concrete results. India has already become the second largest supplier of military equipment and personnel training to Vietnam. The Garden Reach Shipbuilders and Engineers Ltd (GRSE) has finalized the design of a series of 140-tonne fast patrol boats for Vietnam People's Navy (Vinh 2016, pp. 122–23), and Vietnam is exploring the possibility of acquiring Indian-manufactured surveillance equipment such as unmanned aerial vehicles.[6] India may also provide Vietnam with BrahMos supersonic missiles in the future. In terms of training, India is providing comprehensive underwater combat operation training to Vietnamese submariners (Ghosh 2014), which plays an important role in improving the operational capabilities of Vietnam's newly-acquired *Kilo*-class submarine fleet. In addition to the provision of training in information technology and English language skills to Vietnamese military officers, India was also reportedly offering training to Vietnamese Su-30MK2 fighter jet pilots.

In the coming years, new areas in the expanding defence cooperation between Delhi and Hanoi include bilateral cooperation in U.N. peacekeeping missions; shipbuilding; weapons system modernization; and research and application of hi-tech defence systems. As mentioned above, Vietnam has given green light for India to set up a satellite tracking and imaging centre in southern Vietnam. India currently has eleven earth observation satellites on the orbit that can provide military intelligence, with existing ground stations in the Andaman and Nicobar Islands, Brunei, Biak in eastern Indonesia, and Mauritius (Murdoch 2016). Vietnam highly values India's capabilities and the cooperation on tracking facilities as they will give Hanoi access to pictures from Indian earth observation satellites that cover Asia, including China and the South China Sea. This cooperation initiative is yet another prime example of how their strategic interests in the South China Sea converge.

Fifth, Modi showcased the cultural and civilizational dimension of his foreign policy during his Vietnam visit. He underlined the connections between Buddhism and the monuments of the Hindu Cham civilization in Central Vietnam. He also visited and offered prayers at the Quan Su Pagoda in Hanoi. Interacting with the monks, Modi said that "while some came to make war, India had come with the message of peace — the message of Buddha, which has endured", for which he received a rousing reception (Press Information Bureau

2016). During Modi's visit, India launched a scholarship programme for members of the Vietnamese Buddhist Sangha to pursue advanced Buddhist studies and the study of Sanskrit at Indian universities. Modi also announced that an Indian Culture Centre would be opened in Hanoi soon, and that the Archaeological Survey of India would start the conservation and restoration work of Cham monuments in My Son, which are a cluster of ruined Hindu temples constructed between the fourth and the fourteenth century in Central Vietnam (*Madhyamam* 2016).

Embedding Bilateral Ties into Trilateral Frameworks: The Way Forward?

Recognizing the important role that India and the United States play in promoting the security and prosperity of the Indo-Pacific region, leaders of both countries have emphasized that India's Act East Policy and the United States' rebalance to Asia provide opportunities for India, the United States, and other Indo-Pacific countries to work closely to strengthen regional cooperation. The U.S.–India Joint Strategic Vision for the Asia-Pacific and Indian Ocean Region affirms the importance of safeguarding maritime security and ensuring freedom of navigation and over-flight throughout the region, especially in the South China Sea (The White House 2015). There was indeed a new level of "comfort and candour" in the conversations between Indian and American leaders. Speaking at the U.S. Congress in June 2016, for example, Modi called the U.S. "an indispensable partner", adding that a strong India–U.S. partnership could anchor peace, prosperity and stability in the Indo-Pacific region and help "ensure security of the sea lanes of commerce and freedom of navigation on seas" (Ministry of External Affairs 2016*a*). This view was echoed by U.S. Secretary of Defence James Mattis in his remarks at the Shangri-La Dialogue in Singapore on 3 June 2017. Mattis quoted Prime Minister Modi on freedom of navigation and the interlinked geography of the Indo-Pacific in his speech. He also underlined India as "a major defence partner" and Delhi's indispensable role in maintaining stability in the maritime domain (U.S. Department of Defence 2017).

The United States under the Obama administration also planned to better secure the Indo-Pacific region by deploying different assets there, including a new long-range stealth bomber and advanced aircraft and ships (Schwartz 2015, p. 3). It also successfully negotiated the landmark Logistics Exchange Memorandum of Agreement (LEMOA) and the Defence Technology and Trade Initiative (DTTI) with India. Under the LEMOA, India's Reliance Defence and Engineering Limited signed a major contract in February 2017 with the U.S. Navy to provide repair and alteration services for ships of the Seventh Fleet. The LEMOA and DTTI add significant substance to the bilateral strategic partnership, and will facilitate future defence cooperation initiatives between the two countries in the Indo-Pacific region.

The United States also worked with some regional countries, such as India, Japan and Australia, in trilateral frameworks to promote an open, balanced and inclusive security architecture in the region. Regarding the U.S.–India–Japan trilateral framework, Modi and U.S. President Barack Obama underlined the importance of cooperation between the three countries to identify and promptly implement projects of common interest. They also decided to explore the possibility of holding the dialogue among their foreign ministers (Ministry of External Affairs 2015). More importantly, they stressed their commitment to promote regional dialogue on key political and security issues and to invest in trilateral cooperation arrangements with other like-minded countries in the region.

As such, there is a potential for embedding the India–Vietnam partnership into the India–U.S. bilateral framework, or other trilateral frameworks in which both India and the United States are members. Such arrangements will be facilitated by the convergent security interests of these countries, especially in the development of open and inclusive security structures that ensure the peaceful management of regional tensions, including in the maritime domain. Indeed, certain trilateral cooperation initiatives have been put forward. For example, India and the United States are reportedly exploring possibilities to work with Vietnam to help strengthen the country's ground forces.[7] The milestone visit by U.S. President Barrack Obama to Vietnam in May 2016, in which the United States lifted a longstanding lethal arms embargo on Vietnam, further strengthened mutual trust (Hiep 2016) and facilitated future security and defence cooperation between the two countries, including the possible inclusion of Vietnam in Washington's strategic cooperation frameworks with India and other partners.

Similarly, India and Japan are exploring a trilateral framework for cooperation with Vietnam. In fact, Delhi, Tokyo and Hanoi have reached an understanding to work in a trilateral format to coordinate positions on regional security and economic policies (Bagchi 2014). According to a senior Vietnamese scholar, "India, Vietnam and Japan have already signed a trilateral cooperation agreement in December 2014."[8] This trilateral agreement, which is mainly focused on defence technology cooperation and intelligence sharing, could be helpful for the technological modernization of Vietnam's armed forces.[9] Given their shared maritime interests in the South China Sea, India and Japan could also work with Vietnam to help strengthen the Vietnamese Navy's submarine operational capabilities.

The integration of the India–Vietnam strategic cooperation into regional mini-lateral frameworks, if successful, will not only strengthen bilateral ties but also contribute to the emergence of a "principled security network" that the Obama administration once proposed. Such a network will supplement the existing ASEAN-led regional security arrangements as well as the U.S.-led alliance systems to further bolster security and stability in the Indo-Pacific region.

Conclusion

Under the Modi government, India–Vietnam ties have gained a stronger momentum. While Vietnam sees India as a natural ally, India also regards Vietnam as one of its most trusted partners. Modi's visit to Vietnam in September 2016 was a pragmatic step to further strengthen bilateral ties, especially in the area of strategic cooperation. While strengthening ties with India is part of Vietnam's broader foreign strategy of "diversification and multilateralization" to enhance its strategic posture, especially in the South China Sea, a stronger partnership with Vietnam also contributes to the implementation of Modi's Act East Policy as well as the *Panchamrit* concept of the ruling BJP's foreign policy. The elevation of bilateral relations to the Comprehensive Strategic Partnership level in 2016 is therefore a natural outcome of the increasing convergence of the two countries' strategic interests.

The strengthening partnership between Delhi and Hanoi may play a role in the emergence of the Indo-Pacific geopolitical landscape in the coming years. For example, Vietnam–India defence and strategic cooperation, either in bilateral or mini-lateral frameworks, will contribute to the maintenance of the regional balance of power against the backdrop of gigantic geostrategic shifts due to the rise of China. At the same time, Vietnam can also help strengthen the ties between India and ASEAN, thereby engaging India deeper into the Southeast Asian region. As Carlyle Thayer aptly remarks, "Vietnam is poised to play a greater role in facilitating India's Act East Policy both as a formal strategic partner and as the next ASEAN country coordinator for relations with India. India's new role should be welcomed by ASEAN members as it will add ballast to ASEAN's efforts to maintain regional autonomy in Southeast Asia and a multi-polar balance in ASEAN's relations with external powers" (Thayer 2014).

The regular and increasing interactions between the two countries in recent years are a clear indication of progress in the relationship. Bilateral cooperation is guided by both countries' long-term economic and strategic interests that extend far beyond the South China Sea issue. However, while there is ample room for the two countries to further promote their strategic partnership, they will also have to overcome certain challenges along the way. For example, India is still preoccupied with its domestic and near-broad security issues, especially terrorism and the perceived threats from Pakistan. As such, India's implementation of the Act East Policy, including its investment into developing ties with Vietnam, will likely be constrained. Meanwhile, despite Vietnam's increasing interest in a stronger strategic partnership with India, its wish to maintain a stable relationship with China will discourage Hanoi from taking drastic measures to promote defence and security ties with Delhi. Moreover, in order to create a stronger foundation for their relations, the two countries will also need to invest more efforts in strengthening bilateral trade and investment ties, which, despite recent progress, remain rather limited.

NOTES

1. This is based on the findings of Indian Council for Research on International Economic Research (ICRIER) project titled, "The National Interest Project". This project examined India's national interest and relations with the outside world, in respect of both economic growth and security. The author was part of the project team.

2. At the 12th ASEAN–India Summit held in Nay Pyi Taw, Myanmar, in November 2014, Prime Minister Modi formally enunciated the Act East Policy.

3. The idea of an Indo-Pacific region involves recognizing that the growing economic, geopolitical, and security connections between the Western Pacific and the Indian Ocean regions are creating a single "strategic system". The term "Indo-Pacific" is also being used by the Indian government in speeches and joint statements. For example, Indian Prime Minister talked about it at the Second Raisina Dialogue in New Delhi.

4. For example, the Indian Navy has actively participated in HADR operations in the aftermath of the tsunami in 2004, Cyclone SIDR in Bangladesh in 2007, Cyclone Nargis in Myanmar in 2008, Non-combatant Evacuation Operations (NEO) in Yemen in 2015, Sri Lanka's flood and Cyclone Mora in Bangladesh, both in May 2017.

5. Although Vietnam has never clarified the criteria for these partnerships, it generally considers comprehensive strategic partnership as the most important, followed by strategic ones and then comprehensive ones. These countries generally fall into one or more of four major categories — political powers, economic powerhouses, military powers, and countries that play significant roles in the management of the South China Sea disputes (Hiep 2013*b*, p. 357).

6. Interview with a senior Vietnamese scholar, 10 March 2015.

7. Interview with a senior Vietnamese scholar in March 2015. However, it was difficult to verify this claim independently.

8. Interview with a senior Vietnamese scholar in March 2015 who wanted to remain anonymous.

9. Interview with a senior Vietnamese scholar in March 2015; interview in 2015 and 2016 with Indian and Japanese experts who wanted to remain anonymous.

REFERENCES

Bagchil, Indrani. "India Ignores China's Frown, Offers Defence Boost to Vietnam". *Times of India*, 29 October 2014. Available at <http://timesofindia.indiatimes.com/india/India-ignores-Chinas-frown-offers-defence-boost-to-Vietnam/articleshow/44965272.cms> (accessed 4 September 2017).

Bharatiya Janata Party (BJP). "Resolution on Foreign Policy Passed in BJP National Executive Meeting at Bengaluru (Karnataka)", 3 April 2015. Available at <http://www.bjp.org/en/media-resources/press-releases/resolution-on-foreign-policy-passed-in-bjp-national-executive-meeting-at-bengaluru-karnataka> (accessed 4 September 2017).

Binh, Ngo Xuan. "Vietnam–India Economic Ties: Challenges and Opportunities since 2007". *China Report* 52, no. 2 (2016).

Brewster, David. "India's Strategic Partnership with Vietnam: The Search for a Diamond on the South China Sea?" *Asian Security* 5, no. 1 (2009): 24–44.

Chaturvedy, Rajeev Ranjan. "Shoring up Maritime Security Cooperation". *Diplomatist* 2, no. 4 (2014): 47–48.

———. "India's Neighbourhood Policy Under Modi". *FPRC Journal* 1 (2015): 89–95.

———. "Five Reasons the World Needs to Pay Heed to India's New Maritime Security Strategy". *The Wire* (22 December 2015). Available at <http://thewire.in/2015/12/22/five-reasons-the-world-needs-to-pay-heed-to-indias-new-maritime-security-strategy-17741/> (accessed 31 August 2017).

Chaulia, Sreeram. *Modi Doctrine: The Foreign Policy of India's Prime Minister*. New Delhi: Bloomsbury, 2016.

Chellaney, Brahma. "Modi Reshapes India's Foreign Policy". *Deutsche Welle* (30 December 2014). Available at <http://www.dw.com/en/opinion-modi-reshapes-indias-foreign-policy/a-18159829> (accessed 29 August 2017).

Das, Gurudas and C. Joshua Thomas, eds. *Look East to Act East Policy: Implications for India's Northeast*. Oxon and New York: Routledge, 2016.

deSouza, Peter R. "Modi and his Chakravyuh". *The Hindu*, 20 May 2015. Available at <http://www.thehindu.com/opinion/op-ed/modi-and-his-chakravyuh/article7224435.ece> (accessed 29 August 2017).

Doan, Xuan Loc. "Why India, Vietnam Upgraded Their Ties". *Asia Times*, 10 September 2016. Available at <http://www.atimes.com/why-india-vietnam-upgraded-their-ties/> (accessed 4 September 2017).

Duong, Nguyen Nam. "Engaging the 'Traditional Friend': Vietnam's Approach to India in the ASEAN Context". In *India and ASEAN: Partners at Summit*, edited by P.V. Rao. New Delhi: Knowledge World, 2008.

Embassy of India in Vietnam. "India–Vietnam Relations", May 2017. Available at <http://indembassy.com.vn/cms.php?id=8> (accessed 4 September 2017).

Ghosh, P.K. "India's Strategic Vietnam Defence Relations". *The Diplomat*, 11 November 2014. Available at <http://thediplomat.com/2014/11/indias-strategic-vietnam-defense-relations/> (accessed 4 September 2017).

Hiep, Le Hong. "Vietnam's Domestic–Foreign Policy Nexus: *Doi Moi*, Foreign Policy Reform, and Sino–Vietnamese Normalization". *Asian Politics & Policy* 5, no. 3 (2013*a*): 387–406.

———. "Vietnam's Hedging Strategy against China since Normalization". *Contemporary Southeast Asia* 35, no. 3 (2013*b*): 333–68.

———. "Obama's Visit to Vietnam Gave Many Important Immediate and Long-term Outcomes". *ISEAS Perspective* 29 (2016).

Hoang, Nguyen Huy. "India–Mekong Cooperation: Vietnam Perspective". In *ASEAN–India: Deepening Economic Partnership in Mekong Region*, edited by Prabir De. New Delhi: RIS, 2014.

Jaitley, Arun. "Foreword". In *The Modi Doctrine: New Paradigms in India's Foreign Policy*, edited by Anirban Ganguly, Vijay Chauthaiwale and Uttam Kumar Sinha. New Delhi: Wisdom Tree, 2016.

Jha, Pankaj Kumar. "India's Defence Diplomacy in Southeast Asia". *Journal of Defence Studies* 5, no. 1 (2011): 47–63.

Kumar, Rajiv. "India and Vietnam Must Preserve the Ties of Trade and Friendship". *Mail Online India*, 29 October 2014. Available at <http://www.dailymail.co.uk/indiahome/indianews/article-2812002/India-Vietnam-preserve-ties-trade-friendship.html> (accessed 4 September 2017).

Kumar, Rajiv and Santosh Kumar. *In the National Interest: A Strategic Foreign Policy for India*. New Delhi: Business Standard Books, 2010.

Madhyamam. "India Offers $500-mn Defence Credit Line to Vietnam", 3 September 2016. Available at <http://www.madhyamam.com/en/national/2016/sep/3/india-offers-500-mn-defence-credit-line-vietnam> (accessed 4 September 2017).

Mansingh, Lalit. "The Look East Policy and Its Implications for Eastern India". In *Two Decades of India's Look East Policy: Partnership for Peace, Progress and Prosperity*, edited by Amar Nath Ram. Delhi: Manohar Publishers, 2012.

Medcalf, Rory. "Reimagining Asia: From Asia-Pacific to Indo-Pacific". *The ASAN Forum* (26 June 2015). Available at <http://www.theasanforum.org/reimagining-asia-from-asia-pacific-to-indo-pacific/#6> (accessed 4 September 2017).

Ministry of Defence. *Ensuring Secure Seas: Indian Maritime Security Strategy*. New Delhi: Indian Navy Naval Strategic Publication, 2015.

Ministry of External Affairs. "Joint Statement During the Visit of President of USA to India", 25 January 2015. Available at <http://mea.gov.in/incoming-visit-detail.htm?24726> (accessed 4 September 2017).

———. "Indian Prime Minister's Remarks at the U.S. Congress", 8 June 2016a. Available at <http://www.mea.gov.in/Speeches-Statements.htm?dtl/26886/> (accessed 4 September 2017).

———. "Press Statement by Prime Minister During His Visit to Vietnam", 3 September 2016b. Available at <http://www.mea.gov.in/Speeches-Statements.htm?dtl/27363/> (accessed 4 September 2017).

———. "Prime Minister's Address at International Fleet Review 2016", 7 February 2016c. Available at <http://www.mea.gov.in/Speeches-Statements.htm?dtl/26333/> (accessed 29 August 2017).

———. "Speech by India's Foreign Secretary at Raisina Dialogue in New Delhi", 2 March 2016d. Available at <http://mea.gov.in/Speeches-Statements.htm?dtl/26433> (accessed 4 September 2017).

————. "ASEAN–India Relations", 2 March 2017*a*. Available at <http://www.mea.gov.in/aseanindia/20-years.htm> (accessed 29 August 2017).

————. "Inaugural Address by Prime Minister at Second Raisina Dialogue, New Delhi", 17 January 2017*b*. Available at <http://www.mea.gov.in/Speeches-Statements.htm?dtl/27948/> (accessed 4 September 2017).

Modi, Narendra. "Full Speech: Shri Narendra Modi at the BJP National Council Meet, Delhi", 19 January 2014. Available at <http://www.narendramodi.in/full-speech-shri-narendra-modi-at-the-bjp-national-council-meet-delhi-2814> (accessed 29 August 2017).

Mohan, C. Raja. *Samudra Manthan: Sino–Indian Rivalry in the Indo-Pacific*. Washington, D.C.: Carnegie Endowment for International Peace, 2012.

————. "An Uncertain Trumpet? India's Role in Southeast Asian Security". *India Review* 12, no. 3 (2013): 134–50.

————. "Maritime Asia: An Indian Perspective". In *The Changing Maritime Scene in Asia: Rising Tensions and Future Strategic Stability*, edited by Geoffrey Till. London: Palgrave Macmillan, 2015*a*, pp. 49–58.

————. "Modi and the Indian Ocean: Restoring India's Sphere of Influence". *ISAS Insights* 277 (2015*b*).

Mukherjee, Rohan and Clara M. O'Donnell. "Challenges of a Multipolar World: The United States, India, and the European Union in the Asia-Pacific". *GMF Young Strategists Forum Series*, 11 July 2013. Available at <http://www.gmfus.org/publications/challenges-multipolar-world-united-states-india-and-european-union-asia-pacific> (accessed 4 September 2017).

Muni, S.D. "The Turbulent South-China Sea Waters: India, Vietnam and China". *ISAS Insights* 140 (11 October 2011).

————. "Look East Policy: Beyond Myths". In *Two Decades of India's Look East Policy: Partnership for Peace, Progress and Prosperity*, edited by Amar Nath Ram. New Delhi: Manohar & ICWA, 2012.

Murdoch, Lindsay. "Vietnam to Gain Satellite Views of South China Sea Thanks to Indian Agreement". *The Age*, 26 January 2016. Available at <http://www.theage.com.au/world/vietnam-to-gain-satellite-views-of-south-china-sea-thanks-to-indian-agreement-20160126-gme23v.html> (accessed 4 September 2017).

Prakash, Arun. "Maritime Security of India: Future Challenges", 26 November 2013. Available at <https://idsa.in/keyspeeches/MaritimeSecurityOfIndiaFutureChallenges> (accessed 3 September 2017).

Prasad, Kailash K. and Rani Mullen. "India–Vietnam Relations: Deepening Bilateral Ties for Mutual Benefit", 5 August 2013. Available at <http://www.cprindia.org/sites/default/files/policy-briefs/India-Vietnam%20Backgrounder.pdf > (accessed 4 September 2017).

Press Information Bureau. "English Rendering of the Prime Minister's Media Statement during the Visit of Prime Minister of Vietnam to India", 28 October

2014. Available at <http://pib.nic.in/newsite/PrintRelease.aspx?relid=110863> (accessed 4 September 2017).

————. "PM Visits Quan Su Pagoda in Hanoi, Interacts with Monks", 3 September 2016. Available at <http://pib.nic.in/newsite/PrintRelease.aspx?relid=149506> (accessed 4 September 2017).

Ram, Amar Nath., ed. *Two Decades of India's Look East Policy: Partnership for Peace, Progress and Prosperity.* New Delhi: Manohar and ICWA, 2012.

————. *India's Asia-Pacific Engagement: Impulses and Imperatives.* New Delhi: Manohar and ICWA, 2015.

Sardesai, D.R. *Indian Foreign Policy in Cambodia, Laos, and Vietnam 1947–1964.* Berkeley and Los Angeles: University of California Press, 1968.

Schwartz, F. "Pentagon Voices China Concerns". *The Wall Street Journal* XXXIX, no. 152 (2015): 3.

Sibal, Kanwal. "India's Look East Again Policy". In *Two Decades of India's Look East Policy: Partnership for Peace, Progress and Prosperity*, edited by Amar Nath Ram. Delhi: Manohar Publishers, 2012.

Singh, Abhijit. "India's Strategic Stakes in the South China Sea". *Asia Policy* 21 (2016).

Singh, Mahendra. "Niti Aayog Plans to Turn Nation into 'Blue Economy'". *The Economic Times*, 27 September 2016. Available at <http://economictimes.indiatimes.com/news/economy/policy/niti-aayog-plans-to-turn-nation-into-blue-economy/articleshow/54539874.cms> (accessed 29 August 2017).

Thayer, Carlyle A. "India and Vietnam Advance their Strategic Partnership". *The Diplomat*, 11 December 2014. Available at <http://thediplomat.com/2014/12/india-and-vietnam-advance-their-strategic-partnership> (accessed 4 September 2017).

The White House. "U.S.–India Joint Strategic Vision for the Asia-Pacific and Indian Ocean Region", 25 January 2015. Available at <https://www.whitehouse.gov/the-press-office/2015/01/25/us-india-joint-strategic-vision-asia-pacific-and-indian-ocean-region> (accessed 4 September 2017).

Times of India. "India, Vietnam Sign Nuclear Pact, Three Other Agreements", 10 December 2016. Available at <http://timesofindia.indiatimes.com/india/India-Vietnam-sign-nuclear-pact-three-other-agreements/articleshow/55905769.cms> (accessed 4 September 2017).

Townshend, Ashley and Rory Medcalf. "Shifting Waters: China's New Passive Assertiveness in Asian Maritime Security". *Lowy Institute Report*, 29 April 2016. Available at <https://www.lowyinstitute.org/publications/shifting-waters-china-s-new-passive-assertiveness-asian-maritime-security>.

U.S. Department of Defence. "Remarks by Secretary Mattis at Shangri-La Dialogue", 3 June 2017. Available at <https://www.defense.gov/News/Transcripts/Transcript-View/Article/1201780/remarks-by-secretary-mattis-at-shangri-la-dialogue/> (accessed 4 September 2017).

Vinh, Vo Xuan. "India's Strategic Partnership: A Perspective from Vietnam". In *India's Approach to Asia: Strategy, Geopolitics and Responsibility*, edited by Namrata Goswami. New Delhi: Pentagon Press and IDSA, 2016.

Yahuda, Michael. "China's New Assertiveness in the South China Sea". *Journal of Contemporary China* 22, no. 81 (2013): 446–59.

7

Vietnam–Russia Relations: Glorious Past, Uncertain Future

Anton Tsvetov

Out of Vietnam's multiple major partners, Russia is perhaps the most ambiguous in terms of strategic value to Vietnam's current foreign strategy. The rich history of bilateral relations has created a profound basis for the current partnership, but apart from several traditional spheres of cooperation, Russia–Vietnam ties have not seen many breakthroughs in recent times. Moreover, as Vietnam develops its relations with various powers such as China, the United States, Japan, India, South Korea, Australia and the European Union (EU), whether Russia can play a key role in Vietnam's foreign policy in the long run remains an open question.

After the Ukraine crisis broke out, Russia has seen its relations with the United States and European states deteriorate. This has provided Russia with new incentives to intensify its relations with Asia-Pacific countries (Lo 2014). While China has been the focus of such efforts (Gabuev 2015), the Russian leadership also acknowledges the need for diversification. Japan and South Korea, albeit important partners for Moscow, are both U.S. treaty allies, which creates impediments for Russia's diplomatic manoeuvring. Against this backdrop, Vietnam, as an increasingly important economic and strategic player in the region, has emerged as a promising target of Moscow's "pivot to Asia".

This chapter examines Russia–Vietnam relations, their recent history, contemporary state and future prospects. The first section reviews the historical ties between Russia's predecessor, the Union of Soviet Socialist Republics (USSR), and Vietnam. The section accordingly examines how the bilateral Cold War ties have shaped certain aspects of Vietnam's current relations with Russia. The second section looks into the modern Russia–Vietnam relations, starting from Vladimir Putin's third presidency in 2012. Finally, the third section analyses how the substance of this partnership fits into the broader foreign policy of Russia and Vietnam, as well as its future prospects.

Russia–Vietnam Relations from 1975 to 2002

1975–86: The Alignment Sets In

During the formative years of the contemporary Vietnamese statehood — from 1945 to 1975 — the USSR was an active supporter of the Democratic Republic of Vietnam (DRV). First interactions between the Soviet Union and the revolutionary movement in Vietnam date back to the 1920s, and later on, Soviet support was instrumental in Vietnam's struggle against France and the United States for its national independence and unification (Glazunov, Kazakevich, Mkhitaryan, and Solntsev 1982, Chapter VI).

During the First and Second Indochina Wars, Vietnam enjoyed the support of both the USSR and the People's Republic of China, even after the two powers split in the 1960s. The DRV even sought to mediate the Sino–Soviet divide (Birgerson 1997, p. 218). However, the defining moment for this triangular relationship came in the swift and dramatic events of 1978–79. Tensions between China and Vietnam intensified due to border skirmishes and Vietnam's policy towards ethnic Chinese. This, along with Vietnam's looming military inter- vention in Cambodia, caused China–Vietnam relations to deteriorate quickly, prompting Hanoi to strengthen its ties with Moscow.

The USSR–Vietnam Treaty of Friendship and Cooperation was signed in late 1978. For USSR, it was, as Robert Scalapino (1982, p. 71) put it, "the linchpin of USSR drive to contain China". Facing increasing pressures from China, Vietnam also saw the Soviet Union as a key source of support to protect its national security. The China–Vietnam war of 1979 sealed this new geopolitical arrangement. Although Soviet reactions to the Chinese invasion of Vietnam in 1979 were limited to verbal support, strategic manoeuvring and continuing aid,[1] the USSR remained Vietnam's key global partner and donor until the former's collapse in 1991.

From Moscow's perspective, Vietnam was then also a key element of the global socialist movement, a manifestation of the universal nature of communist ideology and its applicability to East Asia. At the same time, Hanoi was central to the Soviet geopolitical strategy in the Asia Pacific as the longstanding Sino–Soviet divide turned Vietnam into a necessary counterweight against China. These considerations brought about the most important Soviet–Vietnamese military arrangement after 1975: the Soviet access to the Cam Ranh Bay. Although Vietnam was reluctant to grant special rights in Cam Ranh to any one foreign power right after its reunification (Storey and Thayer 2001), there seemed to be no other option after 1978. Vietnam granted the USSR with exclusive rights to the Cam Ranh naval base until 2004 in a secret protocol signed several months after the 1978 Treaty (Largo 2002). Starting from the spring of 1979, the Soviet Union started deploying new capabilities at the base and upgrading the existing equipment, eventually turning Cam Ranh into Moscow's largest naval facility outside the Warsaw Pact countries (Bernstein and Gigot 1986).

1986–91: The Two Perestroikas

The mid-1980s brought significant changes to both the Soviet Union and Vietnam. Transformations in domestic and foreign policies in the two countries and the changing geopolitical context affected the bilateral relations and ultimately led to their "disconnection" (Buszynski 2006, p. 278) in the early 1990s.

In the USSR, Mikhail Gorbachev's ascension to power in 1985 was marked by reformist policies known as *perestroika*. Aimed primarily to improve Soviet economic performance, this new agenda included a re-evaluation of the Soviet economic system, introduction of market-based economic practices, and more openness to internal criticism (*glasnost*). In terms of foreign policy, Gorbachev sought to defuse the global ideological confrontation, foster relations with non-communist developing states, and shift towards pursuing national security through political and economic means as opposed to military might.

Gorbachev's foreign policy also involved efforts to improve relations with Asian countries. His well-known 1986 Vladivostok speech elaborated the Soviet desire to rebuild relations with China, achieve rapprochement with Japan, South Korea and ASEAN states, and play a peaceful and meaningful role in the broader Asia-Pacific region (Gorbachev 1986; Konboy 1988). Gorbachev also suggested that if the United States withdrew from Subic and Clark military bases in the Philippines, the Soviet Union would be ready to withdraw from Cam Ranh Bay in return.

In order to improve ties with China, the United States and ASEAN, Gorbachev not only had to withdraw troops from Afghanistan, but also pushed Vietnam to end its military presence in Cambodia. As the Soviet Union sought stronger ties with other Asian states, Vietnam's position within Soviet foreign policy also declined relatively. At the same time, Vietnam suffered from Moscow's efforts to reduce its external economic and military burden under *perestroika*.

Tectonic shifts in Soviet domestic and foreign policy contributed to changes in Vietnam. The sixth national congress of the Communist Party of Vietnam (CPV) in late 1986 launched the *Doi Moi* policy, which, among other things, introduced market-based economic reforms and gradually opened up the country's external relations. The CPV's decision was partly driven by its attempt to respond to the scaling-down of Soviet political, military and economic support.[2]

Between 1986 and 1991, Soviet–Vietnam relations were thus suffering from significant setbacks. The alignment was built upon a clear patron–client set of overlapping interests. New Soviet policies sought to eliminate the very confrontations that the Soviet–Vietnam alignment was meant to service. Meanwhile, economic assistance, a key instrument to maintain this alliance, could be considered as the very "waste" that Gorbachev's new economic strategy was supposed to end.

As a consequence, the Soviet–Vietnam relationship after 1986 failed to meet the expectations of both partners. Although the Soviet Union announced increased aid to Vietnam in 1986 (Stoecker 1989, p. 13), assistance in practical terms was gradually reduced to a "negligible" amount by 1990 (Jeffries 2002, p. 243), and Soviet technical experts also started to leave the Vietnamese facilities that they deemed inefficient (Szalontai 2008, p. 241).

Political support was also getting weaker. In 1988 when China and Vietnam engaged in a naval skirmish over Johnson South Reef in the Spratlys, where the latter lost sixty-four soldiers, the Soviet reaction was weak as Moscow refrained not only from supporting any party, but also from denouncing Chinese conduct (Emmers 2009, p. 71).

As Moscow became increasingly disinterested in supporting Hanoi economically and politically, the CPV started to embrace a more diversified foreign policy. Despite the 1988 clash, Vietnam sought to restore its relations with China, and efforts were also made to normalize ties with the United States. Both of these objectives could not be achieved without Vietnam withdrawing its troops from Cambodia, which was well understood by the CPV leadership (Stoecker 1989, p. 26). Vietnam's move towards gaining more independence from the USSR became clear with the emergence of a "multidirectional foreign policy" concept in 1988 (Ciorciari 2010, p. 83).

Despite such challenges, the period 1986–91 created certain important foundations for the current Russia–Vietnam relationship. In 1986, Vietsovpetro, an oil and gas joint venture, was launched and is considered the flagship of bilateral economic cooperation up to the present. The late 1980s also saw major Vietnamese industrial projects funded by Soviet aid, such as the Hoa Binh and Tri An hydropower plants and the Pha Lai thermal power plant. The importance of Soviet-sponsored and engineered facilities in Vietnam's industrial production during this period remained undisputed. For example, such facilities accounted for 47 per cent of energy, 85 per cent of coal, and 50 per cent of cement output in 1985 (Tien 2008, p. 16). It should also be noted that the decline in Soviet–Vietnam relations was not visible in trade statistics. As shown in Figure 7.1, bilateral trade turnover increased from 5.7 billion roubles in 1981–85 to 8.9 billion roubles in 1986–90, partly due to the weakening of the rouble.

FIGURE 7.1
Soviet–Vietnam Bilateral Trade Turnover (in million Soviet roubles and million USD), 1979–90

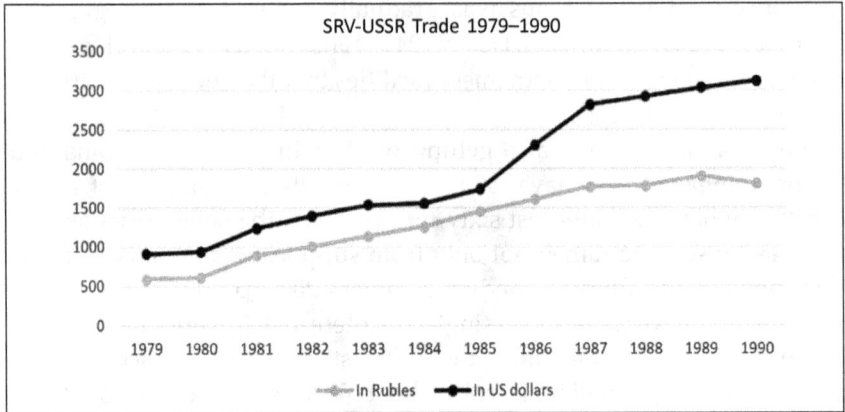

SRV-USSR Trade 1979–1990

Source: Author's calculation based on data from USSR's annual external trade reports (*Vneshnyaya torgovlya SSSR*) and Russian Central Bank (*Ofitsial'nie kursy Gosbanka SSSR*).

1991–2002: Decline and Restoration

After the Soviet Union collapsed, Russia was engulfed in domestic issues and its foreign policy was primarily aimed at creating favourable relations with the West and overcoming the negative legacies of the Cold War. Against this backdrop, "Russia's leadership had prepared for a tidy exit from Southeast Asia, while preserving certain residual and profitable interests" (Buszynski 2006, p. 279).

It could be argued that Vietnam would be the most obvious partner in which Russia would seek to maintain such "residual and profitable interests". In 1994, Vietnamese Prime Minister Vo Van Kiet visited Russia and the two sides signed a treaty on fundamental principles of their relations, which was set to replace the 1978 Treaty of Friendship and Cooperation. Although the document was supposed to give reassurance to bilateral ties, it was virtually an affirmation of the "new normal" in which the two countries were not quasi-allies anymore. Instead, they had become two countries in distant parts of the world with a narrow set of common interests and a positive history.

As such, during the 1990s, the Russia–Vietnam relationship was essentially reduced to a small set of flagship cooperation areas, including the Vietsovpetro joint venture, the Cam Ranh Bay issue, arms trade, and the settlement of Soviet-era debts.

Vietsovpetro started functioning as a self-financed company in 1991 and expanded through the 1990s, with the third oil field opened in 1994. Its annual production increased from around 1 million tons in 1978–79 to 5 million tons in 1993 (Buszynski 2006, p. 280; 2014, p. 203; Vinogradov 1993). Vietsovpetro became the most efficient Russia-Vietnam cooperation project and the cornerstone of Russian presence in Vietnam in the 1990s (Chesnokov 2011).

Unlike the stable development of Vietsovpetro, the Russian naval facility in Cam Ranh was suffering from a gradual decline in the 1990s. Russia's need for such a base had disappeared after the Cold War ended, and it thus became a burden to Moscow. The number of Russian personnel and family members living at the base decreased from 6,000 in 1987 to 700 in the early 1990s. In 1992, the two parties began negotiating about the future of the facility. Vietnam was initially interested in maintaining a certain level of Russian military presence for strategic reasons vis-à-vis China, but later wanted to commercialize the arrangement, suggesting an annual fee of US$360 million starting from 2004 (Buszynski 2006, p. 280). The severe maintenance issues in Cam Ranh became apparent in 1995 when three Russian Su-27 fighter jets crashed near the Cam Ranh airfield. The accident exposed obsolete equipment of the base and struck a reputational blow to Russian military presence in Vietnam (Chesnokov 2011, p. 99). As Vietnam's relations with China improved and Russian interest in Cam Ranh dwindled, Russia decided to leave the facility in 2002.

As Russia was trying to make use of its large defence production capabilities inherited from the Soviet era, Russia's military exports to Vietnam emerged as a key component of bilateral ties during this period. For example, in 1993, Vietnam ordered five Su-27SKs and one Su-27UBK for US$150 million. Another purchase in 1996 was for two Su-27SKs and four Su-27UBKs. Vietnamese Su-22M4 bombers also underwent upgrades during this decade. In terms of naval equipment, Russia sold Vietnam *Molniya*-class missile boats in 1999 (*Armstrade.org* 2010). Given the weak overall economic ties,[3] arms trade was an important channel for maintaining commercial contact. In 1995, for example, helicopters, aircraft spare parts and other military components accounted for 66 per cent of all Russian exports to Vietnam (Mosyakov 2014a, p. 42).

Another key issue which was discussed during Vo Van Kiet's visit to Moscow in 1994 and remained high on the bilateral agenda throughout the 1990s was the repayment of Vietnam's debt to Russia. Most of Vietnam's military equipment acquired and industrial facilities built in the 1980s were funded by Soviet loans. By 1994, Vietnam's debt to Russia amounted to about US$9 billion (Buszynski 2006, p. 280). During the 1990s, Vietnam exported goods and services worth up to US$100 million per year to Russia to service its debt, which was not sufficient to solve the issue in a meaningful manner. Eventually, during Prime Minister Phan Van Khai's visit to Russia in 2000, around 85 per cent of the total debt (US$9.53 billion out of US$11.03 billion) was written off. The rest is payable during the period 2016–22 (*Kommersant* 2013).

The Significance of Historical Ties

The significant wartime aid provided by the USSR was crucial for Hanoi's military victory as well as the CPV's rule. At the same time, Vietnam was also the closest and most important Asian partner of the Soviet Union during its last thirty years of existence. This period of unprecedented friendship has both practical and psychological implications.

The Soviet "material" footprint in Vietnam has been immense. A significant proportion of military hardware, industrial and infrastructure capacities in Vietnam was created or modernized by the USSR. As a result, Russia is still the preferred partner for Vietnam in upgrading these capabilities, as Vietnam seeks to avoid the additional costs of switching to other suppliers.

At the same time, deep people-to-people connections were created over time, especially before the collapse of the Soviet Union, with Russian delegations and experts travelling to Vietnam on a regular basis, and dozens of thousands of Vietnamese working and studying in the Soviet Union. Frequent cultural exchanges and Soviet influence on Vietnam's education system also caused a generation of Vietnamese to cherish fond memories of Russia and the Russian people.

However, the close historical ties also tend to create expectations of "special treatment" on the part of Russia in its cooperation with Vietnam. Moreover, the 1990s have also left some negative perception among Russians about certain Vietnamese traders who lived illegally and traded counterfeit goods in ethnic markets in urban Russia.

Within the official narratives, the bilateral relationship reached its peak during the Vietnam war and the post-war reconstruction years. It is especially true for Russia as that was also the period during which Soviet global influence peaked. Russia's political and economic upheavals in the 1990s as well as its declining global status caused bilateral ties to languish. Russia was even seen to "abandon" Vietnam as manifested in its withdrawal from Cam Ranh in 2002. In a sense, the reinvention of bilateral relations since the 2000s is presented by Moscow as one of the indications of Russia's re-emergence as a global power.

Vietnam–Russia Relations from 2002 to the Present

2002–12: Shaping the Strategic Partnership

After becoming President of Russia in 2000, Vladimir Putin started to implement political, economic and foreign policy changes. Responding to domestic demands for economic and political stability and the restoration of Russia's international status, he saw a proactive foreign policy to be the next step after economic reforms. Such a foreign policy was meant to help Russia rejoin the club of power centres within a new polycentric world. Against this backdrop, the Asia Pacific emerged as a new focus of Putin's foreign policy, which was partly manifested by his visits to China, Japan, India and North Korea during the first two years of his presidency.

Putin visited Vietnam in February 2001, just one year after he came to power. Putin announced that Vietnam was a "traditional" partner and that bilateral relations had reached the level of a strategic partnership. In response, Vietnamese President Tran Duc Luong also stated that the two countries were "seeking ways to bring [...] economic, trade, and technological cooperation to a higher and more effective level, to match [the] fine political relations" (*AP* 2001). The official rhetoric used in bilateral documents and statements, including references to the "traditional" nature of the relations, their deep historical roots, the "friendship" between the two peoples, and Vietnam's special position in Russia's Asia policy, has remained almost unchanged ever since. These statements were reiterated during various high-level visits by the two countries' heads of state or party leaders during the 2000s. The high frequency of these meetings (see Table 7.1)

TABLE 7.1
Bilateral Official Visits by Heads of State/Party Leaders of Vietnam and Russia, 2001–11

Month/Year	Russian Leaders' Visit to Vietnam	Vietnamese Leaders' Visit to Russia
Feb 2001	President Vladimir Putin	
May 2004		President Tran Duc Luong
Nov 2004	President Vladimir Putin	
Nov 2006	President Vladimir Putin	
Oct 2008		President Nguyen Minh Triet
Dec 2009	President Dmitry Medvedev	
Jul 2010		General Secretary Nong Duc Manh
Oct 2010	President Dmitry Medvedev	

Note: The table does not include occasional meetings at international events, such as the APEC summits in 2005 and 2011.
Source: Author's compilation.

also points to the significance that the two countries accorded to each other in their foreign policy.

After Putin's first visit to Vietnam, bilateral trade started to pick up. In 2002, bilateral trade turnover exceeded US$400 million and more than doubled in 2005 to reach US$900 million. Between 2001 and 2005, the total trade turnover was 2.3 times higher than that of the period 1996–2000, amounting to US$2.8 billion. Bilateral trade turnover continued to increase by 2.6 times between 2006 and 2010. During this period, Vietnam's export growth helped bring down its trade deficit with Russia from US$1.8 billion in 2001–5 to US$133 million in 2006–10 (see Figure 7.2).

During President Tran Duc Luong's visit to Moscow in 2004, a Russia–Vietnam Business Forum was created, and after Vladimir Putin's visit to Vietnam in 2006, the two countries set up a joint venture bank aimed at supporting bilateral business transactions. By 2004, Russia's had invested US$1.7 billion in about 300 projects in Vietnam, and the two parties were even discussing Russia's help in building a subway

FIGURE 7.2
Russia–Vietnam Trade Turnover in the 2000s (in million USD)

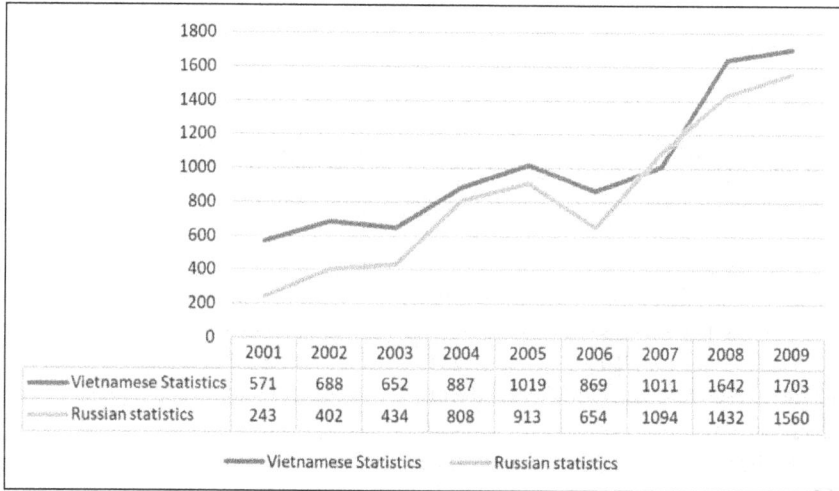

	2001	2002	2003	2004	2005	2006	2007	2008	2009
Vietnamese Statistics	571	688	652	887	1019	869	1011	1642	1703
Russian statistics	243	402	434	808	913	654	1094	1432	1560

Source: General Statistics Office of Vietnam and Russian Federal Customs Service (cited in Lan 2012).

system in Ho Chi Minh City (Kazakov 2004). However, despite such positive dynamics, by the late 2000s, Vietnam only accounted for 0.4 per cent of Russia's external trade, while Russia accounted for just 1.3 per cent of Vietnam's (Lan 2012).

After Dmitry Medvedev was elected president of Russia in 2008, Vladimir Putin assumed the position of Prime Minister and retained significant influence on the country's foreign policy. Seeking to increase Russia's global influence while avoiding direct confrontation with the West, the Russian leadership paid more attention to multilateral institutions and forums. These bodies were expected to emphasize Russia's strengthening posture on the international arena and at the same time promote a multi-polar world order that suits Russia's interests.

In this regard, Russian policymakers found Vietnam a helpful and friendly partner. Vietnam was supportive of Russia's accession to the World Trade Organization (WTO) and acknowledged the country's market economy status in 2007, thereby contributing to Russia's eventual accession to the organization in 2012. Vietnamese diplomats also supported Russian participation in regional arrangements such as the Asia-Pacific Economic Cooperation (APEC) forum, ASEAN Regional Forum (ARF), Asia-Europe Meeting (ASEM), and the East Asia Summit (EAS) (Kozyrev 2014, p. 8).

Russia–Vietnam arms trade also witnessed significant expansion in the 2000s. In December 2003, Vietnam ordered four Su-30MK jets for US$150 million. Military-technical cooperation was further boosted in 2008 during Vietnamese President Nguyen Minh Triet's visit to Russia when a memorandum of understanding (MOU) on defence cooperation was signed. In the same year, the value of signed contracts exceeded US$1 billion and reached US$3.5 billion the next year, including Vietnam's order for eight more Su-30MK2s, *Molniya*-class boats, *Gepard*-class frigates, and, most importantly, six *Kilo*-class submarines. Vietnam was also reportedly interested in maintenance services, spare parts and air defence systems from Russia. By 2010, Russian Defence Ministry officials were referring to Vietnam as the third largest importer of Russian arms after China and India (Klyuchanskaya 2011, p. 61).

In 2010, Atomstroyexport, a subsidiary of Russia's state-owned Rosatom, won the bid to construct Vietnam's first nuclear power plant in Ninh Thuan province. The project was financed by a US$8 billion loan from Russian banks (*RIA Novosti* 2011). However, the Fukushima nuclear disaster in 2011 created new concerns over the safety of the project, and its implementation was therefore delayed several times. In 2016, additional concerns about the project's economic viability and Vietnam's expanding budget deficit[4] led to Hanoi's decision to shelve the project.

Putin's Third Presidency and Bilateral Relations after 2012

In 2012, when Vladimir Putin was elected President of the Russian Federation for the third term, his narrative contained a strong defensive element against perceived external pressures exerted on Russia.[5] Indeed, part of his campaign platform was to strengthen Russia's international posture, including a more proactive foreign policy in Asia.

Immediately after assuming office, Putin signed a series of decrees known as the May Decrees, which outlined his key policies in crucial areas, including Decree No. 605 "On Measures to Implement the Foreign Policy of the Russian Federation". Despite the very general nature of the document, it was particularly significant to Vietnam–Russia relations as only three of Russia's Asian partners were named directly:

China, India and Vietnam. This was widely seen as an indication of Vietnam's growing importance in Russian foreign policy (see, for example, Mazyrin and Kobelev 2015; Mosyakov 2014*a*).

Another breakthrough in bilateral relations came soon afterwards. In July 2012, during Vietnamese President Truong Tan Sang's visit to Moscow, the two sides announced the establishment of a "comprehensive strategic partnership". Putin's visit to Vietnam in November 2013 further consolidated the partnership which has been characterized by frequent high-level interactions, strong military cooperation, and growing trade and investment ties.

Meetings between heads of state or government currently take place at least once a year, either during bilateral visits or on the sidelines of international events.[6] At the working level, the key mechanism for interaction is the Russia–Vietnam Strategic Dialogue (chaired by Deputy Foreign Ministers, with nine rounds as of late 2017) and the Intergovernmental Commission on Trade and Investment Cooperation that convenes annually. The two sides' relevant authorities also hold regular consultations on various issues ranging from human rights, law enforcement to economic cooperation, in addition to themed consultations between the two foreign ministries. Visits by local and provincial leaders also take place on a regular basis and are usually associated with specific local business interests. There are also inter-party ties between the Communist Party of Vietnam and the Communist Party of the Russian Federation (KPRF), as well as the ruling United Russia party.

Regarding military cooperation, two most important issues are the new arrangement for Russia's access to Cam Ranh Bay, and Russia's arms export to Vietnam. In 2014, during President Truong Tan Sang's visit to Moscow, the two sides signed an agreement that allows Russia to have unlimited port calls to Cam Ranh through simplified administrative procedures (*TASS* 2014). The Russian air force was also reportedly using the Cam Ranh airfield for its refuelling aircraft that service Tu-95 Bear long-range nuclear-capable bombers (*Reuters* 2015).[7] Meanwhile, Russian media have reported that joint exercises were planned in 2016 (*Sputnik News* 2015), but there has been no confirmation that they have taken place.

In terms of arms trade, despite Vietnam's efforts to diversify its sources of military equipment, Russia remains the key supplier. By early 2017, all six *Kilo*-class submarines had been delivered to the Vietnamese Navy. Vietnam also reportedly acquired fifty anti-ship *Klub* missiles that can be installed on the submarines and have a range of up to 300 km. In addition, Vietnam is said to be negotiating the purchase of Russia's modern S-400 air defence system (Malyasov 2016). If the deal is done, Vietnam will be the second foreign buyer of the system after China.

As seen in Figure 7.3, bilateral trade, while still modest, has been growing steadily during this period. Russia's main exports to Vietnam include machinery, equipment, metals and lubricants, while Vietnam's main exports are electronics, garments, footwear, agricultural produce and seafood. However, similar to previous periods, despite the positive growth in bilateral trade, Vietnam currently accounts for only 0.8 per cent of Russia's total foreign trade (up from 0.4 per cent in 2011), while the share of trade with Russia in Vietnam's total trade stands at 1.2 per cent. In terms of investment, by 2015, Russia's accumulative stock of investment in Vietnam had been US$2.06 billion with 113 projects, while Vietnam had invested US$2.4 billion in 18 projects in Russia (Russian Embassy in Vietnam 2016).

FIGURE 7.3
Russia–Vietnam Bilateral Trade, 2010–16 (in million USD)

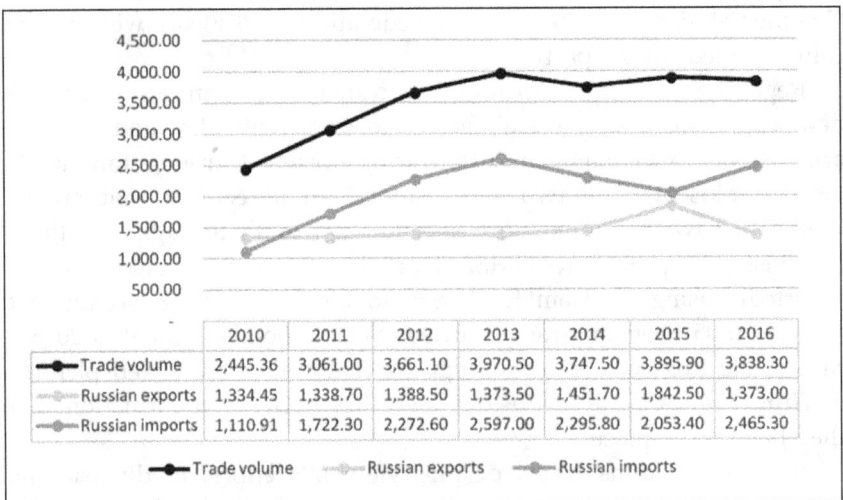

	2010	2011	2012	2013	2014	2015	2016
Trade volume	2,445.36	3,061.00	3,661.10	3,970.50	3,747.50	3,895.90	3,838.30
Russian exports	1,334.45	1,338.70	1,388.50	1,373.50	1,451.70	1,842.50	1,373.00
Russian imports	1,110.91	1,722.30	2,272.60	2,597.00	2,295.80	2,053.40	2,465.30

Trade volume — Russian exports — Russian imports

Source: Author's compilation based on data from the Russian Federal Customs Service.

Among major areas of bilateral economic cooperation, oil and gas remain the most significant one. Vietsovpetro continues to be a successful joint venture and is often portrayed as a symbol of continuity in bilateral relations. In 2012, the two governments signed an agreement to extend the joint venture's operation until 2030. Russia's state-owned gas giant Gazprom is also conducting operations in Vietnam with exploration projects at blocks 112, 129–132, 05–2 and 05–3. Meanwhile, another Russian state corporation, Rosneft, is extracting natural gas condensates at Hai Thach and Moc Tinh gas fields, and extracting oil at blocks 06.1 and 05.2/11. Rosneft also owns a 33 per cent stake in the Nam Con Son pipeline that conveys gas from blocks 06.1, 11.2 and 12W to Dinh Co Gas Processing Plant in Southern Vietnam (*Offshore* 2016).

PetroVietnam has also invested in several oil and gas projects in Russia. Specifically, the Rusvietpetro joint venture between Zarubezhneft and PetroVietnam is exploring for oil in the Nenets Autonomous Region in Northern Russia. Gas condensate is also being exploited and processed by Gazpromviet in the Yamalo-Nenets Region and at the Nagumanovsk facility in the Orenburg region in Southern Russia. In April 2015, the two countries signed an MOU to expand oil and gas cooperation to the Pechora Sea (Russian Embassy in Vietnam 2016).

Outside the oil and gas industry, however, Russia–Vietnam economic cooperation remains modest. Therefore, the two countries are trying to boost bilateral trade and investment through new initiatives. Most significant is perhaps the Eurasian Economic Union (EAEU)–Vietnam Free Trade Agreement (FTA) which was signed on 31 May 2015 and entered into force in October 2016. It is the first FTA of the EAEU and the choice of Vietnam can be seen as a testimony to Vietnam's rising political and economic significance to Russia. The agreement reduces or abolishes tariffs for almost 90 per cent of goods, and contains provisions to facilitate investment and trade in services as well (Eurasian Economic Commission 2016).

An important factor that helps strengthen bilateral people-to-people connections is tourism. The number of Russian tourist arrivals in Vietnam increased from just around 50,000 in 2009 to 380,000 in 2014. After an 11 per cent drop in 2015, the number increased again to reach 434,000 in 2016.[8] The number of Vietnamese tourists visiting Russia is not statistically significant, but Russian authorities are planning to attract more Vietnamese tourists by choosing Vietnam as one of the first countries where the Visit Russia office was opened (Fedorov 2016).

However, such people-to-people connections are also facing constraints. For example, according to official statistics, about 30,000 Vietnamese were living in Russia in 2015 (Dinh 2015). Although they contribute to the strengthening of bilateral connections, regular televised exposures of illegal production facilities run by Vietnamese migrants are also damaging their image among the Russian public (Ryazantsev and Pismennaya 2016). At the same time, while Russia used to host tens of thousands of Vietnamese students before the collapse of the Soviet Union, the number of Vietnamese studying at Russian universities has fallen to about 6,000 in the recent years (Sokolov 2014). Moreover, although certain senior Vietnamese officials are Soviet-educated, this cohort is gradually losing their influence to the younger, English-speaking and Western-trained officials.

The Geopolitical Context and Prospect of Bilateral Ties

Having reviewed the historical background of contemporary Russia–Vietnam relations, the chapter will now assess the significance of the relationship for each country's foreign strategy. The subsequent analyses show that each country plays certain important roles in the other's external policy, although these roles have clear limitations. Understanding these limitations is essential for assessing how the relationship will develop in the near future.

Russia's Asia Pivot

One key aspect relevant to Vietnam in Russia's contemporary foreign policy is Moscow's so-called "pivot to Asia" which arguably started in 2012 when Russia assumed the chairmanship of APEC.[9] The 2012 APEC Leaders' Meeting was widely advertised domestically as a manifestation of Russia's multifaceted foreign policy and increased focus on the Asia Pacific. Russia's "pivot" to the region was further accelerated after the outbreak of the Ukraine crisis and the significant deterioration of Russia's relations with the West.

Russia's "pivot to Asia" is aimed at several targets. *First*, Russia is seeking alternative foreign markets and sources of capital to cope with structural economic issues and the fallouts of economic sanctions imposed by the West. *Second,* Russia aims to diversify and strengthen its relations with Asian countries to enhance its bargaining position vis-à-vis the West. *Third,* Moscow also wants to enhance the socio-economic development of the Far East. The Russian leadership understands that this will not be achievable without engaging Asian states, especially those with capital, technology and market power. *Fourth,* Russia considers the ability to influence outcomes in various regions of the world as an attribute of a great power, a status Russia feels it is denied by the "collective West".[10]

Within this policy, Southeast Asia appears to be of secondary significance to Russia due to a number of reasons. Most importantly, the Northeast Asian trio of China, Japan and South Korea hold the bulk of capital Russia seeks to tap into. Moreover, Russia has already had a certain level of cooperation with these three countries, which creates strong foundation for future cooperation.[11] Nevertheless, Southeast Asia remains important to the Russian pivot in a number of ways. Strengthened relations with this region allow Russia's Asian policy to be portrayed as a diversified and multifaceted one. Southeast Asian countries are also potential markets for Russian technologies that are unlikely to be in high demand in Japan and South Korea or even China, all of which have already had or are developing similar technological platforms of their own. As such, Russia tends to pay greater attention to its relations with ASEAN states, which is manifested in such grand initiatives as the 2016 Russia–ASEAN Summit in Sochi and the Russian proposal for an EAEU–ASEAN FTA.

Vietnam is the most suitable partner with whom Russia can work to promote its interests in the region. Solid historical foundations, high level of mutual trust, strong political, military and economic ties, as well as Vietnam's enhanced role in ASEAN, make Vietnam an important entry point for Russia to deepen its engagement with Southeast Asian states and ASEAN as a whole. At the same time, strengthening its traditional ties with Moscow also serves Vietnam's strategic calculations, especially its policy of deepening ties with the major powers to deal with rising tensions in the South China Sea.

Vietnam's Diversification Policy

Given its bitter Cold War experiences, the CPV currently shies away from alliances and upholds a non-alignment policy based on the so-called "three no's" principle: no foreign military bases on Vietnamese soil, no participation in military alliances, and no reliance on one country to challenge another. At the same time, Vietnam maintains the policy of *đa dạng hóa, đa phương hóa* [diversification and multilateralization], while deepening ties with some selected partners.

Under this approach, the Vietnamese leadership seeks to hedge against China's rise by developing closer ties with the United States. However, there is an obvious drawback to Hanoi's rapprochement with Washington as it creates concerns in Beijing due to the rising strategic rivalry between the United States and China. U.S.–Vietnam relations are thus limited by how far Vietnam is prepared to lean towards Washington at the expense of its relations with Beijing. Given this constraint, Vietnam needs to develop ties with not only the United States but also other major powers. It is within this context that Russia emerges as one of the preferred partners of Vietnam.

To some extent, Russia is important to Vietnam's quest for an independent foreign and security policy, not least because of Russia's supply of weapons and military equipment to Vietnam. These weapons and equipment obviously enhance Vietnam's deterrence capabilities against potential aggressors. More importantly, the relationship with Moscow also enhances Vietnam's strategic posture as well as its bargaining position vis-à-vis foreign partners, including China. Unlike the United States, Russia does not present a threat to Vietnam's political system, and strengthened ties with Moscow helps to dispel the perception that Vietnam is becoming increasingly reliant on the United States to challenge China's maritime and territorial ambitions. Due to the newfound Russia–China intimacy, Beijing would seem to prefer Russia arming Vietnam rather than the United States given China's increasing ability to influence Russia's decisions.

Risks for Russia–Vietnam Ties

While the increasing convergence of national interests facilitates the deepening of Hanoi–Moscow relations, there are also significant risks to bilateral ties. Vietnam's diversification policy means that although there is a lot of room for the future development of its relations with Russia, Vietnam may also seek to diversify away from Russia as well, especially if Vietnam's reliance on Russia in certain aspects becomes excessive or exposes Vietnam to potential risks. A case in point is Vietnam's efforts to diversify its sources of arms imports away from Russia. Vietnam's push for the lifting of the U.S. lethal arms embargo as well as its strengthened cooperation with Israel, India and several European countries in terms of defence procurement are part of this ongoing effort.

Another risk originates from Russia's Asia policy, which needs to acquire more strategic depth, comprehensiveness, and credibility. If Russia's relations with the West are restored, for example, Moscow's pivot to Asia may be weakened. Moreover, Moscow's ongoing engagements in the Ukraine and the Middle East may also distract the Russian leadership away from Asia. Under this scenario, Southeast Asia, including Vietnam, may be neglected as Russia will naturally prioritize its relationship with more important Asian partners, such as China, Japan and South Korea.

Another notable constraint on Russia–Vietnam relations is Russia's perceived embrace of China. Russia has explicitly maintained a neutral stance on the territorial and maritime disputes in the South China Sea. Specifically, Moscow does not take side on sovereignty matters and has called for self-restraint, peaceful dispute resolution, and an early conclusion of a binding Code of Conduct for the South China Sea. However, Moscow has also occasionally opposed the internationalization of the South China Sea issue (Lavrov 2015; Zakharova 2016). Specifically, Russian officials have criticized "extra-regional powers", a clear hint at the United States, for using the South China Sea disputes as a means to serve their own geopolitical ends (Lavrov 2015). Moreover, in September 2016, Russian President Vladimir Putin also expressed support for China's non-recognition of the landmark ruling issued two months earlier by an arbitral tribunal in The Hague on the Philippines' case against China over the disputes (Russian Embassy in China 2016). In both cases, China's alleged pressure as well as Moscow's wish to warm up to Beijing may be a major reason accounting for Russia's skewed position regarding the issue.[12] At official levels, Russia's relations with Vietnam seemed not to be affected by such statements. However, some Vietnamese journalists, experts and civil servants in private conversations with the author have expressed dissatisfaction with Russia's position, describing Russia–Vietnam relations as being "strained" in 2015–16.

Conclusion

Contemporary Vietnam–Russia relations are based on a solid historical foundation and have been strengthened over the past decade thanks to the two countries' increasingly convergent economic and strategic interests, including Russia's pivot to Asia and Vietnam's attempt to diversify and deepen its relations with the major powers. However, there are also certain obstacles that the two sides will need to overcome to further promote bilateral ties.

In the short term, Russia–Vietnam relations are likely to maintain their current trajectory given the continuity in each country's foreign policy as well as the current dynamics of the regional geostrategic and economic environment. Various bilateral cooperation initiatives, such as the EAEU–Vietnam FTA, oil and gas projects, as well as Russia's arms transfer to Vietnam, are still providing strong momentum for the relationship.

However, in the long run, certain scenarios, including Russia's improved relations with the West or its tighter embrace of China, may cause the two countries to attach less importance to their relationship. Russia's influence in Vietnam may even relatively decline if cooperation initiatives do not gain traction. Vietnam's decision to shelve its nuclear power projects, for example, has already dealt a blow to bilateral ties. If oil prices continue to fall and cause bilateral oil and gas projects to stall, the momentum of bilateral ties will also be sapped. At the same time, although Russia currently remains Vietnam's most important source of arms imports, Moscow's position may be undermined if Hanoi's efforts to reduce its reliance on Russian weapons and military equipment meet with success in the long term.

Another trend that may also negatively affect bilateral ties in the future is the decline of Russia's soft power base in Vietnam. As Soviet-trained policymakers and business elite are gradually superseded by the younger and Western-trained generations of policymakers and business leaders, and memories of Soviet war-time assistance fade away, Russia may risk losing its most important source of influence in Vietnam. Therefore, while bilateral ties have seen a glorious past, their future remains somehow uncertain.

NOTES

1. The role of the Soviet Union in the 1979 Sino–Vietnamese border war is a matter of academic and political debate. The official narrative of Russia–Vietnam relations and some scholars (see, for example, Glazunov et al. 1982, Chapter V; Mosyakov 2014b; Tien 2008) underlines Russian support for Vietnam. Other authors, mostly Western (for example, Elleman 1996; Stoecker 1989), point out that the 1978 Treaty of Friendship and Cooperation was worded in such a manner that allowed the USSR to avoid getting involved in Vietnam's potential armed conflicts. They argue that the way Moscow reacted to the Chinese invasion of Vietnam was a demonstration of how weak the Russia–Vietnam alignment actually was.

2. The internal and external motivations of *Doi Moi* are deeply intertwined. Overcoming economic stagnation called for broader economic cooperation with foreign partners. As the socialist bloc sank into economic crises, a more open foreign policy also became necessary for Vietnam.

3. In the period 1995–2001, the annualized bilateral trade turnover was merely US$260 million, partly as a consequence of the 1997–98 Asian financial crisis that also hit Russia (Lan 2012).

4. Another possible reason for Vietnam to shelve the nuclear power plant projects is the domestic politicization of environmental issues in Vietnam. The growing sensitivity of the issues was due to the 2016 environmental disaster caused by a Taiwanese steel mill in Ha Tinh province that triggered social instability in four affected provinces and throughout the country.

5. For a discussion of these factors, see Tsvetov (2016a).

6. The two countries emphasize cooperation in multilateral forums. Vietnam is often referred to as Russia's influence base in ASEAN and an advocate of Russian engagement with the region. For example, Vietnam supported Russia's admission to the East Asia Summit and the two countries frequently interact with each other at, among others, the ASEAN Regional Forum, the ASEAN Defense Ministers Meeting Plus, and APEC meetings.

7. However, there are indications that this arrangement has been halted after *Reuters'* leak (Thayer 2017).

8. Data collected from the Vietnam National Administration of Tourism (VNAT), available at <www.vietnamtourism.gov.vn>.

9. There has hardly ever been an announced "pivot to Asia", since the official government narrative holds that the Asia Pacific has always been one of the cornerstones of Russian foreign policy.

10. For a detailed discussion of these motivations, see Tsvetov (2016a).

11. In 2015, China accounted for 12 per cent of Russian foreign trade, Japan 4.1 per cent, and South Korea 3.4 per cent, while ASEAN states accounted for merely more than 2.7 per cent. Increasing trade with ASEAN members

will involve working with ten individual states and require much more effort than dealing with one of the three Northeast Asian states (Federal Customs Service 2016).

12. Russia's opposition to the internationalization of interstate conflicts is a traditional element of Russian diplomacy and is closely linked to the perceived interference of the United States into regional issues. In addition, the support for China's non-recognition of the PCA ruling is connected to Russia's similar position on the *Arctic Sunrise* case and probable lawsuits filed by the Ukraine over the waters surrounding the Crimean Peninsula (Tsvetov 2016*b*).

REFERENCES

AP Archive. "Vietnam: Russian President Putin Visit", 1 March 2001. Available at <http://www.aparchive.com/metadata/youtube/e9586fe97351d7e36fcdd893f1850510> (accessed 6 September 2017).

Armstrade.org. "Vzaimodeistvie RF i Vietnama v sfere VTS vyhodit na uroven' strategicheskogo partnerstva" [Russia–Vietnam Arms Trade Cooperation is Reaching the Level of a Strategic Partnership], 29 October 2010. Available at <http://www.armstrade.org/includes/periodics/mainnews/2010/1029/10276232/detail.shtml> (accessed 6 September 2017).

Bernstein, Alvin H. and Paul Gigot. "The Soviets in Cam Ranh Bay". *The National Interest* 3 (1986): 17–29.

Birgerson, Susanne. "The Evolution of Soviet Foreign Policy in Southeast Asia: Implications for Russian Foreign Policy". *Asian Affairs: An American Review* 23, no. 4 (1997): 212–34.

Buszynski, Leszek. "Russia and Southeast Asia: A New Relationship". *Contemporary Southeast Asia* 28, no. 2 (2006): 276–96.

———. *Gorbachev and Southeast Asia*. London and New York: Routledge, 2014.

Chesnokov, A. "Rossiyskaya dinastiya vo Vietname: Istoria i sovremennost" [The Russian Dynasty in Vietnam: History and Current Affairs]. *Vestnik Chelyabinskogo gosudarstvennogo universiteta* 21 (2011).

Ciorciari, John D. *The Limits of Alignment: Southeast Asia and the Great Powers since 1975*. Washington, D.C.: Georgetown University Press, 2010.

Dinh, H.M. "Istoria I razvitie vietnamskoy diaspory v Rossii" [History and Development of the Vietnamese Diaspora in Russia]. *Teoria i praktika obshestvennogo razvitia* 20 (2015).

Elleman, Bruce. "Sino–Soviet Relations and the February 1979 Sino–Vietnamese Conflict", 20 April 1996. Available at <https://www.vietnam.ttu.edu/events/1996_Symposium/96papers/elleviet.php> (accessed 6 September 2017).

Emmers, Ralf. *Geopolitics and Maritime Territorial Disputes in East Asia*. London and New York: Routledge, 2009.

Eurasian Economic Commission. "Free Trade Agreement between the Eurasian Economic Union and Vietnam to Enter into Force on October 5", 19 August 2016. Available at <http://www.eurasiancommission.org/en/nae/news/Pages/19-08-2016.aspx> (accessed 6 August 2017).

Federal Customs Service. "Vneshnaya torgovlya Rossiyskoy Federatsii po osnovnym stranam za yanvar-dekabr 2015" [Russian Federation Foreign Trade with Key Countries in January–December 2015], 2016. Available at <http://www.customs.ru/index2.php?option=com_content&view=article&id=22580:-2015-&catid=125:2011-02-04-16-01-54&Itemid=1976> (accessed 7 August 2017).

Fedorov, Gleb. "Visit Russia Tourism Office Opens in Hanoi". *Russia Beyond The Headlines*, 19 April 2016. Available at <http://rbth.com/news/2016/04/19/visit-russia-tourism-office-opens-in-hanoi_586255> (accessed 6 August 2017).

Gabuev, Alexander. "A 'Soft Alliance'? Russia–China Relations after the Ukraine Crisis". *European Council on Foreign Relations* 126 (2015).

Glazunov, E.P., I.S. Kazakevich, S.A. Mkhitaryan, and V.M. Solntsev. *Vietnam v bor'be* [Vietnam at War]. Moscow: Nauka, 1982.

Gorbachev, Mikhail. "Speech in Vladivostok". *Izbr. rec'i i stati* 4 (1986): 9–34.

Jeffries, Ian. *Socialist Economies and the Transition to the Market: A Guide*. London and New York: Routledge, 2002.

Kazakov, I. *Rossisko-V'etnamskie interesy: Neft, Energetika, I Oruzhie* [Russia–Vietnam Interests: Oil, Energy and Arms], 18 May 2004. Available at <http://www.strana.ru/print/215580.html> (accessed 5 August 2017).

Klyuchanskaya, Svetlana. "Russia and Southeast Asia: Cooperation in Strategic Areas". *Security Index* 17, no. 1 (2011): 37–52.

Kommersant. "Komu Rossiya proshala dolgi" [Whose Debt Russia Wrote Off], 12 December 2013. Available at <http://www.kommersant.ru/doc/2364889> (accessed 5 September 2017).

Konboy, Kenneth J. "After Vladivostok: Gorbachev's Asian Inroads". *Asian Backgrounder (The Heritage Foundation)* 73 (1988).

Kozyrev, Vitaly. "Russia–Vietnam Strategic Partnership: The Return of the Brotherhood in Arms?" *Russian Analytical Digest* 145 (2014).

Lan, N.T.C. "Tendentsii i struktura vnesheekonomicheskikh svyazey Rossii i Vietnama" [Trends and Structure of Russia–Vietnam Economic Ties]. *Rossiyskiy vneshneekonomicheskiy vestnik* 3 (2012).

Largo, V. *Vietnam: Current Issues and Historical Background*. New York: Nova Science Publishers, 2002.

Lavrov, Sergey. "Russian Foreign Minister Sergey Lavrov's Interview with the Channel NewsAsia". MFA of the Russian Federation, 5 August 2015. Available at <http://www.mid.ru/en/foreign_policy/news/-/asset_publisher/cKNonkJE02Bw/content/id/1635121> (accessed 5 September 2017).

Lo, Bobo. "Russia's Eastern Direction: Distinguishing the Real from the Virtual". *Russie. Nei. Reports* 17 (2014).

Malyasov, Dylan. "Vietnam is Negotiating to Buy S-400 Triumph Anti-aircraft Missiles". *Defence Blog*, 4 July 2016. Available at <http://defence-blog.com/news/vietnam-is-negotiating-to-buy-s-400-triumph-anti-aircraft-missiles.html> (accessed 5 September 2017).

Mazyrin, V. and E. Kobelev. "Rossia–Vietnam: 20 predlozheniy po povisheniyu effektivnosty vseob'emlyushego strategicheskogo partnerstva" [Russia–Vietnam: 20 Propositions for Increasing the Efficiency of the Comprehensive Strategic Partnership]. *RIAC Working Paper* 23 (2015).

Mosyakov, D. "Perspektivy rossiysko–vietnamskogo ekonomicheskogo sotrudnichestva" [The Prospects for the Russian–Vietnamese Economic Cooperation]. *Yugo-Vostochnaya Azia: Aktualnie Problem Razvitia* 25 (2014*a*).

———. "Rol' SSSR v otrazhenii agressii Kitaya protiv Vietnama v 1979 g." [Role of the USSR in Repelling Chinese Aggression Against Vietnam in 1979]. *Yugo-Vostochnaya Azia: Aktualnie Problem Razvitia* 25 (2014*b*).

Offshore. "Gazprom, Rosneft Strengthen Offshore E&P Links with Vietnam", 17 May 2016. Available at <http://www.offshore-mag.com/articles/2016/05/gazprom-rosneft-strengthen-offshore-e-p-links-with-vietnam.html> (accessed 5 August 2017).

Reuters. "U.S. Asks Vietnam to Stop Helping Russian Bomber Flights", 11 March 2015. Available at <http://www.reuters.com/article/us-usa-vietnam-russia-exclusive-idUSKBN0M71NA20150311> (accessed 6 September 2017).

RIA Novosti. "Russia to Grant $8 Bln Loan to Vietnam to Build First Nuke Plant", 23 November 2011. Available at <http://en.ria.ru/world/20111123/168971366.html> (accessed 6 August 2017).

Russian Embassy in China. "V.Putin Press-Conference Following G20 Summit in Hangzhou", 6 September 2016. Available at <http://www.russia.org.cn/en/news/v-putin-press-conference-following-g20-summit-in-hangzhou/> (accessed 6 September 2017).

Russian Embassy in Vietnam. "Rossiysko-vietnamskie otnosheniya" [Russia–Vietnam Relations], 2016. Available at <http://vietnam.mid.ru/rossijsko-v-etnamskie-otnosenia> (accessed 8 August 2017).

Ryazantsev, S. and E. Pismennaya. "Vietnamskie migranty na rossiyskom rynke truda" [Vietnamese Migrants on the Russian Labour Market]. *Zluzhba zanyatosti* 3 (2016).

Scalapino, Robert A. "The Political Influence of the USSR in Asia". In *Soviet Policy in East Asia*, edited by Donald S. Zagoria. New Haven: Yale University Press, 1982.

Sokolov, A. "Rossiysko-vietnamskor sotrudnichestro v oblasi obrazovania" [Russia–Vietnam Educational Cooperation]. *Yugo-Vostochnaya Azia: Aktualnie Problem Razvitia* 25 (2014).

Sputnik News. "Russia, Vietnam Will Hold 1st Joint Drills on Vietnamese Territory in 2016", 26 November 2015. Available at <https://sputniknews.com/military/20151126/1030777476/russia-vietnam-military-drills.html> (accessed 7 August 2017).

Stoecker, Sally W. *Clients and Commitments: Soviet–Vietnamese Relations, 1978–1988 (No. RAND/N-2737-A)*. Santa Monica: RAND Corp, 1989.

Storey, Ian J. and Carlyle A. Thayer. "Cam Ranh Bay: Past Imperfect, Future Conditional". *Contemporary Southeast Asia* 23, no. 3 (2001): 452–73.

Szalontai, Balazs. "The Diplomacy of Economic Reform in Vietnam". 아세아연구 51, no. 2 (2008): 199–252.

TASS. "Russia, Vietnam Agree on Simplified Cam Ranh Port Entry for Russian Warships", 27 November 2014. Available at <https://push.tass.ru/en/world/763988> (accessed 6 August 2017).

Thayer, Carlyle A. "Russia: A Military Base at Cam Ranh Bay?" *Thayer Consultancy*, 20 February 2017. Available at <http://www.viet-studies.net/kinhte/Thayer_RussiaCamRanh.pdf> (accessed 6 August 2017).

Tien, Nguyen Thanh. "Vai net ve quan he Viet Nam – Lien Xo tu nam 1975 den nam 1990" [On Vietnam–USSR Relations in 1975–1990]. *Tap Chi Khoa Hoc DHSP TP.HCM* 13, no. 12 (2008): 12–22.

Tsvetov, Anton. "After Crimea: Southeast Asia in Russia's Foreign Policy Narrative". *Contemporary Southeast Asia* 38, no. 1 (2016a): 55–80.

———. "Russia's Strategy and Tactics in the South China Sea". *Asia Maritime Transparency Initiative*, 1 November 2016b. Available at <https://amti.csis.org/russias-tactics-strategy-south-china-sea/> (accessed 12 September 2017).

Vinogradov, B. "Kak Rossiya okalazalas' 'vne konkurentsii' na neftyanom shelf'e V'etnama" [How Russia was Left Without Competition on Vietnam's Shoal]. *Izestiya* 30 (January 1993).

Zakharova, Maria. "Briefing by Foreign Ministry Spokesperson Maria Zakharova". MFA of the Russian Federation, 14 July 2016. Available at <http://www.mid.ru/en/foreign_policy/news/-/asset_publisher/cKNonkJE02Bw/content/id/2354135> (accessed 7 September 2017).

8

Vietnam's Foreign Policy Towards its Smaller Neighbours

Vannarith Chheang

After three decades of *Doi Moi* (Renovation), Vietnam's role in the region has been remarkably strengthened, particularly after its accession to Association of Southeast Asian Nations (ASEAN) and diplomatic normalization with the United States in 1995. Vietnam's foreign policy has been restructured, readjusted and reoriented in response to the fast-changing global and regional geostrategic and economic landscape. With its growing economic and geopolitical weight, Vietnam is gradually becoming an important strategic actor in Southeast Asia as well as the Asia Pacific.

Available studies on Vietnam's foreign policy mainly focus on Hanoi's relations with the major powers, such as China, the United States, Japan and Russia, and its foreign policy towards regional institutions, especially ASEAN. Few studies have been conducted on Vietnam's relations with its smaller neighbours. To fill the gap, this chapter aims to examine Vietnam's foreign policy towards Cambodia and the Lao People's Democratic Republic under *Doi Moi*.

The chapter argues that Vietnam is incrementally asserting its leadership role in the Mekong subregion by tightening its traditional ties with the two neighbours through comprehensive engagement with a multi-pronged and multi-layered approach, including strengthening political and security cooperation, economic integration, and socio-cultural exchanges. As long as Vietnam can secure its presence and influence in Cambodia and Laos, its foreign policy, especially its hedging strategy against China, will provide better outcomes with greater returns and fewer risks.

The chapter starts by reviewing Vietnam's foreign policy, objectives and approaches towards Cambodia and Laos within the context of Hanoi's foreign policy reforms and its pursuit of regional integration under *Doi Moi*. It then analyses the achievements, challenges, and remaining issues in Vietnam's relations with the two neighbours.

Vietnam's Foreign Policy: An Overview

Doi Moi, which was introduced in 1986, marked a critical turning point in Vietnam's foreign policy. The end of the Cold War enabled Vietnam to enlarge its strategic space through the normalization and cementing of ties with all major powers, particularly with China in 1991 and the United States in 1995. Vietnam also gained membership in key regional and global institutions, most notably ASEAN in 1995, Asia-Pacific Economic Cooperation (APEC) in 1998, and World Trade Organization (WTO) in 2007. Vietnam has since adopted a robust regional integration strategy in tandem with its domestic economic reforms and bureaucratic capacity building.

Vietnam's foreign policy trajectory is also moving from internal development to external engagement. Accordingly, the country gradually expands its diplomatic focus from securing favourable external conditions for domestic development to enhancing its national status through active engagement with major partners and international institutions. During this process, striking a stable balance between China and the United States is becoming an increasingly challenging task for Vietnam, especially given the heightened strategic competition and rivalry between the two powers (Hiep 2012*a*). Intensifying disputes between Vietnam and China over the South China Sea, especially after the *Haiyang Shiyou* 981 oil rig crisis in 2014, have forced Vietnam to move closer to the United States, yet Vietnam cannot afford to have a hostile relationship with China due to various reasons, including the geographical proximity, the ideological affinity between the two ruling parties, as well as the growing economic interdependence between the two countries (Hiep 2015).

Against this backdrop, Vietnam has smartly practised "bamboo diplomacy" and strategic sturdiness to avoid being "entrapped" in the complicated rivalry among big powers. Diversifying strategic partners is therefore regarded as the key strategy (Do 2014). As argued by Thayer, "Vietnam will continue to pursue a policy of multi-polar balancing — diversification and multilateralization of relations — rather than a narrower policy of balancing relations between China and the United States in the years following the twelfth party congress" (Thayer 2015).

However, it is an uphill struggle for Vietnam to have an equi-proximate relationship with all the major powers amid increasing regional power competition and rivalry as well as the intensifying tensions in the South China Sea. As such, Hanoi's balancing act may encounter more pains and risks (Brennan 2013). As pointed out by McCornac (2013), "whenever China or the U.S. swings the tightrope more aggressively, Vietnam finds itself in a more precarious position, not knowing which end of the rope is the safest point of refuge. If the Vietnamese government is to continue to stay upright it must avoid too close an alignment with one country at the expense of ties with the other".

ASEAN is regarded by Hanoi as a shield, even more so amid rising global uncertainty, to protect the sovereignty and interests of its member states. Vietnam underscores the role of ASEAN in maintaining its neutrality and independence through the strengthening of the ASEAN-centred regional architecture and the promotion of rules-based international relations. Accordingly, Vietnam appreciates ASEAN norms and principles, such as non-interference, equal sovereignty, peaceful coexistence, and peaceful settlement of disputes. Moreover, Vietnam believes that a strong ASEAN can "ward off possible aggression, especially from China" (Yeong 1992, p. 257). In a speech at the Asia Society in New York on 24 September 2014, Foreign Minister Pham Binh Minh also stressed that Vietnam needs to, among other things, promote an ASEAN-led regional order so that it can secure a favourable international posture (Do 2015).

Apart from ASEAN and the major powers, Vietnam also attaches significance to its relations with neighbouring countries (Government of Vietnam 2006). The Political Report of the Communist Party of Vietnam (CPV)'s eighth national congress in 1996, for example, considers the strengthening of Vietnam's relations with neighbouring countries and ASEAN member states as the country's top foreign policy priority (*Nhan Dan* 1996). Cambodia and Laos are strategically and economically important to Vietnam due to the geographical proximity, economic connectivity, historical memory of their common struggle against colonial powers, and the three countries' complex security interdependence. In particular, increasing Chinese presence and influence in Cambodia and Laos are presenting a new security challenge for Vietnam from the West at a time when tensions are also rising in the East due to the South China Sea disputes.

Vietnam's Foreign Policy towards Cambodia and Laos

This section discusses Vietnam's foreign policy towards Cambodia and Laos after the launch of *Doi Moi*, focusing on Vietnam's national interest calculations and its strategy. Towards this end, the section analyses the continuity and changes in Vietnam's perception of and approaches towards Cambodia and Laos within the context of the changing regional geopolitics and geoeconomics. It argues that Vietnam has paid closer attention to Cambodia and Laos by undertaking a relatively comprehensive engagement with the two countries across different sectors and at different levels over the past decade. This effort by Hanoi has partly been driven by ASEAN's regional integration and community building process. At the same time, it can also be interpreted as Hanoi's reaction to China's rising power and influence in the two countries.

Interests

In Vietnam's strategic thinking, Cambodia and Laos are critical neighbours, and the backbone of its national security and defence. Vietnam's experience of using logistic supports and military bases in Laos and Cambodia to conduct its war against America, and Vietnam's vulnerabilities during the Khmer Rouge regime, are primary examples of the significance of the two neighbours to Vietnam's peace and stability. By extension, political changes in Cambodia and Laos also carry significant security implications for Vietnam. Vietnam therefore strives to maintain its traditional friendship with both countries. At the same time, Hanoi also tries to expand its benign influence over the two countries through political and economic means to pre-empt any potential threats that may arise to its national security.

Ensuring a stable and peaceful borderline with neighbouring countries constitutes one of the core elements of Vietnam's foreign policy, as this creates a stable environment for Vietnam to successfully implement its socio-economic and political reforms. With a combined population of 20 million and a fast growing middle class, Cambodia and Laos are also potential markets for Vietnamese products and services. Vietnam is now one of the main trading partners of both Cambodia and Laos. Bilateral trade volume, investment flow, and people movement have increased significantly since the beginning of the 2010s. At the subregional level, the Cambodia–Laos–Vietnam Development Triangle has contributed to the economic development and poverty reduction in the three countries' border provinces. Having more financial resources and technical expertise, Vietnam is taking a leadership role in promoting subregional cooperation and integration (Chheang and Wong 2014). As Vietnam is projecting itself to become the hub of subregional production network and supply chains, Cambodia and Laos are the two main connecting dots for Vietnam.

However, territorial disputes with Cambodia and Laos pose a challenge to Hanoi's pursuit of its foreign policy goals regarding the two neighbours. While Vietnam has successfully negotiated and demarcated its land border with Laos based on an agreement in 1977, its efforts to manage its border with Cambodia is less so (Amer and Thao 2009). Although Vietnam has convinced the ruling Cambodian People's Party (CPP) to respect the border agreement between the two countries (Hoang 2007), which was concluded in 1985 and later supplemented by another treaty in 2005, the unfinished demarcation of the bilateral border as well as the historical resentment of certain segments of the Cambodian population against Vietnam have allowed anti-Vietnam nationalism to grow in Cambodia. An early completion of the border negotiation and demarcation is therefore in the interest of both countries.

Strategy

Vietnam is intensifying its relations with Cambodia and Laos at multiple levels and across various sectors with the aim to maintain frequent high-level dialogues, deepen economic cooperation and integration, strengthen security and defence cooperation, and promote cultural exchanges and people-to-people contacts. Without stepping up its efforts to gain political and economic leverage in Cambodia and Laos, Vietnam risks being contained by China if bilateral tensions over the South China Sea worsen.

The end of the Cold War and the successful resolution of the Cambodian conflict in the early 1990s opened up new opportunities for regional cooperation and integration in Southeast Asia. Vietnam, Laos, and Cambodia joined ASEAN in 1995, 1997, and 1999, respectively, marking the end of the Cold War confrontation between ASEAN and Indochina. ASEAN is regarded by the three countries as the most important regional institution that can help them not only protect their independence and sovereignty, but also promote their domestic socio-economic development, especially through regional economic integration. As such, the three countries have attached great importance to their ASEAN membership and strived to play an active and constructive role in the Association. As the earliest ASEAN member among the three, Vietnam has endorsed the admission of Laos and Cambodia into ASEAN. Vietnam has also assisted the two countries in chairing ASEAN summits and related meetings, implementing regional and subregional integration blueprints, and promoting human resources development. Hanoi hopes that the three countries' stronger role in the Association will improve their common status, as well as their bargaining power both within ASEAN and vis-à-vis external powers.

As subregional cooperation projects contribute to the realization of the ASEAN community, Vietnam has taken a leadership role in forging closer ties among Mekong countries through various subregional cooperation initiatives and mechanisms. For example, the Cambodia–Laos–Vietnam Development Triangle has significantly contributed to the maintenance of border security of the three countries, while facilitating their trade, investment, poverty reduction, and economic as well as socio-cultural development (Hoang 2007).

Vietnam's efforts in maintaining its traditional influence over Indochina have been challenged by China who has the ambition to create its own regional sphere of strategic influence. Fluctuations in Vietnam–China relations significantly shape the foreign policy as well as the domestic politics of Cambodia and Laos (Storey 2004). Over the past decade, China has gained increasing political and economic influence in Cambodia and Laos through the promotion of its "charm offensive", including the provision of concessional loans and grants, the deepening of bilateral trade and investment ties, and the promotion of educational and cultural exchanges. In particular, China views Cambodia as the most reliable and loyal friend in Southeast Asia, and has a strong interest in strengthening Phnom Penh's role in the Mekong region.

In addition, China initiated the Lancang–Mekong Cooperation (LMC) mechanism in 2015 to further project its regional leadership role by strengthening comprehensive partnerships with the lower Mekong countries. At the second LMC Foreign Ministers' Meeting in Cambodia in 2016, China committed US$300 million to support the Mekong countries. Regional and national secretariats will also be created to implement LMC initiatives.

China is now the top trading partner and foreign investor of both Cambodia and Laos. In 2015, China's trade turnover with Cambodia and Laos reached US$4.4 billion and US$4 billion, respectively. Cambodia's exports to China include rice, dry rubber, cassava, fishery, and apparels, while its major imports from China are garment input materials, machinery, vehicles, foodstuffs, electronics, medicines and cosmetics. By the same year, China's accumulated investment in Cambodia had reached more than US$10 billion, while that in Laos was more than US$5 billion. As economic ties with China strengthen, the economic reliance of Cambodia and Laos on China has increased, giving Beijing growing political clout over the two countries. As long as Cambodia and Laos define economic development and poverty reduction as their top national interests, China will remain their most important strategic and development partner.

As a result, Cambodia and Laos are reluctant to take any position that may harm their good relations with China despite the fact that such an approach may hurt their bilateral relations with Vietnam. The differences over the South China Sea disputes and the controversy over the construction of hydropower dams along the main stem of the Mekong River are the cases in point. The 45th ASEAN Foreign Ministers Meeting in July 2012 failed to issue a joint communiqué for the first time in the Association's history because Cambodia, as the host of the meeting, refused to include references to South China Sea incidents in the communiqué despite pressures from some ASEAN members, especially the Philippines and Vietnam. China's influence seems to have played an important role in Cambodia's decision. As Hiep (2012*b*, p. 45) argues, the incident may have been "a move by China to split Vietnam and Cambodia. As good relations with Cambodia are also essential to Vietnam's security, it seems that China knows how to inflict pain on Hanoi if it fails to pay due attention to Beijing."

After the incident, although Cambodia tried to justify that the failure was due to unreasonable demands from the Philippines and Vietnam to bring bilateral disputes into the joint statement, Cambodia's international image was largely dented. Cambodia was accused of being a proxy of China. At the same time, as diplomatic tension between Vietnam and Cambodia ran high, foreign ministers of both countries did not comfortably see eye to eye.

In a more recent episode, after visiting Brunei and Cambodia in late April 2016, Chinese Foreign Minister Wang Yi wrapped up his Southeast Asian tour in Laos, the chair of ASEAN in 2016, and declared that the four countries reached a four-point consensus on the South China Sea.[1] Again, this move by China is perceived by some regional analysts as a strategy to divide ASEAN over differences related to the South China Sea disputes. Tang Siew Mun, for example, argues that "regardless of China's intentions, the four-point consensus will be perceived as an attempt to break ASEAN's solidarity and cohesiveness on South China Sea" (Tang 2016).

Vietnam has strengthened its "special relations" [*quan hệ đặc biệt*] with Cambodia and Laos with the hope that these two countries will stay neutral and independent of China. However, Vietnam does not have enough resources and capacity to compete with China and to counterbalance its influence over these two neighbours. Consequently, China's aggressive "charm offensive" in the region may present Vietnam with the risk of being isolated in the South China Sea disputes.

To deal with this prospect, Vietnam has actively engaged and encouraged the United States and Japan to pay closer attention to the Mekong region. Indeed, from the perspective of Vietnamese policymakers, the United States and Japan are the only two major powers that have sufficient resources as well as political will and strategic incentives to assist Laos and Cambodia to stay neutral and independent. Although the United States is slow in engaging Indochina after the end of the Cold War, it has paid serious attention to this subregion after the launch of its strategic rebalance towards East Asia in early 2011. Then

Secretary of State Hillary Clinton visited Cambodia in 2010 and Laos in 2012; and in January 2016, her successor John Kerry also visited the two countries to further strengthen bilateral ties as part of Washington's efforts to counterbalance the increasing influence of China over the region.

Meanwhile, Japan has taken more robust diplomatic moves in the Mekong region. For example, in 2009, Japan hosted the first annual Mekong–Japan Summit attended by leaders from Cambodia, Laos, Myanmar, Thailand, and Vietnam. Since then, Japan's relations with the Mekong countries have gained new momentum after the New Tokyo Strategy for Mekong–Japan cooperation was adopted in 2015. The strategy outlines four pillars of development, namely industrial infrastructure, industrial human resource, sustainable development towards the realization of a green Mekong, and coordination with various stakeholders. During his visit to Thailand in April 2016, Japanese Foreign Minister Fumio Kishida pledged US$7 billion to support the Mekong countries. Japan's economic presence and development assistance are seen by Vietnam as an effective measure to balance against the risk of China's economic dominance over the region.

Vietnam–Cambodia Relations

The relationship between Cambodia and Vietnam is built on multiple factors, including geographical proximity, the tradition of solidarity and mutual assistance during their struggle for national liberation and construction, and now increasingly the benefits of economic cooperation. Personal ties between leaders of the CPV and the CPP are also the backbone of the post-1979 Cambodia–Vietnam friendship. The official foreign policy discourse of the two countries highlights the objective of enhancing bilateral relations under the slogan of good neighbours, traditional friendship, comprehensive cooperation, and long-term stability.

Cambodia and Vietnam officially established diplomatic relations on 24 June 1967. Before 1993, bilateral ties mainly focused on security issues. Since 1993, the relationship has expanded to include the deepening of economic and cultural cooperation. The wartime political trust and camaraderie remain a critical foundation of the bilateral relationship. In particular, the CPP and the CPV continue to enhance their ties via frequent high-level visits and bilateral dialogues, through which mutual political understanding and the habit of cooperation have been developed. Both countries also frequently exchange views on national and regional issues of mutual concern. An important point that both sides have emphasized as a basis for mutual trust is that each country will not allow any hostile forces to use its territory to undermine the security of the other.

In tandem with strong political ties, bilateral defence and security cooperation has also been strengthened over the years. Vietnam has assisted Cambodia in military training and capacity building, defence infrastructure development, and the supply of military equipment. Both countries also hold annual high-level dialogues between defence ministers to review past activities and set direction for future cooperation. In December 2015, the two sides inked an agreement to foster bilateral defence and security cooperation, with a focus on high-ranking delegation exchanges, deputy-ministerial-level defence policy dialogue, young officer exchanges, joint sea patrols, search and collection of remains of Vietnamese soldiers who fell in Cambodia, and bilateral coordination to manage the borderline of the two countries.

In terms of economic relations, bilateral trade has increased significantly in recent years. In 1998, the total two-way trade turnover stood modestly at about US$117 million. Since then, it has gradually increased to US$585 million in 2004, US$940 million in 2006, US$3.29 billion in 2014, and US$3.37 billion in 2015. Vietnam's main exports to Cambodia are petroleum, steel, fertilizer, machinery, consumer goods, and food products. Meanwhile, Cambodia's exports to Vietnam include mainly agricultural products, such as rice, cashew nuts, rubber, and wood. Vietnam has also become one of the top five foreign investors in Cambodia. By the end of 2015, Vietnam had invested nearly US$3 billion in Cambodia in such sectors as rubber plantation, mining, telecommunications, finance and banking, and tourism industry.

Educational and cultural exchanges constitute yet another important foundation of the long-term friendship between the two countries. Annually, Vietnam offers 120 scholarships to Cambodian students to study at various universities and institutions in Vietnam. Vietnam also ranks among Cambodia's top five sources of tourist arrivals. In 2015, for example, 987,792 Vietnamese tourists visited Cambodia, accounting for 20.7 per cent of the kingdom's total tourist arrivals in the same year. Meanwhile, cultural exchanges, particularly performing arts, have also gained more attention and support from both governments.

Despite such positive developments, however, Vietnam–Cambodia relations still face certain significant challenges deriving from the dynamics of Cambodia's domestic politics. Most notably, opposition parties in Cambodia generally perceive Vietnam as the main external threat to Cambodia's sovereignty and security, and view Vietnam as an expansionist power. Anti-Vietnam nationalism has increased over the years along with the widening political power base of the main opposition party, the Cambodia National Rescue Party (CNRP). As such, border demarcation and cross-border irregular immigration are the two thorny issues that need to be carefully addressed by both governments. Otherwise, they risk being over-politicized, allowing ultra-nationalism to further grow and undermine bilateral relations.

Vietnam's border negotiation with Cambodia is much more complicated than its negotiation with Laos due to some disagreements over the boundary demarcation maps, and Cambodia's complex domestic politics and nationalism (Chheang 2015). According to a report by the National Police of Cambodia in March 2016, 90 per cent of the border demarcation had been completed, with 283 out of 314 border posts having been planted. Nevertheless, the opposition parties, particularly the CNRP, have accused the CPP of ceding land to Vietnam and failing to protect Cambodia's territorial integrity.

From the government's point of view, such accusations are baseless and politically motivated. In August 2012, Prime Minister Hun Sen spent five hours at the National Assembly explaining the border issues and the process of border demarcation between the two countries. Yet, he still failed to convince the opposition party's members and supporters of the government's commitment to defend Cambodia's national interests. The CNRP's lack of trust in the CPP government, however, may have partly derived from its strategy of exploiting anti-Vietnam sentiments to gain electoral support from certain segments of the Cambodian population.

Border tensions have flared up several times in recent years with violence taking place in contested border areas in May and June 2015. The Cambodian government took a firm position by sending Hanoi diplomatic notes that demanded the latter to halt construction activities in the contested area. Prime Minister Hun Sen told visiting CPV Politburo Member Le Hong Anh on 9 June 2015 that pending the demarcation of the border, the areas that had not been demarcated should not be changed. At the same time, as the two countries used maps prepared by the French colonial authorities as the basis for the demarcation of their border, the Cambodian government asked the United Nations, France, the United Kingdom, and the United States to help verify the authenticity of the maps. This was to invalidate the opposition party's allegation that the government was using maps prepared by Vietnam for the demarcation. In the wake of the incidents, two members of parliament from the opposition CNRP were arrested and jailed for stirring up border tension with Vietnam.

Protestant indigenous Montagnards from Vietnam's Central Highlands who cross the border into Cambodia to seek refugee status is another lingering issue for Cambodia to deal with. As a party to the 1951 Convention Relating to the Status of Refugees and its 1967 Protocol, Cambodia is mandated to protect the rights of these asylum seekers. However, doing so will upset Vietnam. At the request of Hanoi, Cambodia often deports them back to Vietnam on the basis that they are illegal economic migrants. As noted by Vietnam analyst Carlyle Thayer, "Vietnam will not be pleased if highland ethnic minorities who [seek] asylum in Cambodia are given refugee status... This will impact on Vietnam's international standing and also act as stimulus for other ethnic minorities to flee Vietnam... Vietnam will make its displeasure known through diplomatic channels but is unlikely to take any further steps because this would draw even more international attention to this issue" (quoted in Crane 2015).

Finally, the divergent national interests and differences in their approach to the South China Sea disputes are also constraining Vietnam–Cambodia relations. Cambodia maintains that the disputes should be resolved through direct bilateral channels or multilateral dialogues among claimant states. ASEAN does not have a mandate to resolve these disputes. However, Vietnam is of the view that helping to solve or manage the South China Sea disputes is within ASEAN's mandate, as the disputes have significant security implications for not only claimant states but also other ASEAN non-claimant members and the broader region. Failing to address the disputes will also call the ASEAN centrality in the regional security architecture into question. As such, Vietnam wishes to see ASEAN play a stronger role in managing tensions and preventing conflicts in the South China Sea. At the same time, Vietnam also seeks the constructive engagement of such major powers as the United States, Japan, and India in the region to counterbalance China's assertiveness in the South China Sea. Meanwhile,

Cambodia tends to share China's view that the intervention of external powers into the South China Sea is further complicating the disputes and should be avoided. Such differences tend to be an enduring irritant to bilateral relations given China's increasing influence over Cambodia as well as the rising tensions between Vietnam and China in the South China Sea.

Vietnam–Laos Relations

The modern relationship between Vietnam and Laos has been developed since the inception of the Communist Party of Indochina in 1930, and especially during their subsequent joint struggle against colonialism and imperialism. Formal diplomatic relations between the two countries were established on 5 September 1962. During the Vietnam War, the Lao People's Revolutionary Party (LPRP) granted permission to North Vietnam to construct parts of the Ho Chi Minh Trail in Lao territory, which was used by the North Vietnamese government to send troops, weapons and supplies to South Vietnam.

After the Vietnam War and the proclamation of the Lao People's Democratic Republic in 1975, Vietnam–Laos relations started a new phase of development, which was partly based on the strong personal ties between the leaders of the two countries. Vietnam and Laos forged a "special relationship" in 1976 and signed a Treaty of Friendship and Cooperation in July 1977. Designed to deepen the "special relationship" between the two countries and peoples, the twenty-five-year mutual security agreement allowed Vietnam to station a small number of troops in Laos until Vietnam decided to withdraw all of its troops out of Cambodia and Laos in the late 1980s. Vietnamese advisers and technicians were also sent to assist Laos in running its government ministries and agencies (*Global Security* 2013).

The "special relationship" between the two countries and their ruling communist parties has survived beyond the end of the Cold War and the collapse of communism in the Soviet Union and Eastern Europe. Indeed, shared concerns about national and regime security have facilitated bilateral cooperation as the leaderships in both Hanoi and Vientiane have a strong conviction that their national and regime security is interconnected. As a result, they have closely coordinated and cooperated in preventing "hostile forces" from stirring up political instability, and from using the territory of one country to mount security threats against the other.

To stabilize bilateral relations, the two sides have made the settlement of border issues a priority. Bilateral border negotiation and demarcation were conducted smoothly. On 18 July 1977, Laos and Vietnam signed a treaty on their land boundary. Following the completion of the demarcation process, a supplementary treaty was signed on 24 January 1986. In March 1990, an additional protocol and an agreement on border regulations were signed. From 2008 to 2014, the two governments oversaw a project to increase the number of border markers between their twenty adjoining provinces over a distance of 2,337 km. A total of 1,002 markers were installed along the shared border. In March 2016, both countries marked the completion of the project at a ceremony held in Hanoi and attended by Vietnamese Deputy Prime Minister and Minister of Foreign Affairs Pham Binh Minh and his Lao counterpart Thongloun Sisoulith. The successful demarcation of the shared border has contributed to the enhancement of mutual trust and further facilitated cooperation between the two countries, especially along border areas.

Furthermore, since the late 1980s, when Vietnam undertook its economic overhaul under *Doi Moi*, Laos has also gradually opened up its economy along market lines. Apart from increasing bilateral trade and investment, Laos also looks to Vietnam as a source of experiences for its domestic reforms. Economic cooperation has therefore played an increasingly important role in cementing the bilateral relationship.

Two-way trade turnover has increased continuously in recent years, reaching US$1.3 billion in 2015, and is targeted to reach US$3 billion by 2020. In terms of investment, Laos has licensed 413 projects to Vietnamese investors with the total registered capital of over US$5.2 billion by 2015. Vietnamese investment in Laos has been concentrated in the sectors of energy, mining, telecommunications, services, infrastructure, and agriculture (Potkin 2016). At the same time, Vietnam is the third largest source of tourist arrivals for Laos, only after China and Thailand. In 2014, more than 1.1 million Vietnamese tourists accounted for 26.7 per cent of the total number of tourist arrivals in Laos (Lao Ministry of Tourism 2015).

Vietnam considers the special solidarity and comprehensive cooperation with Laos as "invaluable assets". CPV General Secretary Nguyen Phu Trong stated that "the Vietnam–Laos special solidarity has become more critical than ever, given complicated developments around the world. Vietnam and Laos have been doing their utmost to make this relationship last forever" (*Voice of Vietnam* 2016b). Vietnam and Laos have therefore nurtured their relationship by maintaining frequent exchanges of high-level visits and people-to-people ties, and regularly consulting each other on national and international issues of mutual concern. The two countries hold annual meeting of the Vietnam–Laos Intergovernmental Committee, which is composed of representatives from central ministries and agencies and local governments from both sides, to coordinate bilateral cooperation. At the 38th meeting of the Committee in 2016, for example, the two sides discussed and adopted measures for promoting bilateral cooperation in 2016 as well as the period 2016–20.

In recent years, local governments, especially those along the shared border, have remarkably strengthened their friendship and cooperation to ensure border security, stability and economic development. Bilateral cooperation at the local level has been particularly strong between major cities and provinces such as Hanoi, Ho Chi Minh City, Ha Tinh, and Quang Tri in Vietnam, with Vientiane, Bolikhamsai, Savannakhet, and Khammouane in Laos. With the permission from Hanoi and to promote its foreign trade activities, cooperation with Vietnam's local governments has also facilitated Laos' access to Vietnam's seaports, such as the Vung Ang Port in Ha Tinh province. In the coming years, the construction of the Hanoi–Vientiane Highway will further strengthen infrastructure connectivity and economic cooperation between local governments of the two countries.

In terms of education exchanges, each year, about 600 Lao students are granted scholarships by the Vietnamese government to study at various universities in Vietnam. In 2011, the two sides signed an agreement on human resources development for the period 2011–20 to help Laos strengthen its human capital. Vietnam has also been providing political training for Lao officials at the Ho Chi Minh National Academy of Politics and Public Administration. From the perspective of Hanoi, training Lao students and government officials helps Vietnam maintain some political leverage over its neighbour, especially given the fact that China is becoming a more attractive destination for Lao students and officials thanks to its deeper pocket.

China is stepping up its competition with Vietnam for political influence in Laos not only through the provision of scholarships to

Lao students and officials but also economic and security cooperation. With its stronger economic clout, China will likely gain upper hand in the long run as its higher level of trade, investment and economic assistance will gradually translate into stronger political leverage in Vientiane. A primary example of China's growing influence in Laos, or to put in differently, Laos' growing reliance on China, is the US$6 billion rail link connecting Vientiane with Laos–China border, which is mostly financed by China. Although Laos is trying to diversify its external relations with the major powers, it falls short of diplomatic flexibility and development strategy to reduce its overdependence on China's economic powerhouse (Fujimura 2009).

However, the power reshuffle after the tenth congress of the LPRP in January 2016 resulted in a leadership team believed to have closer relations with Vietnam. Bounnhang Vorachith, who was educated and trained in Vietnam, replaced Choummaly Sayasone as the General Secretary of the Party and President of the country. Sayasone was appointed as the Party chief in 2006, which was seen as the beginning of Laos' shift towards China (McCartan 2008).[2] With the rise of Vorachith, Vietnam is expected to be in a better position to counter the rising influence of China over Laos (Potkin 2016).

In his first official visit to a foreign country after the Party congress, Vorachith went to Vietnam to further cement bilateral ties. The visit underscores "the significance of the traditional friendship, special solidarity and comprehensive cooperation" between the two nations (*Vietnamnet* 2016b). A senior Lao official described the visit as a testimony of Laos' high regard for its relationship with Vietnam and that "Laos is a strategic friend, and a country that has a special, rare, and loyal relationship with Vietnam" (*Voice of Vietnam* 2016a). During the visit, Vietnam also urged Laos to work closely with ASEAN to maintain peace and stability in the South China Sea, and to take practical measures to effectively manage the Mekong River.

Currently, the biggest challenge for bilateral relations is perhaps the two countries' divergent interests regarding the construction of hydropower dams along the main stem of the Mekong River. Laos' construction of two major dams — the US$3.8 billion Xayaburi dam and the US$300 million Don Sahong dam — has already caused concerns for Vietnam as the dams may generate adverse impact on food security and the livelihood of millions of Vietnamese in the downstream of the river. According to Nguyen Ngoc Tran, former Deputy Chairman of Vietnam National Assembly's Committee of Science and Technology, the mainstream hydropower projects on the Mekong River caused a loss of US$231 million in seafood and agriculture output to the Mekong Delta (*Vietnamnet* 2016*a*). Although Vietnam has expressed concern and even protested against Lao's construction of these dams, Lao proceeded with the projects for its own economic interests and its ambition to become "the battery of the region". If Laos continues to build more dams and causes more damages to Vietnam in the future, bilateral relations may suffer.

Conclusion

While striving to promote its relations with the major powers and international institutions, Vietnam has also paid great attention to fostering ties with Laos and Cambodia. Vietnam's foreign policy towards its two smaller neighbours is shaped by not only its security and economic calculations but also the dynamics of regional and subregional integration as well as Vietnam's efforts to hedge against China.

By and large, Vietnam has successfully built strong bilateral relations with both Cambodia and Laos. Historical memories and personal trust between Vietnamese leaders and their Cambodian and Lao counterparts play a crucial role in maintaining these traditional friendships. But such social and political capital may decrease as the future leadership generations will not share similar historical memories and the same level of trust. Vietnam will therefore face mounting challenges in maintaining its traditional influence in these two important neighbours.

At the same time, domestic politics, border disputes, irregular immigration, and Mekong water resources management may further strain Vietnam's relations with Cambodia and Laos. These issues should be collectively and holistically addressed. Towards this end, Vietnam needs to develop innovative ways to maintain its traditional friendship with the two countries through the deepening of comprehensive engagement and cooperation, and particularly the strengthening of people-to-people ties.

Vietnam also faces challenges arising from the increasing political and economic clout of China in Cambodia and Laos. Apart from its own efforts to further cultivate ties with the two neighbours to offset

China's "charm offensive", Vietnam believes that the active and constructive engagement with these two countries by the major powers, especially the United States and Japan, as well as the ASEAN centrality in regional affairs, are critical for the maintenance of the regional order against the backdrop of China's rising power and influence. At the same time, the South China Sea disputes continue to cloud Vietnam's relations with the two neighbours. Vietnam should not expect the two countries to always act in its favour. If Hanoi pushes Phnom Penh and Vientiane too hard on the issue, it may backfire and prove counter-productive to its relations with the two neighbours.

NOTES

1. The four points are: *First,* the South China Sea disagreements are not disputes between China and ASEAN, and the matter should not affect China–ASEAN relations. *Second,* the rights of all countries to independently choose the way to resolve the dispute in accordance with international law should be affirmed. The imposition of a unilateral approach would be wrong. *Third,* in accordance with Article IV of the 2002 Declaration on Conduct of Parties in the South China Sea (DOC), China and the three states believe that the parties involved should resolve disputes over their territorial and maritime rights and issues through dialogue and consultation. *Fourth,* China and ASEAN states have the capacity to jointly safeguard peace and stability in the South China Sea, and external parties should play a constructive role, rather than the reverse (*Xinhua* 2016).
2. Sayasone was not a revolutionary war veteran when the communists took over the country in 1975, and he studied in the Soviet Union rather than in Vietnam.

REFERENCES

Amer, Ramses and Nguyen Hong Thao. "Regional Conflict Management: Challenges of the Border Disputes of Cambodia, Laos, and Vietnam". *Current Research on Southeast Asia* 2, no. 2 (2009): 53–80.

Brennan, Elliot. "Vietnam's Foreign Policy: Fewer Enemies, More Friends". *The Interpreter*, 29 November 2013. Available at <http://www.lowyinterpreter. org/post/2013/11/29/Vietnams-foreign-policy-Fewer-enemies-more-friends. aspx> (accessed 1 July 2017).

Chheang, Vannarith. "Nationalism Drives Border Disputes Between Cambodia and Vietnam". *East Asia Forum* (16 October 2015).

Chheang, Vannarith and Wong Yushan. "Cambodia–Laos–Vietnam: Economic Reforms and Sub-regional Integration". *Kyoto Sangyo University Economic Review* 1 (2014): 225–54.

Crane, Brent. "Cambodia's Montagnard Problem". *The Diplomat*, 8 September 2015. Available at <http://thediplomat.com/2015/09/cambodias-montagnard-problem/> (accessed 1 July 2017).

Do, Thuy T. "Is Vietnam's Bamboo Diplomacy Threatened by Pandas?" *East Asia Forum* (3 April 2014). Available at <http://www.eastasiaforum.org/2014/04/03/is-vietnams-bamboo-diplomacy-threatened-by-pandas/> (accessed 1 July 2017).

———. "Vietnam's Moderate Diplomacy Successfully Navigate Difficult Waters". *East Asia Forum* (16 January 2015). Available at <http://www.eastasiaforum.org/2015/01/16/vietnams-moderate-diplomacy-successfully-navigating-difficult-waters/> (accessed 1 July 2017).

Fujimura, Kazuhiro. "The Increasing Presence of China in Laos Today". *Ritsumeikan Journal of Asia Pacific Studies* 27 (2009): 65–83.

Global Security. "Laos–Vietnam Relations", 2013. Available at <http://www.globalsecurity.org/military/world/laos/forrel-vn.htm> (accessed 1 July 2017).

Government of Vietnam. "Viet Nam's Present Foreign Policy", 7 November 2006. Available at <http://www.chinhphu.vn/portal/page/portal/English/strategies/strategiesdetails?categoryId=30&articleId=3036> (accessed 1 July 2017).

Hiep, Le Hong. "Vietnam's Strategic Trajectory: From Internal Development to External Engagement". *Strategic Insight* (June 2012a): 1–20.

———. "Vietnam's Balancing Act". *American Review* 10 (2012b): 38–46.

———. "The Vietnam–US–China Triangle: New Dynamics and Implications". *ISEAS Perspective* 45 (2015).

Hoang, Vu Le Thai. "Vietnam's Quest for Influence and Its Implications for the Management of Border Disputes with Laos and Cambodia". *Current Southeast Asian Affairs* 26, no. 2 (2007): 5–37.

Lao Ministry of Tourism. "Top Markets (Regional Visitors) with Forecast to 2020", 2015. Available at <http://www.tourismlaos.org/> (accessed 2 July 2017).

McCartan, Brian. "From China and Vietnam Square Off in Laos". *Asia Times*, 30 August 2008. Available at <http://www.atimes.com/atimes/Southeast_Asia/JH30Ae01.html> (accessed 1 July 2017).

McCornac, Dennis C. "Vietnam's Foreign Policy Tightrope". *East Asia Forum* (12 October 2013). Available at <http://www.eastasiaforum.org/2013/10/12/vietnams-foreign-policy-tightrope/> (accessed 1 July 2017).

Ministry of Foreign Affairs (MOFA), Vietnam. *Diplomatic Bluebook 2015*. Hanoi: National Political Publishing House, 2016.

Nhan Dan. "Du thao Bao cao Chinh tri cua Ban Chap hanh Trung Uong Dang Khoa VII trinh Dai hoi lan thu VIII cua Dang", 10 April 1996.

Potkin, Fanny. "Is Laos Moving Away from China with its Leadership Transition". *The Diplomat*, 3 February 2016. Available at <http://thediplomat.com/2016/02/is-laos-moving-away-from-china-with-its-leadership-transition/> (accessed 1 July 2017).

Storey, Ian. "China and Vietnam's Tug of War over Laos". *Jamestown Foundation China Brief* 5, no. 13 (2004).

Tang Siew Mun. "China's Dangerous Divide and Conquer Game with ASEAN". *TODAY* (27 April 2016).

Thayer, Carlyle A. "Why Vietnam's Foreign Policy Won't Change After Its Party Congress". *The Diplomat* (8 December 2015). Available at <http://thediplomat.com/2015/12/why-vietnams-foreign-policy-wont-change-after-its-party-congress/> (accessed 1 July 2017).

Vietnamnet. "Hydropower Dams Cause $231 Million in Damage to Mekong Delta", 6 March 2016a. Available at <http://english.vietnamnet.vn/fms/environment/152083/hydropower-dams-cause--231-mln-in-damage-to-mekong-delta.html> (accessed 2 July 2017).

———. "Vietnamese, Lao Leaders Underscore Bilateral Friendship", 26 April 2016b. Available at <http://english.vietnamnet.vn/fms/government/155541/vietnamese--lao-leaders-underscore-bilateral-friendship.html> (accessed 1 August 2017).

Voice of Vietnam. "Enhancing Vietnam, Laos Ties", 25 April 2016a. Available at <http://vovworld.vn/en-US/current-affairs/enhancing-vietnam-laos-ties-430681.vov> (accessed 1 July 2017).

———. "Milestones in Vietnam's 2016 Foreign Affairs", 14 December 2016b. Available at <http://vovworld.vn/en-us/Current-Affairs/Milestones-in-Vietnams-2016-foreign-affairs/496040.vov> (accessed 2 July 2017).

Xinhua. "China Reaches Consensus with Brunei, Cambodia, Laos on South China Sea Issue", 23 April 2016. Available at <http://news.xinhuanet.com/english/2016-04/23/c_135306137.htm> (accessed 2 July 2017).

Yeong, Mike. "New Thinking in Vietnamese Foreign Policy". *Contemporary Southeast Asia* 14, no. 3 (1992): 257–67.

9

Vietnam's Decision to Join ASEAN: The South China Sea Disputes Connection

Nguyen Vu Tung and Dang Cam Tu

As the 1991 Paris Peace Accords brought an end to the Cambodian conflict, the normalization of Vietnam's relations with China appeared to be just a matter of time. Yet, China's seizure of the Paracels in 1974 and its encroachment into the Spratlys in 1988 continued to complicate the Sino–Vietnam relationship. Therefore, while trying to promote friendly relations with China, Vietnam remained vigilant and endeavoured to enhance its comprehensive national power to cope with the latter's territorial and maritime ambitions. Against this backdrop, some scholars argued that if Vietnam became an Association of Southeast Asian Nation (ASEAN) member, Hanoi could improve its strategic position vis-à-vis China as Beijing would have to deal with not only Vietnam, but also ASEAN as a whole (Johnston 2003, p. 28; Tuan 1994). It was therefore possible that Hanoi did have China in mind while pursuing ASEAN membership, which seemed to be even more sensible given the rising "China threat" thesis in the early 1990s (Betts 1995; Betts and Christensen 2000; Brown 1997).

This chapter, based on Vietnam's diplomatic archive and interviews with Vietnamese foreign policymakers and diplomats, traces thoughts of policymakers in Hanoi as to whether, while considering to join ASEAN, they were serious about enlisting ASEAN's support to bolster Vietnam's position in the South China Sea disputes with China. The chapter also examines if Hanoi viewed its bid for ASEAN membership as a measure to improve ties with the United States, thereby gaining leverage vis-à-vis China in the South China Sea.

The chapter contends that although the South China Sea disputes became an increasingly central security concern for Vietnam in the 1990s, Hanoi did not seriously consider its prospective ASEAN membership as a strategic tool to counter China's expansion in the South China Sea.[1] This was because Hanoi realized that ASEAN was indeed not a military organization, and ASEAN members, as well as the United States, did not want to antagonize China by supporting Vietnam in the South China Sea disputes.

The chapter is divided into three sections. The first analyses shifts in Vietnam's perception of the China threat in the late 1980s and early 1990s when Vietnam was pursuing ASEAN membership. The second looks into four major incidents in the South China Sea during this period to find out how the South China Sea disputes factored into Vietnam's decision to join ASEAN. Finally, the third section examines the link between Vietnam's bid to join ASEAN and its quest for normalization with the United States, and whether Vietnam pursued these foreign policy projects with the South China Sea disputes in mind.

Shifts in Vietnam's Perception of the China Threat

Before 1986, Vietnam considered China as a main threat to its security. For example, the 1980 Constitution even called China a "direct and dangerous" enemy of Vietnam. Yet, Hanoi's perception of the China threat became increasingly nuanced ever since. Assessing that China became preoccupied with the Four Modernization Program, and although tensions on Sino–Vietnamese borders persisted, another border war with China looked unlikely, Hanoi began to embrace the view that the military threat from China had eased. A document of the Ministry of Foreign Affairs (MOFA) entitled "On the Situation in Southeast Asia and Guidelines for Our Diplomatic Struggle" in October 1981 observed,

China is big, but it is not strong. Internally, it is not stable; externally, it has contradictions with most of the countries in the world, especially in Asia and Southeast Asia. Therefore, China's scope of actions, especially in the military field, will be limited in nature and will take place only under very specific conditions (MOFA 1981*b*, p. 4).

MOFA's 1981 Annual Report wrote, "The possibility that China would teach [Vietnam] a second lesson is increasingly limited" (MOFA 1981*a*, p. 16). When there were signs of Sino–Soviet rapprochement in 1982, MOFA claimed that "relatively peaceful and stable conditions in Southeast Asia already exist" (MOFA 1982 p. 3). Moreover, partly due to improvements in Sino–Soviet relations, Hanoi began making efforts to mend the fence with China since 1980. According to a MOFA document, between 1980 and 1987, Hanoi made eighteen attempts to resume talks on normalization of relations with Beijing (MOFA 1990, p. 14). In October 1988, Hanoi sent a congratulatory message to the People's Republic of China (PRC) on its 39th National Day, in which it officially recognized that the PRC was still a socialist country. In December 1988, it removed the reference to China as Vietnam's "dangerous and direct enemy" from the 1980 Constitution. Following the secret bilateral summit held in Chengdu in September 1990, the normalization process accelerated and bilateral relations were fully restored in November 1991.

Vietnam's improved perception of China since 1986 was due to both the ease of global tensions among the great powers and Vietnam's radical domestic changes. Politburo Resolution No. 13 in May 1988 identified "economic backwardness and political isolation" as "the biggest threat to Vietnam's security and independence". At the Communist Party of Vietnam (CPV)'s mid-term conference in January 1994, Hanoi introduced a list of four major threats to the regime's security: lagging behind other states in economic terms; corruption and inefficient bureaucracy; peaceful evolution; and deviation from the socialist path. In other words, due to the post-Cold War global setting and the on-going reforms in Vietnam, Hanoi's threat perception had changed, reflecting the fact that its concerns over regime survival had trumped those over state security.[2]

Moreover, in a Resolution issued by the third plenum of the CPV Central Committee in 1992, China, Laos, Cambodia, and ASEAN states were, for the first time, put in the same category of close neighbours with whom friendship must be cultivated (Tung 1993, pp. 88–90).

Therefore, when Hanoi decided to pursue ASEAN membership, China had ceased to be a threat to Vietnam in the conventional sense. As a result, the need to rely on ASEAN to balance China was not the main reason for Hanoi to improve relations with the bloc. This logic is all the more plausible given the fact that Beijing was not against Vietnam's ASEAN membership. Commenting on the ASEAN decision to admit Vietnam as a member at the 27th ASEAN Ministerial Meeting (AMM), Chinese Foreign Minister Qian Qichen told his Vietnamese counterpart Nguyen Manh Cam in Bangkok that "China welcomes Vietnam's membership in ASEAN because this will contribute to peace and stability in the region" (MOFA 1994*a*, p. 10).

While Beijing may indeed have had some reservations about Vietnam's ASEAN membership as it might constitute a balancing act against China in the long run, Hanoi had realized that any effort to rally ASEAN support to counter China had serious limitations because ASEAN countries did not want to confront Beijing. Following the normalization of Indonesia–China relations in 1990, all ASEAN countries started to strengthen their relations with China in various fields. Furthermore, China became increasingly important for ASEAN countries, as Vietnamese Ambassador to Singapore Nguyen Manh Hung observed in 1994, "Recent statements by Lee Kwan Yew and other high-ranking officials have shown that China is becoming more important to Singapore economically, politically, and strategically" (Hung 1994). As a result, ASEAN did not want to let tensions in Sino–Vietnamese relations negatively affect ASEAN–China relations. In 1994, after attending the 27th AMM as an observer and learning that Vietnam would join ASEAN the following year, Foreign Minister Nguyen Manh Cam also observed,

> While accelerating the process of admitting Vietnam into ASEAN, the organization also upgraded its relations with China, granting the latter with the consultative partner status and establishing the ASEAN–China joint cooperative commission. Related to the Eastern Sea (South China Sea) problems, ASEAN tried to avoid confrontation with China and dismissed the impression that ASEAN was critical of China (MOFA 1994*a*, p. 10).

In addition, Hanoi also became increasingly aware that ASEAN was indeed not a military organization. A MOFA memo submitted to the Politburo on 1 November 1992 stated: "Military cooperation between ASEAN countries is of bilateral nature; among ASEAN countries, there are no mechanisms for multilateral military cooperation." Deputy Minister of Foreign Affairs Vu Khoan, who led a delegation visiting ASEAN member countries and the ASEAN Secretariat from 3–14 October 1994 to "study in depth the ASEAN modes of cooperation, cooperative mechanisms within ASEAN, and possibilities for Vietnam to take part in ASEAN cooperation", wrote,

> First and foremost, ASEAN is not a military organization. Officials in all the countries that the delegation visited stressed the political and economic nature of ASEAN cooperation, and confirmed that ASEAN did not have collective military cooperation. *ASEAN is not a military organization* and *has never intervened into disputes that involved member states [original italics]*; security cooperation in ASEAN is bilateral and trilateral only (MOFA 1994b, p. 2).

The new understanding helped leaders in Hanoi realize that there was no chance for Vietnam to develop military cooperation with ASEAN or to rely on military cooperation within ASEAN frameworks to strengthen its posture vis-à-vis a third party. One member of the delegation told the author that the ASEAN emphasis on the non-military nature of ASEAN cooperation seemed to convey to Hanoi the message that ASEAN did not expect Vietnam to seek military support from the Association. The same official also commented that if Hanoi had previously misunderstood ASEAN as a collective defence alliance, it now became clear that Hanoi could no longer hope to turn ASEAN into a military bloc to defend Vietnam. Therefore, Vietnam's decision to join ASEAN was not based on the hope that ASEAN could strengthen Vietnam's military posture.[3] Furthermore, even when ASEAN might eventually agree on building a united armed force of its own, which is highly unlikely, ASEAN's military strength would not be able to match that of China. As Vietnamese Ambassador to the Philippines Vu Quang Diem wrote in a cable to Hanoi: "Even if all Southeast Asian countries could stand together, their forces could not compete with those of China. Moreover, at the present and in the future, there is no such a desire by Southeast Asian countries to stand together, due to their different interests" (Diem 1995b).

In sum, given Hanoi's realization that ASEAN was indeed not a military organization, its weakened perception of the China threat, and its efforts to improve relations with China, Vietnam's pursuit of ASEAN membership should not be seen as an effort on the part of Vietnam to balance against China through ASEAN.

The South China Sea Disputes Connection

As Sino–Vietnamese political and economic ties improved following normalization, the two sides embarked on negotiations to settle territorial and maritime disputes. In 1999, the two countries concluded an agreement on land border demarcation. The following year, they signed another agreement on the maritime delimitation of and fishery cooperation in the Tonkin Gulf. Yet, disputes about sovereignty and maritime jurisdiction over the Paracels and the Spratlys remain unsolved as both sides showed no signs of compromise.[4] The South China Sea disputes have therefore become one of the most salient issues in the bilateral relationship.

As three other ASEAN countries, namely Malaysia, the Philippines and Brunei, are also involved in the Spratlys dispute, it may be argued that seeking ASEAN support could be one of the drivers behind Hanoi's quest for ASEAN membership. Specifically, Hanoi might have wished to take advantage of its ASEAN membership to consolidate its bargaining power vis-à-vis China as other ASEAN claimant states might agree to join Hanoi in forming a united front to deal with China's expansionism. However, again, the following four empirical cases suggest that Hanoi did not take that prospect into serious consideration when it decided to join ASEAN.

The Sino–Vietnamese Naval Clash, 1988

In mid-March 1988, China sent warships to the Spratlys. Following a brief but fierce naval clash at the Johnson South Reef that claimed sixty-four Vietnamese lives, China seized three of the features from Vietnam. By mid-April 1988, China had occupied seven features, and for the first time set its foot in the Spratly Islands.

On 17 March 1988, Hanoi sent diplomatic notes to ASEAN countries to inform them of the incident and asked its ambassadors posted to regional capitals to assess reactions of the host countries and to mobilize their support for Vietnam. Hanoi soon found out that although ASEAN countries were concerned about China's move, they generally remained aloof, wishing to distance themselves from the Sino–Vietnamese dispute and refraining from openly supporting Hanoi and criticizing Beijing. On 18 March, the Director General of the ASEAN Department in Malaysia's MOFA told Vietnamese Ambassador Tran Le Duc, "We sympathize and agree with Vietnam's position. We closely follow the developments and hold that Vietnam's proposal to solve the dispute through negotiations is in accordance with our position" (Duc 1988). On 17 March, the Philippine Department of Foreign Affairs issued a statement expressing concerns over the Sino–Vietnamese conflict. However, in Hanoi's assessment, as a matter of self-interest, Manila did not want to worsen its ties with Beijing. According to a report by the Asia-3 Department,

> Being one of the claimants and currently occupying eight islands, the Philippines is concerned about the clash and therefore agrees with the measures [of solving the dispute peacefully] that we have proposed. But as preparations for the coming visit to China by President Aquino are underway, Manila cannot openly voice its support for us (MOFA 1988, pp. 1–2).

Indonesia also remained silent for a host of reasons. According to the report, "although Indonesia dislikes China, it shows no support for us. If Jakarta supports us, it will have trouble with Malaysia and the Philippines, the two ASEAN states that have claims to the Spratlys. In addition, Jakarta's relations with Beijing will be affected. Last but not least, Indonesia may be more preoccupied with its domestic politics." As a result, the report concluded that Indonesia "made no public statement in order not to displease any party concerned" (MOFA 1988, p. 2).

Neither was Thailand supportive of Vietnam. On 21 March, Ambassador Le Mai met Thai Foreign Ministry's Director General in charge of political affairs to inform the latter of Hanoi's 17 March diplomatic note. The Thai interlocutor said: "We wish that there would be a solution to this matter. But we find it difficult to voice our opinion, because apart from China and Vietnam, there are other claimants in the dispute as well" (Mai 1988). Hanoi then believed that Thailand wanted to take advantage of the Sino–Vietnamese clash because following the incident, Vietnam would face more pressure and have to solve the Cambodian problem in a way that benefited Thailand (MOFA 1988, p. 2).

Singapore also kept silent over the incident. According to Hanoi, it was because Singapore "is not involved in the dispute. In addition, this is a sensitive and complicated issue on which Singapore finds it difficult to publicly voice its opinion. Therefore, Singapore remained silent and adopted a wait-and-see approach to avoid getting involved and displeasing any party concerned" (MOFA 1988, p. 3).

In short, during the 1988 Sino–Vietnamese naval clash in the Spratlys, ASEAN countries, including claimant states, did not openly criticize Beijing and support Hanoi. The failure of ASEAN countries to stand united to endorse the principle of peaceful dispute resolution, their unwillingness to complicate relations with China, together with existing tensions between Vietnam and ASEAN over the Cambodian problem, had dispelled expectations from Hanoi that it could rely on ASEAN to counter China's expansionism in the South China Sea.

First Crestone and Tu Chinh Bank Incident, 1992

On 22 July 1992, after Vietnam had acceded to the Bali Treaty and become an ASEAN observer, ASEAN countries signed the ASEAN Declaration on the South China Sea. The Declaration, among other things, called on parties concerned to exercise self-restraint and resolve all disputes pertaining to the South China Sea by peaceful means; to explore possibilities of maritime cooperation; and to employ the principles of the Bali Treaty as the basis for establishing a code of international conduct in the South China Sea. Hanoi welcomed this Declaration.

The Declaration was signed after China's National Offshore Oil Corporation entered into an agreement in May 1992 with Crestone Energy Corporation, a U.S. company, under which the latter was allowed to explore for oil and gas in the Tu Chinh (Vanguard) Bank — an area within Vietnam's exclusive economic zone (EEZ) and continental shelf. In addition, the Chinese government even promised to provide military protection to Crestone's operation in the area (Odgaard 2002, pp. 3, 85). Policy planners in Hanoi therefore thought that the Declaration represented a positive joint effort by ASEAN to stop China from using force to impose its claims in the South China Sea. One MOFA document even surmised that although the ASEAN decision to grant Vietnam and Laos with observer status in July 1992 might be influenced by the need for more regional cooperation, "the immediate impulse was the Chinese actions in the South China Sea" (MOFA 1992*a*, p. 5). Hanoi also believed that because ASEAN succeeded in forging such a collective position, Beijing had to show its support for the Declaration (MOFA 1994*a*). If it was the case, Hanoi now might not find itself standing alone against China's pressure as it did in 1988. The benefits of joining ASEAN would therefore be vindicated.

But there have also been different explanations as to why ASEAN adopted the Declaration. Some MOFA researchers, for example, argued that when ASEAN countries emphasized the principle of peaceful resolution of the South China Sea disputes, they in fact also expected Hanoi not to use force to advance its claims against Malaysia and the Philippines.[5] A MOFA report stressed that as Hanoi was not a signatory of the Declaration, ASEAN was anxious to know if Hanoi accepted it (MOFA 1992*a*, p. 5). One researcher even argued that the accession to the Bali Treaty and the Declaration marked the beginning of a new difficult phase for Vietnam's foreign relations in which Hanoi had to learn to live by the ASEAN Way. This meant Hanoi effectively had to stop thinking of using force and start learning to rely on negotiations to solve the disputes with ASEAN claimant states.[6] Therefore, the ASEAN's stress on the peaceful resolution of disputes was believed by some Vietnamese observers to have put constraints on Hanoi's future freedom of action in the Spratlys.

More importantly, the 1992 ASEAN Declaration on the South China Sea did not lay a strong foundation for concerted actions by ASEAN to cope with China. Instead, ASEAN adopted a non-confrontational approach toward China, and the parties concerned preferred to begin talks with Beijing to seek bilateral solutions. As one observer concluded, although Hanoi share with ASEAN countries "mutual interests in countering Chinese advances in the South China Sea", ASEAN's "non-provocative stance toward China" was positive for Hanoi when it also attached great importance to the improvement of its relations with Beijing (Ramses Amer quoted in Odgaard 2002, p. 127). In addition, Chinese actions in the South China Sea in May 1992 did not have a direct link with Hanoi's accession to the Bali Treaty, as Hanoi had already decided to accede to the Treaty in June 1991. Although it could still be surmised that Chinese actions might have provided greater impetus for Hanoi to join ASEAN,[7] the consensus in Hanoi at the time was that ASEAN membership would not be immediate. In other words, Hanoi's early efforts to pursue ASEAN membership were not directly related to developments in the South China Sea.

Second Crestone and Tu Chinh Bank Incident, 1994

Another wave of tensions emerged between Vietnam and China in April 1994 when Benton (formerly Crestone) planned to undertake another oil and gas exploration operation in the Tu Chinh Bank under a license granted by China. Hanoi was successful in preventing the operation from being conducted. Yet, in retaliation, Beijing sent warships to the area to harass a rig of Vietsovpetro (a joint venture between Vietnam and Russia) that was drilling there (Odgaard 2002, p. 85).

By that time, Vietnam's accession to ASEAN was only a matter of procedure, and in April 1994, Vietnamese President Le Duc Anh announced that Vietnam was preparing to join ASEAN at an early date. But despite Hanoi's efforts, it failed to secure ASEAN's support. In a cable, Vietnamese Ambassador to Beijing Dang Nghiem Hoanh wrote,

> Following the Ministry's instructions, on 26 April, I went to see the Malaysian Ambassador who had just returned to Beijing from Kuala Lumpur. The Ambassador told me the followings: (i) Malaysia is very concerned because this affects not only Sino–Vietnamese relations, but the whole region as well; (ii) But Malaysia supports negotiated solutions, which should require great patience because there is no other alternative (Hoanh 1994c).

Dang Nghiem Hoanh also met with the Indonesian Ambassador to Beijing, who said: "The situation involving Tu Chinh is very sensitive. The two sides should find common points to start negotiations. Indonesia supports the prevention of conflicts in the South China Sea and the promotion of regional cooperation" (Hoanh 1994a). Reactions from other ASEAN countries were similar. Vietnamese Ambassador to the Philippines Vu Quang Diem cabled from Manila that: "On 3 May, Philippine Deputy Foreign Minister Severino told me, 'We [the Philippines] are concerned about the latest dispute, but hope that Vietnam and China could solve it in an amicable way. Only after this, all the parties concerned could proceed with negotiations on a multilateral basis to solve the problem" (Diem 1994b).

On 18 May 1994, Ambassador Dang Nghiem Hoanh cabled Hanoi again, this time about the talks in Beijing between Malaysian Prime Minister Mahathir Mohamad and his Chinese counterpart Li Peng:

> The Malaysian Ambassador in Beijing informed me about the talks, stressing that Mahathir and Li Peng had agreed that the two sides had a common need for the improvement of friendship and cooperation. As far as the Spratly Islands are concerned, Mahathir "expressed his entire support for the Chinese position of peacefully resolving the disputes, showed his opposition to the internationalization of the disputes, and stressed that parties concerned should first and foremost make efforts through conducting bilateral negotiations and improving bilateral relations to find solutions to the disputes" (Hoanh 1994b).

When Dang Nghiem Hoanh asked whether the two Prime Ministers discussed the Chinese proposal to "shelve the disputes and promote joint exploitation", the Malaysian Ambassador replied: "Mr. Mahathir did not mention this proposal. But in principle, Malaysia thinks that this proposal can be discussed" (Hoanh 1994*b*).

Cables sent from Kuala Lumpur also helped Hanoi better understand ASEAN's position. For example, on 28 May, Vietnamese Ambassador Ngo Tat To met with the Director of the Southeast Asian Affairs Department of the Malaysian Foreign Ministry to learn about Malaysia's position on the dispute. Reporting his meeting to the MOFA, he wrote,

> the country's [Malaysia's] policies are, (i) to consider China as a friend, not an enemy, because if China is approached otherwise, it will be a self-fulfilling prophecy; (ii) with regard to the South China Sea, Malaysia supports negotiated settlements and joint exploitation. Malaysia referred to the Thai–Malaysian agreement to shelve sovereignty disputes and promote joint exploration and exploitation as an 'example' that others should follow (To 1994).

In short, individual ASEAN countries did not support Hanoi. And by suggesting bilateral solutions, they also implied that ASEAN countries could not forge a collective position to support Vietnam on this matter.

Hanoi, however, still tried to seek ASEAN's support. On 20 May 1994, Minister of Foreign Affairs Nguyen Manh Cam sent a letter to his ASEAN counterparts to state Vietnam's position and explore if ASEAN could support it. But MOFA's records showed that it took a month for ASEAN countries to reply to this letter. Moreover, the replies revealed that ASEAN countries did not take side in the dispute. In his reply dated 21 June to Mr Cam's letter, the Malaysian Foreign Minister wrote,

> Disputes involving questions of sovereignty and jurisdiction are sensitive and complex. I would like to assure your Excellency that Malaysia remains firmly committed to the settlement of all disputes peacefully, through negotiations. Malaysia notes that all parties involved in the territorial disputes in the South China Sea have expressed similar commitments. I would also like you to know that Malaysia, in cooperation with all parties concerned, will work to promote adherence to this principle. Indeed, all parties have a particular responsibility to ensure that peace and stability of the area remain undisturbed.

The reply dated 25 June by the Foreign Minister of Brunei was almost similar. It read,

> Brunei Darussalam is guided by the principles contained in the ASEAN Declaration on the South China Sea of 1992 which emphasize the need to resolve all sovereignty and jurisdictional issues by peaceful means without resort to force. We are of the view that all parties should refrain from undertaking any activity in the disputed areas as it may complicate matters further.

In the same vein, the letter dated 13 June from the Singaporean Foreign Minister mentioned that all countries which were parties to the disputes or had an interest in the South China Sea should exercise restraint and work constructively to seek the peaceful resolution of the disputes. Meanwhile, the letter dated 29 June 1994 by the Philippine Foreign Minister stressed that the Philippine government put an emphasis on the necessity to resolve all sovereignty and jurisdictional issues pertaining to the South China Sea through peaceful means and urged "all member nations concerned to exercise restraint with the view to creating a positive climate for the eventual solution of all disputes".

Given the timing of these replies and their similar content, it was possible that ASEAN countries had consulted one another before reaching a consensus to stay away from the Sino–Vietnamese dispute.

There were also signs that ASEAN — as an organization — did not want to get involved into the Sino–Vietnamese dispute over the South China Sea either. To Vietnam's disappointment, ASEAN failed to discuss the Tu Chinh Bank incident in their official meetings. Reporting on the outcomes of the ASEAN Regional Forum (ARF) Senior Official Meeting (SOM) on 25 and 26 May 1994, Vietnamese Ambassador to Thailand Le Cong Phung wrote that "although there were discussions about Chinese actions in the South China Sea in general and Tu Chinh in particular, the SOM reached a consensus not to include the South China Sea issue in the ARF agenda although countries may raise it on an individual basis" (Phung 1994).

In a report on the 27th AMM and ARF Meeting, MOFA also noted, "On several occasions, issues related to the South China Sea were raised. Yet, all the countries tried to address them indirectly and make the impression that they did not criticize China by name" (MOFA 1994a, p. 7). A report covering the third quarter of 1994 by the Southeast Asian and South Pacific Affairs Department commented: "On the one hand,

ASEAN countries agreed to accept Vietnam's full membership in 1995 and reiterated the principles spelled out in the ASEAN Declaration on the South China Sea. Yet, on the other hand, there have been signs that some countries, including Malaysia and the Philippines, wanted to avoid confrontation and seek bilateral agreements with China."[8]

In sum, by 1994, Hanoi became increasingly aware that for a variety of reasons, ASEAN was not eager to side with Hanoi in its maritime disputes with China, and ASEAN claimant states also preferred to deal with China on a bilateral basis. Consequently, Hanoi found it difficult to make use of its improved relations with ASEAN to strengthen its position vis-à-vis China in the South China Sea.

The Mischief Reef incident, 1995

In February 1995, the Philippines discovered that China had occupied the Mischief Reef, a low-tide elevation (LTE) within the Philippines' EEZ, and started to construct permanent structures there. The Philippines released a strong statement against China and tensions were mounted between Manila and Beijing at some point (Odgaard 2002, pp. 4, 83–84). That was the first time Beijing had directly antagonized a member state of ASEAN over the South China Sea disputes. As Vietnam was due to become an ASEAN member in five months' time, Hanoi was curious to observe how Manila and ASEAN would react to China's encroachment.

Indeed, ASEAN showed some collective support for the Philippines, albeit belatedly. Nguyen Trung Thanh, Deputy Director General of MOFA's ASEAN Department cabled from Jakarta, informing the headquarters what he learned about the contents and the mood of the ASEAN–China SOM in Hangzhou in April 1995. He wrote,

> ASEAN Secretary General Ajit Singh, who had just returned from the Meeting, informed me as follows:
>
> – China made it clear in the unofficial meeting held from 9:30 PM to 11:00 PM the previous evening that it did not support the inclusion of the South China Sea in the Meeting's agenda. ASEAN, however, asked to have a session on the South China Sea.
> – ASEAN stressed that there were in fact disputes over sovereignty in the South China Sea and asked that China should show a certain level of transparency about its policy on this issue, especially about the base line according to which China's jurisdiction in the South China Sea was defined. The Chinese Foreign Minister, however, refused to do so.

- ASEAN made it clear that ASEAN was not against the idea of joint exploitation and development in the South China Sea. Yet, this would be implemented within the ASEAN–China frameworks, and not on any bilateral basis.
- ASEAN proposed that China utilize ASEAN–China SOM frameworks for continued discussions on the South China Sea (Thanh 1995).

Thanh also highlighted comments by Singh: "This is the first time after the 1992 Manila Declaration that ASEAN has had *a concerted action* [original italics] vis-à-vis China on the South China Sea, which has succeeded in forcing China to recognize that its action in the area caused real concerns for ASEAN" (Thanh 1995).

But before the Hangzhou meeting, Hanoi had learned that tensions between Manila and Beijing abated mainly due to bilateral efforts. On 25 February, Ambassador Vu Quang Diem sent a cable to MOFA explaining that "the Philippines is in a weak position because it gets very little regional and international support. As a result, although unwillingly, Manila has to enter into negotiations with Beijing and will be pushed around because of its weak position. Manila is alone in this fight, and there is a real risk that Manila has to compromise, especially when Beijing proposes joint exploration and exploitation." In the same cable, he informed Hanoi that "the Philippines has agreed to enter into bilateral talks with China in March 1995 in Bangkok" (Diem 1995a). Therefore, in light of these developments, MOFA officials believed that while ASEAN would appreciate Vietnam's membership in the organization, Hanoi would not be able to take advantage of ASEAN to improve its posture in its South China Sea disputes with China because ASEAN's support for the Philippines — a founding member state of ASEAN — was inconsiderable. Meanwhile, Vietnamese Ambassador to the United States Le Van Bang also believed that Chinese actions at the Mischief Reef "might force ASEAN countries to quickly admit Vietnam as a full-fledged member". Yet, on the other hand, he asserted, "China warns us that even when Vietnam has joined ASEAN, China could attack Vietnam because the Mischief Reef [incident] has shown that ASEAN cannot deter China from attacking the Philippines" (Bang 1995).

By the end of 1995, Hanoi became increasingly aware that the Philippines preferred to solve disputes with China bilaterally. When Vietnamese President Le Duc Anh visited the Philippines in December 1995 to explore, among other things, if the two sides could join efforts to improve their position vis-à-vis China in the South China Sea, Manila made it clear that only bilateralism would work. According to a MOFA report on the visit, Philippine leaders informed Le Duc Anh that "the Philippines has reached an eight-point agreement with China with regard to the Spratlys. In addition, a joint legal team and a mechanism for regular bilateral consultations between the Philippines and China were set up. As a result, the situation in the South China Sea has improved." Manila then suggested "Vietnam should do likewise." Manila, according to the report, also showed the willingness "to serve as a bridge between Hanoi and Beijing" (MOFA 1995, p. 4).

MOFA officials were therefore not buying the idea that ASEAN would come to Hanoi's support in its maritime disputes with China. They sought to design a policy that would have elements of accommodation with Beijing. Vu Quang Diem, for example, contended that "we should not have illusions about China. Yet, we should not be hostile towards China. We should have a proper policy and a flexible strategy which could allow us to enjoy friendship with China and, at the same time, to protect our independence and sovereignty" (Diem 1995*b*). They also suggested that Hanoi should take advantage of improved Sino–Vietnamese relations to hold bilateral talks with Beijing to ease tensions and to solve territorial disputes. Vietnamese Ambassador to Beijing Dang Nghiem Hoanh suggested,

> As China continues to diversify its foreign relations and seems to adopt a policy that favours negotiated settlements to disputes, we should seize the opportunity to make important decisions so that by the year 2000 we could have a policy that would [...] further improve our relations with China and limit uncertainties in the Sino–Vietnamese relationship, thereby ensuring stable conditions for industrialization and modernization as well as the protection of our territorial integrity (Hoanh 1997).

In July 1994, when the CPV Politburo held a meeting to make the final decision on Vietnam's accession to ASEAN, the top leadership in Hanoi agreed, "Our purpose in joining ASEAN is not to side with one party to oppose another. We will not harm any third party." The Politburo also instructed, according to the transcripts of the meeting:

> As we join ASEAN, we should improve relations with other countries, especially the neighbouring ones; we should accelerate the implementation of the cooperative projects that we have signed with China; and

we should openly and directly inform China about our decision to join ASEAN so that they understand our position with regard to our membership in ASEAN (CPV 1994).

Once again, the case suggests that Hanoi did not think seriously of rallying ASEAN member states to balance against China when it was considering its ASEAN membership.

The American Connection

A related question worth considering is whether or not Hanoi viewed its ASEAN membership as a tool to improve its relations with the United States, thereby indirectly deterring against Beijing's aggressive moves in the South China Sea. A 1992 report by the MOFA Department of American Affairs seemed to show this calculation. After stressing the predominant role of the United States in the Asia Pacific after the Cold War and pointing out that the containment elements were becoming more prevalent than the engagement ones in Washington's China policy, the report asserts: "The United States wants to maintain peace and stability in Southeast Asia and to improve the region's economic and political postures with a view to preventing any single superpower from dominating the region. Therefore, the U.S. wants to accelerate the integration of Indochinese states into [the broader] Southeast Asia; check the Chinese expansion in the region; encourage improvements in Vietnam–ASEAN relations; and improve its own relations with Vietnam, Laos, and Cambodia" (MOFA 1992b, pp. 7–8). The report then contends that the United States supported Vietnam's accession to ASEAN and its integration into the international and regional communities (MOFA 1992b, p. 11).

Vietnamese Ambassador to Washington D.C. Le Van Bang also noted, "We should 'make friends' with all the superpowers, including the U.S. and China, and welcome the U.S. to contribute to peace, stability, and development in the region." He even supported the exchange of military attachés as well as the strengthening of "military and security relations" between Hanoi and Washington following bilateral normalization (Bang 1995).

Yet, Hanoi soon realized that any attempt to rely on the United States to check China might not be feasible for a variety of reasons. First and foremost, Washington attached more importance to Sino–U.S. relations. A MOFA report on the November 1994 Seattle meeting between Clinton and Jiang Zemin on the sideline of the Asia-Pacific Economic Cooperation (APEC) Summit said that both China and the United States were readjusting their strategies and reducing bilateral tensions. Washington, according to the report, encouraged Beijing to engage in multilateral frameworks in the Asia Pacific, which would serve to accelerate China's reforms and international integration, thereby raising the costs for China's actions that would destabilize the region (MOFA 1993, pp. 3–4). The report also took note that during the meeting, Clinton and Jiang did not mention developments related to the South China Sea and Vietnam. It observed, "President Clinton told the press following the APEC Summit that the U.S. wanted Vietnam to integrate itself into the region after solving, to the fullest extent possible, the MIA issues." According to the report, such a U.S. attitude implied that the South China Sea disputes "do not play an important role in the dynamics of the U.S.–Vietnamese relations" (MOFA 1993, p. 5).

In other words, Hanoi became increasingly aware of Washington's unwillingness to get involved in the territorial disputes in the South China Sea. Instead, Hanoi observed that "The U.S. tried to avoid taking side with any claimant state and only urged the parties concerned to refrain from using force" (MOFA 1993, p. 5). From a broader perspective, the MOFA also believed that the United States was trying not to upset China. According to a report by the Ministry, Sino–U.S. relations were increasingly stabilized after the Cold War. Washington's China policy combined both containment and engagement elements while the "China threat" was still a controversial thesis. China, on its part, also wished to promote cooperation with the United States to gain greater access to U.S. market, technologies, and capital flows. As a result, despite ups and downs, both sides tried to avoid direct confrontation (MOFA 1992b). Furthermore, on 26 April 1994, during the Crestone incident, Ambassador Dang Nghiem Hoanh cabled from Beijing, quoting the American Ambassador in Beijing as telling him that "Crestone is a private company and the U.S. Government does not control it" (Hoanh 1994c).

The U.S. position on the Mischief Reef incident also brought home to Hanoi that if Washington did not want to take side in the Sino–Philippines dispute, it would be even more unlikely for Washington to back Hanoi in the latter's disputes with China. During the incident, the United States adopted a neutral position even though it had a security treaty with Manila. Ambassador Le Van Bang sent a cable from Washington, informing Hanoi that "On 10 February, the U.S. Embassy in Manila made a statement that the U.S.–Philippine security treaty did not cover the Spratly Islands; the U.S. did not want to create tensions with China; and it did not want to take side in the disputes over the Spratly Islands in general and over the Mischief Reef in particular" (Bang 1995). Ambassador Vu Quang Diem also cabled Hanoi from Manila that "According to a confidential document of the Joint Intelligence Centre Pacific (JICPAC), which kept the Philippines informed of the situation in the South China Sea, the U.S. has made it clear that even if Washington takes part in any discussions about the situation in the South China Sea, it does not imply that Washington supports any country in the territorial disputes there" (Diem 1994*a*).

Contacts with American officials further confirmed Hanoi's belief that it would be naïve to expect the U.S. support in any disputes with China. In August 1995, after a meeting with Stanley Roth, Director of the Asian Affairs Bureau in the U.S. National Security Council, Vietnamese Ambassador to the United Nations Ngo Quang Xuan informed Hanoi,

> Mr. Roth reiterated the U.S. neutral position on the Spratly Islands disputes and said that the parties concerned should not waste more time in seeking opportunities for negotiated settlements. With regard to Vietnam, he asserted that the idea to use Hanoi to counterbalance Beijing is short-sighted, and Senator McCain's proposal to normalize relations with Vietnam on the basis that Hanoi could help the U.S. cope with China by military means is an overstatement (Xuan 1995).

In light of developments in Sino–U.S. relations and Washington's unwillingness to take side in territorial disputes in Southeast Asia, although some policymakers in Hanoi seemed to favour better relations with Washington, even in military and security fields, Hanoi did not take into serious consideration any possible type of association with the United States to check Chinese expansionism in the South China Sea. Hanoi did not envisage that the United States would play an important role in prospective solutions to the South China Sea disputes either. This was further evidenced in a policy announcement by Hanoi on the impacts of the normalization of U.S.–Vietnam relations on the South China Sea disputes, which claimed: "We will not let the U.S.–Vietnam relationship harm the interests of any third party. On issues related to the Spratly Islands, our consistent policy is to patiently solve the disputes through peaceful means, through negotiations with the parties concerned, and in accordance with international laws and the 1982 U.N. Convention on the Law of the Sea" (Khoan 1997). As such, it was unlikely that Hanoi saw its pursuit of ASEAN membership as a measure to improve its ties with Washington, and ultimately to check China's ambitions in the South China Sea.

Conclusion

There is little evidence that Hanoi's quest for ASEAN membership in the early 1990s was driven by its desire to balance China in the South China Sea, mainly because ASEAN countries did not want to side with Vietnam at the expense of their relations with Beijing. Similarly, in the early 1990s, the United States did not plan to take advantage of its improved relations with Hanoi as a counterweight to Beijing's increasing regional influence, which invalidates the argument that Vietnam's bid for ASEAN membership was part of its strategy to improve ties with Washington in order to check China's maritime ambitions.

Instead, available evidence suggests that Hanoi's pursuit of ASEAN membership in the early 1990s was part of its foreign policy of "diversification and multilateralization" primarily aimed at creating a favourable external environment for its domestic economic reform under *Doi Moi*. Indeed, economic cooperation with ASEAN countries through trade and investment, as well as through ASEAN-led economic cooperation arrangements with external partners, such as free trade agreements with China, Korea, Japan, India, Australia and New Zealand, have contributed significantly to Vietnam's economic performance over the past thirty years.

That said, Vietnam's ASEAN membership has also enabled the country to strengthen its political and security cooperation with other ASEAN member states, and to elevate its international standing and bargaining power. Although in the early 1990s, when Vietnam decided to join ASEAN, its policymakers did not have a lot of hope for ASEAN's support in its South China Sea disputes with China, ASEAN has now become a linchpin in Vietnam's foreign policy in general and its South China Sea policy in particular. From the 2002 ASEAN–China Declaration on the Conduct of Parties in the South China Sea (DOC) to ASEAN's joint statements following high-level meetings, Vietnam has invested enormous efforts in mobilizing regional support for its South China Sea position, especially its emphasis on the resolution of the disputes through peaceful means and in accordance with international law. At the same time, China's increasing assertiveness in the South China Sea over the past decade has helped Vietnam win a higher level of sympathy and understanding among several ASEAN member states regarding its South China Sea position. Therefore, despite certain setbacks, most notably ASEAN's difficulty in reaching a common position on the issue, Vietnam now attaches great importance to ASEAN as a mechanism to manage the South China Sea disputes, and considers its membership in the Association as one of the key pillars in its hedging strategy against China.

NOTES

1. From this perspective, this chapter reinforces the arguments the author made earlier that the constructivist approach is helpful in providing a more rounded explanation as to why Vietnam decided to join ASEAN. See Tung (2007).
2. For a comprehensive analysis of Hanoi's threat perception, see Tung (2000).
3. Interviews by the author (Hanoi, November 2002).
4. In 1974, China used force to seize the Paracels from the Saigon regime. In 1988, China troops occupied seven features in the Spratlys and the two sides engaged in a brief yet bloody naval clash at the Johnson South Reef.
5. Authors' interview with researchers at MOFA's Institute for International Relations (Hanoi, October 2002).
6. Ibid.
7. For example, the third plenum of the CPV Central Committee in June 1992 mentioned for the first time Vietnam's membership in ASEAN. One month later, the MOFA began to produce a series of memos arguing for ASEAN membership.
8. MOFA Southeast Asian and South Pacific Affairs Department Report covering the third quarter of 1994, p. 8.

REFERENCES

Bang, L.V. Cable from Washington D.C. (18 February 1995).
Betts, Richard K. "Vietnam's Strategic Predicament". *Survival* 37, no. 3 (1995): 61–81.

Betts, Richard K. and Thomas J. Christensen. "China: Getting the Question Right". *National Interests* 62 (2000): 17–29.

Brown, Frederick Z. "U.S.–Vietnam Normalization: Past, Present, Future". In *Vietnam Joins the World*, edited by James Morley and Masashi Nishihara. New York: M.E. Sharpe, 1997, pp. 200–24.

Communist Party of Vietnam (CPV). Concluding Note of the Politburo Discussions on Vietnam's Membership in ASEAN (22 July 1994).

Diem, V.Q. Cable from Manila (5 May 1994*a*).

———. Cable from Manila (6 May 1994*b*).

———. Cable from Manila (25 February 1995*a*).

———. Cable from Manila (30 December 1995*b*).

Duc, T.L. Cable from Kuala Lumpur (18 March 1988).

Hoanh, D.N. Cable from Beijing (17 May 1994*a*).

———. Cable from Beijing (18 May 1994*b*).

———. Cable from Beijing (26 April 1994*c*).

———. Cable from Beijing (19 May 1997).

Hung, N.M. Cable from Singapore (18 April 1994).

Johnston, Alastair I. "Is China a Status Quo Power?" *International Security* 27, no. 4 (2003): 5–56.

Khoan, V. Deputy Foreign Minister Vu Khoan's Report on the ARF Meeting (21 May 1997).

Mai, L. Cable from Thailand (22 March 1988).

Ministry of Foreign Affairs (MOFA), Vietnam. Annual Report: On the World Situation and Our Foreign Policy (1981*a*).

———. On the Situation in Southeast Asia and the Guidelines for Our Diplomatic Offensives (31 October 1981*b*).

———. Memo to Le Duc Tho: On the Diplomatic Activities for the Coming Period (10 June 1982).

———. Asia-3 Department Report: On the Regional Countries' Reactions to the MOFA March 17, 1988 Diplomatic Note on the Spratly Islands (1988).

———. Report: On Some Strategic and Tactical Issues in Our Struggle to Solve the Kampuchea Problem and Improve International Relations (21 December 1990).

———. Report on the 25th ASEAN AMM (4 August 1992*a*).

———. Report on the U.S. Foreign Policy and Vietnam–U.S. Relations (15 September) prepared for the 19th Diplomatic Conference (1992*b*).

———. Report signed by Deputy Minister Le Mai (30 November 1993).

———. Report on the 27th AMM and the First ARF Meeting (1994*a*).

———. Report on the Results of the Visit to ASEAN Countries and the ASEAN Secretariat (18 October 1994*b*).

———. Report on the Outcomes of President Le Duc Anh's Official Visit to the Philippines (5 December 1995).

Odgaard, Liselotte. *Maritime Security between China and Southeast Asia: Conflict and Cooperation in the Making of Regional Order*. Burlington, VT: Ashgate, 2002.

Phung, L.C. Cable from Bangkok (30 May 1994).

Thanh, N.T. Cable from Jakarta (5 April 1995).

To, N.T. Cable from Kuala Lumpur (28 May 1994).

Tuan, Hoang Anh. "Vietnam's Membership in ASEAN: Economic, Political, and Security Implications". *Contemporary Southeast Asia* 16, no. 3 (1994): 259–73.

Tung, Nguyen Vu. "Vietnam–ASEAN Cooperation in Southeast Asia". *Security Dialogue* 24, no. 1 (1993): 85–92.

———. "Vietnam's New Concept of Security in the Context of Doi Moi". In *Comprehensive Security in Asia: Views from Asia and the West on a Changing Security Environment*, edited by Kurt W. Radtke and Raymond Feddema. Boston: Brill, 2000, pp. 405–24.

———. "Vietnam's Membership of ASEAN: A Constructivist Interpretation". *Contemporary Southeast Asia* 29, no. 3 (2007): 483–505.

Xuan, N.Q. Cable from New York (15 August 1995).

Part III
Major Foreign Policy Issues

10

Vietnam's South China Sea Strategy since 2007

Ha Anh Tuan

Over the past decade, territorial and maritime disputes in the South China Sea have become an issue of greater global significance. The disputes, which traditionally involve competing sovereignty and jurisdiction claims by littoral states, have now also encompassed aspects of the intensifying strategic competition between the major powers, especially China, the United States, and Japan. At the same time, the increasing militarization of the disputes by different parties also poses a serious risk to global peace and trading activities.

As one of the key claimant states, Vietnam has since 2007 experienced a new wave of tensions in the South China Sea, with China being the main security challenger. On the economic front, Beijing steps up its patrols in the South China Sea and tries to drive Vietnamese fishermen away from their traditional fishing grounds in the Paracels and the Spratlys. Incidents in which Chinese law enforcement vessels chase, capture, confiscate, or attack Vietnamese fishing boats are frequently reported in the Vietnamese media. Every year, dozens of Vietnamese fishermen are reportedly captured, beaten, or killed by Chinese law enforcement authorities (Tuan 2012). China also puts pressure on international oil companies that operate inside Vietnam's proclaimed exclusive economic zone (EEZ). More importantly, China has since 2014 reclaimed land and built seven artificial islands in the Spratlys. By the end of 2015, China had reclaimed seventeen times more land than the other claimants combined over the preceding forty years, accounting for about 95 per cent of all reclaimed land in the Spratlys (U.S. Department of Defence 2015, p. 16). China has also installed dual-purpose equipment, including helipads, airstrips, and surveillance radars, on its artificial islands.

Against this backdrop, how to manage the disputes in order to protect its legitimate interests against rising threats while preserving peace and stability in the South China Sea has long been a major foreign policy challenge for Vietnam. This chapter examines this challenge and how Vietnam has handled it since 2007 when tensions in the South China Sea began to intensify. The chapter argues that Hanoi considers the South China Sea disputes as a highly complicated security issue that warrants a multi-faceted approach. While seeking to manage the disputes peacefully through diplomatic means between relevant parties, Hanoi is also preparing for worst-case scenarios by employing a strategy of internal and external balancing to respond to emerging security threats.

The chapter first reviews Vietnam's position on the South China Sea issue and its dispute settlement arrangements with neighbouring countries before discussing Vietnam's strategy in response to recent heightened tensions in the South China Sea. Finally, the chapter examines Hanoi's perception of the regional strategic environment after the 2014 oil rig crisis and adjustments in its South China Sea policy.

Vietnam's Position on the South China Sea Issue and Its Dispute Settlement Arrangements

Four key legal documents lay the foundation for Vietnam's maritime claims in the South China Sea. They are:

i. Statement of the Government of the Socialist Republic of Vietnam on the Territorial Sea, the Contiguous Zone, the Exclusive Economic Zone and the Continental Shelf (dated 12 May 1977);[1]

ii. Statement of the Government of the Socialist Republic of Vietnam on the Territorial Sea Baselines of Vietnam (dated 12 November 1982);[2]

iii. Vietnam National Assembly's Resolution on the ratification of the 1982 UNCLOS (dated 23 June 1994); and

iv. The Law of the Sea of Vietnam (passed by the National Assembly on 21 June 2012).[3]

Vietnam's 1977 Statement is a short document consisting of seven points outlining the limits of its territorial sea, contiguous zone, and the EEZ. Although the Statement was made before the 1982 UNCLOS negotiations concluded, it is mostly in line with the regulations set in the Convention thanks to Vietnam's active participation in the negotiation process. However, the Statement does not clarify how Vietnam defines its baseline, which is crucial for determining the legal status of the bodies of water around its mainland as well as the features that Vietnam claims in the South China Sea.

The 1982 Statement supplements the 1977 Statement and defines Vietnam's baseline claims. According to this statement, the baseline of mainland Vietnam is a line connecting eleven points with specific coordinates. With regards to the Paracels and the Spratlys, Vietnam claims sovereignty over the two archipelagos but does not define the baselines and the legal status of the waters surrounding them. Paragraph 4 of the 1982 Statement states that "The baseline for measuring the breadth of the territorial sea of the Hoang Sa [Paracel] and Truong Sa [Spratly] Archipelagos will be determined in a coming instrument in conformity with paragraph 5 of the 12 May 1977 statement of the Government of the Socialist Republic of Vietnam."

The 2012 Law of the Sea of Vietnam is another step that Hanoi has taken to further strengthen the legal grounds for its maritime claims in accordance with the 1982 UNCLOS. The Law, which has fifty-five articles, derives most of its regulations from the Convention. Articles 8 to 53 define territorial waters, contiguous zones, EEZs, islands, the legal status of the surrounding waters, and the legal rights that the country is entitled to under UNCLOS. Concerning Vietnam's position on the baselines, in an explicit reference to the 1982 Statement, Article 8 of the Law states that the baselines have been announced by the Vietnamese government, and that the government will announce the baselines in areas that have not yet been determined by the 1982 Statement after such baselines are ratified by the Standing Committee of the National Assembly.

Taken together, the 1977 and 1982 Statements constitute Vietnam's official position on the limits of Vietnam's claims in the South China Sea. However, Vietnam's view of the legal status of the Paracel and Spratly Islands remains unclear. Hanoi has never officially published its position on whether it considers any features of the two archipelagos as eligible for territorial seas or EEZs.

Since the early 1980s, Vietnam has also made significant efforts to reach agreements with other littoral states in the South China Sea to resolve bilateral maritime disputes and to promote peace and stability in the region. It is notable that most of these agreements were concluded after 1986 when Vietnam started to adopt economic and foreign policy reforms under the banner of *Doi Moi*. These agreements include:

The 1982 Vietnam–Cambodia Agreement on Historic Waters: Vietnam and Cambodia had disputes over the waters and coastal islands in the Gulf of Thailand as the two sides maintained competing views regarding their overlapping territorial seas, EEZs and continental shelves. On 7 July 1982, Vietnam signed an agreement with Cambodia placing an overlapping area of over 8,000 km² between the two countries in the Gulf of Thailand under the status of historic internal waters. The agreement states that the two countries agree to use the Brévié Line, which was drawn by Governor of French Indochina Jules Brévié in 1939, to divide, and thus define their respective sovereignty over, the islands in this maritime area (Dong 2009).

The 1992 Vietnam–Malaysia Memorandum of Understanding for the exploration and exploitation of petroleum in a defined area of the continental shelf involving the two countries: South Vietnam's 1971 claims and Malaysia's 1979 claims gave rise to an overlapping area of 2,800 km² between the two countries in the Gulf of Thailand. In 1992, Hanoi and Kuala Lumpur started their negotiations to settle the issue, leading to the signing of an Memorandum of Understanding (MOU) in June of the same year for the joint exploration and exploitation of oil reserves in the area on the principle of equal rights and obligations. Cooperation between the two countries' national oil companies, PetroVietnam and Petronas, reached a milestone on 29 July 1997 when the first barrel of oil was extracted on a commercial basis (Thao and Amer 2007). In May 2009, Vietnam and Malaysia submitted to the UN a Joint Submission on the Limits of the Continental Shelf beyond 200 nautical miles in the southern part of the South China Sea (Dong 2009).

The 1997 Vietnam–Thailand Agreement on the Delimitation of the maritime boundary between the two countries in the Gulf of Thailand: In 1992, Vietnam and Thailand also entered into negotiations to delimit an overlapping area of 6,074 km² in the Gulf of Thailand. An agreement was reached on 9 August 1997 and came into force on 27 February 1998, granting Vietnam 32.5 per cent of the area. This was Vietnam's first maritime boundary agreement with a neighbouring country since the 1982 UNCLOS took effect. The agreement defines a single boundary delimiting both the EEZ and the continental shelf between Thailand and Vietnam (Dong 2009; Thao 1997).

The 2000 Vietnam–China Agreement on the Delimitation of the territorial seas, EEZs and continental shelves in the Tonkin Gulf: Vietnam and China had overlapping claims in the Gulf of Tonkin, one of the world's largest gulfs with a total area of 126,250 km². There are roughly 2,300 islands and rocks on the Vietnamese side of the Gulf, including Bach Long Vi island, while China possesses a number of small islands in the northeast of the Gulf. The process of bilateral negotiation on the delimitation of the Gulf was first started in 1974 but did not bring any result until after the two countries normalized their diplomatic relations in 1991. In October 1992 and February 1993, Vietnam and China conducted two rounds of negotiation that resulted in an agreement on fundamental principles governing the solution of border and territorial disputes between the two countries (Thao 2005). On the delimitation of the Tonkin Gulf, the two countries pledged to uphold principles of equitability and base their negotiations on international law of the sea and its practice, while taking into consideration all relevant circumstances in the Gulf (Zou 2005). Soon afterwards, bilateral negotiations on the delimitation of the Gulf officially started and lasted until 25 December 2000 when the Agreement was eventually concluded.

The Agreement came into force on 30 June 2004, entitling Vietnam to 53.23 per cent of the Gulf's total area and China 46.77 per cent. Vietnam adopted a rather flexible stance when agreeing to give two of its major islands partial effect in determining the equidistant line. Specifically, Bach Long Vi island (located near the centre of the Gulf) was given 25 per cent effect, while Con Co island (located 13 nautical miles off the Vietnamese coastline) was given 50 per cent effect. At the same time, the two sides also signed an agreement on fishery cooperation in the Gulf, providing for bilateral cooperation on the preservation, management and extraction of living resources in their EEZs. Accordingly, Vietnam and China conducted eleven joint fishing patrols in the Gulf between 2006 and April 2016.

The 2003 Vietnam–Indonesia Agreement on the delimitation of the continental shelf boundary: South Vietnam's 1971 claims and Indonesia's 1968 claims created an overlapping area of almost 37,000 km² of continental shelf. The Saigon regime and Indonesia started negotiations to settle the dispute but no substantial agreements were reached. After Vietnam's reunification in 1975, Hanoi and Jakarta initiated a new round of negotiations, leading to an agreement to settle their overlapping claims. The agreement was signed on 26 June 2003 and came into force on 29 May 2007. Vietnam and Indonesia are currently involved in negotiations on the delimitation of their overlapping EEZs (Dong 2009; Thao and Amer 2007) but have faced opposition from China.

Over the past two decades, Vietnam has also taken part in two multilateral arrangements to foster cooperation in the South China Sea. The first was an agreement between Vietnam, Thailand, and Malaysia. The three countries have an overlapping area of roughly 875 km² in the Gulf of Thailand. This overlapping area was created by Vietnam's 1971 claims, Thailand's 1973 claims and Malaysia's 1979 claims. The three countries reached an agreement on the principle of joint development in the area and are now in discussion regarding the technicalities of joint development plans. The second one was the March 2005 China–Philippines–Vietnam Tripartite Agreement for Joint Marine Scientific Research in Certain Areas in the South China Sea (also known as the Joint Seismic Marine Undertaking). The agreement, however, was in force for only three years and abrogated by the Philippines in 2008. Philippine critics of the agreement contended that it undermines Philippines' sovereignty and violated the constitution "when foreigners, particularly Chinese explorers, were allowed to conduct seismic tests in Philippine territorial waters" (Gatdula 2008).

Vietnam's Responses to Heightened Tensions in the South China Sea

Vietnam's history of national building is essentially a history of wars. During almost two thousand years until the arrival of French colonialism in 1858, Vietnam undertook more than ten wars or uprisings against repeated Chinese invasions and occupation to maintain its independence. Since regaining its independence from France in 1945, the country has engaged in three more devastating wars against France (1946–54), the United States and its allies (1955–75), and China (1979). During the 1980s, Vietnam faced significant economic hardship due to U.S. economic embargoes, high post-conflict expenses, and failed economic policies. At the same time, the country was involved in the Cambodian conflict, which put further strains on the war-torn economy. The long history of wars and the concomitant economic hardship have instilled a deep sensitivity among the Vietnamese about sovereignty and territorial integrity issues, as well as the value of peace.

At the sixth national congress of the Communist Party of Vietnam (CPV), the *Doi Moi* (renovation) policy was introduced. Apart from economic reforms, the policy also called for the gradual opening-up of foreign relations. The three major goals of contemporary Vietnamese diplomacy are to create a favourable external environment conducive to domestic economic development; to safeguard national independence, sovereignty and territorial integrity; and to promote the country's role in international and regional affairs. To meet these objectives, Hanoi has consistently pursued the policy of diversification and multilateralization of its diplomatic relations [*đa dạng hóa, đa phương hóa*]. With this pragmatic foreign policy approach, economic growth has been considered to be more important than ideological purity. Foreign policy documents issued by the CPV state that the country works with partners for mutual benefits wherever there is a convergence of interests, and negotiates or pushes back whenever Vietnam's national interests are challenged (CPV 2003, p. 44).

Since the end of the Cold War, Vietnam has adopted the so-called "three no's" policy, i.e. no foreign bases on Vietnamese soil; no military alliances; and no siding with one country against another. Vietnam believes the best way to preserve its independence in peacetime and to maximize strategic headroom is not to ally with any one country but to create a network of interconnected relationships with the major powers and international institutions (Hayton 2015). The twelfth CPV national congress in January 2016 reaffirmed "the foreign policy of independence, self-reliance, diversification and multilateralization of relations, proactive international integration; maintaining a peaceful and stable environment and creating a favourable international environment conducive to national construction and defence; promoting Vietnam's position and prestige in the region and in the world" (CPV 2016).

Among the most serious challenges to Vietnam's contemporary foreign policy is how to handle intensifying tensions and strategic rivalry between the major powers in the South China Sea. Towards this end, Vietnam has in recent years pursued a comprehensive strategy to protect its sovereignty and maritime interests, while striving to maintain peace and stability in the region. This strategy consists of three main elements: managing relations with China, arguably the key source of tensions in the South China Sea; building up domestic capabilities to deter aggression and handle incidents; and engaging other stakeholders to manage the disputes and rally international support.

Managing Relations with China

Vietnam and China share a long land and sea border. Although the two countries have reached agreements on the demarcation of their land border and the delimitation of the Gulf of Tonkin, bilateral maritime border in other parts of the South China Sea remains disputed.

In the South China Sea, Vietnam and China have long-standing disputes regarding the ownership of the Paracels and the Spratlys, as well as the rights over the waters around the two archipelagos (Nguyen 2015). While territorial disputes over the Paracels involve only Vietnam, China and Taiwan, the disputes over the Spratlys also involve Brunei, the Philippines and Malaysia. In 1974, China invaded and seized control of the western part of the Paracels from the Republic of Vietnam (South Vietnam). China first established its presence in the Spratlys in 1988 after a brief naval clash with Vietnam at the Johnson South Reef, killing 64 Vietnamese soldiers (Pedrozo 2014, p. 25). China has since gradually expanded its presence and currently occupies seven features in the Spratlys. The two countries also contest rights over both living and non-living resources in the South China Sea.

In recent years, Vietnam–China relations have been under strains due to rising tensions in the South China Sea. In May 2014, bilateral ties were seriously damaged after China placed a giant oil rig within Vietnam's claimed EEZ. To mitigate the tensions, Vietnam has made efforts to engage China both politically and economically to improve mutual trust and to discourage China from further escalation (Hai 2017). As noted by Trung and Vu in Chapter 4, Vietnam frequently exchanges visits by high-ranking leaders with China. For example, Chinese President Xi Jinping visited Vietnam in November 2015, and Vietnam's top three leaders, namely Prime Minister Nguyen Xuan Phuc, CPV General Secretary Nguyen Phu Trong, and President Tran Dai Quang, also paid official visits to Beijing in 2016 and 2017. As shown in Table 10.1, Vietnam also maintains a dense network of engagement with China at various levels and through different channels. Economic ties with China have also been promoted by Hanoi to help absorb tensions generated in the South China Sea.

Increasing Self-reliance

Vietnam's strategy to increase self-reliance in dealing with maritime disputes in the South China Sea has four pillars: issuing legal and political documents to strengthen its claims; strengthening naval and maritime law enforcement capabilities; providing special support for fishermen and promoting the development of the marine economy; and preparing for legal actions against hostile activities. Among these, the first two pillars have witnessed the most visible progress.

TABLE 10.1
Major Engagement Mechanisms between Vietnam and China

Mechanism	Channel
High ranking visits; Hot line between high-ranking leaders	Government-to-Government; Party-to-Party
Steering Committee on Vietnam–China Bilateral Cooperation	Government-to-Government
Annual meetings between Central Departments of External Affairs/ Propaganda of the two communist parties	Party-to-Party
Annual consultation meetings between the two Ministries of Foreign Affairs	Government-to-Government
Annual strategic dialogues and hot line between the two Ministries of Defence	Government-to-Government
Annual anti-crime conferences between the two Ministries of Public Security	Government-to-Government
Committee on Bilateral Economic and Trade Cooperation	Government-to-Government
Committee on Bilateral Scientific and Technological Cooperation	Government-to-Government
Joint Committee on Land Border, Joint Working Groups on the South China Sea	Government-to-Government
Agreement on Fishery Cooperation in the Tonkin Gulf; Hot line between the two Ministries of Agriculture on fishery incidents	Government-to-Government
Annual meetings between border provincial governments	Government-to-Government; People-to-People
Vietnam–China Youth Festivals; Vietnam–China Youth Friendship Meetings; Vietnam–China People's Forum	People-to-People

Source: Hiep (2017, p. 168).

Since China stepped up its assertiveness in the South China Sea, Vietnam has issued several important official legal, political, and administrative documents to strengthen its claims in the area. The most comprehensive one is the Law of the Sea of Vietnam adopted by the National Assembly in June 2012. This law represents an effort by the Vietnamese government to bring domestic laws into compliance with the 1982 UNCLOS and to strengthen Vietnam's legal position in the South China Sea. In February 2007, the Central Committee of the CPV issued Resolution 09-NQ-TW on the "Maritime Strategy until 2020", providing a comprehensive blueprint to guide the protection of Vietnam's sovereignty and maritime interests in the South China Sea as well as the development the country's blue economy. This strategy also serves as the basis for a number of political and legal documents on Vietnam's maritime capacity-building, such as the 2008 Ordinance No. 03 on the organization of the Vietnam Marine Police, the 2009 Decree No. 25 on the Management of Maritime Resources and Environment, and the 2010 Decree No. 568 on the Master Plan to Develop the Marine Economy until 2020.

Over the past decade, the Vietnamese military has witnessed substantial modernization. A report by the US-based Centre for Strategic and International Studies (CSIS) concluded that Vietnam's military expenditure grew faster than that of any other Southeast Asian state between 2010 and 2014, registering a 59.1 per cent increase during that period (Abuza 2015). In absolute terms, data from the Stockholm International Peace Research Institute (SIPRI) shows that Vietnam's military expenditure more than doubled from US$1 billion in 2005 to US$2.67 billion in 2010, and nearly doubled again to US$4.57 billion in 2015 (SIPRI 2016a). Given the rising tensions in the South China Sea, it is not surprising that the Vietnam People's Navy has received the lion's share from this increased investment. Between 2011 and 2015, for example, warships accounted for 44 per cent of Vietnam's total defence acquisitions (SIPRI 2016b). Most notably, in 2009, Vietnam reached an agreement with Russia to purchase six *Kilo*-class diesel-electric submarines and all of them have been commissioned. In 2011, Vietnam acquired two *Gepard*-class frigates from Russia, which became the largest and most advanced warships in the Vietnamese navy. Vietnam took delivery of two more frigates of the same class in October 2017 and January 2018. Hanoi also purchased two fast *Molniya* missile attack ships from Russia which were delivered in 2007 and 2008, and secured the license to build ten more in Vietnam.

Hanoi has also been expanding and improving the capabilities of its maritime law enforcement agencies. In 2013, the marine police force was renamed the Vietnam Coast Guard (VCG) and has since received significant investments. By 2014, the force had been equipped with approximately thirty-eight vessels ranging from 120 tons to 2,500 tons, including four Damen (DN-2000) patrol vessels (Thayer 2014*b*, p. 13). Other notable additions since then include six new US-made Metal Shark high-speed patrol boats transferred from the United States in May 2017 under Washington's Maritime Security Initiative; one second-hand Hamilton-class cutter (3,250 tons) transferred from the U.S. Coast Guard, six patrol boats transferred from Japan, and one off-shore patrol vessel transferred from South Korea. In 2016, during Indian Prime Minister Narendra Modi's visit to Vietnam, India pledged to provide a US$500 million line of credit for Vietnam to purchase Indian weapons and military equipment, of which roughly US$100 million will be spent on patrol boats. At the same time, Vietnam has also invested to build the capacity for the Vietnam Fisheries Surveillance Force. On 4 June 2014, for example, Prime Minister Nguyen Tan Dung announced that the government would allocate US$200 million to build four large fisheries surveillance vessels for the force (Thayer 2014*b*, p. 14). The expanded naval and maritime law enforcement capabilities will enable Vietnam to better handle incidents and deter against hostile activities by foreign forces in the South China Sea.

Developing Ties with ASEAN and Engaging Regional Stakeholders

As one of Vietnam's priorities in its external relations, ASEAN is seen by Hanoi as a venue for regional countries to pool their leverage in dealing with the major powers and to strengthen their cooperation for regional peace and prosperity. Vietnam therefore considers ASEAN and ASEAN-led mechanisms, such as the ASEAN Regional Forum and the East Asia Summit (EAS), as relevant and important platforms to discuss regional security issues, including the South China Sea disputes. Hanoi is of the conviction that ASEAN should be actively involved in the management of the disputes because the South China

Sea lies at the heart of Southeast Asia and only by doing so can ASEAN maintain its relevance and claim its centrality in regional affairs. As such, Vietnam often brings up South China Sea issues at different ASEAN and ASEAN-led meetings.

However, Hanoi does not have any illusions that the disputes could be settled through ASEAN-led frameworks. ASEAN members have different interests and thus different positions on the disputes. Moreover, ASEAN's consensus-based decision making mechanism makes it difficult for ASEAN members to reach substantial agreements on the disputes. From Hanoi's perspective, ASEAN's failure to issue a joint communiqué at its 45th ASEAN Ministerial Meeting (AMM) in Phnom Penh in 2012 and its silence about the 2016 tribunal award on the Philippines' case against China are clear examples of limitations in ASEAN's management of the disputes.

Apart from ASEAN and ASEAN-led arrangements, Vietnam is also active in engaging major regional countries at the bilateral level. Hanoi has established strategic partnerships with Indonesia, Singapore, Malaysia, Thailand, and the Philippines between 2013 and 2015. In 2009, Vietnam and Malaysia jointly submitted a claim for extended continental shelves in the South China Sea to the UN Commission on the Limits of the Continental Shelf. In recent years, Vietnam has also participated in a number of joint exercises with regional countries and has sent observers to the 35th and 36th Cobra Gold military exercise co-hosted by Thailand and the United States in 2016 and 2017.

As security in the South China Sea is vital for the broader regional and international trade, peace, and stability, Vietnam has actively engaged other regional and extra-regional stakeholders in managing the South China Sea disputes. The most important extra-regional power for Vietnam to engage in this effort is the United States. Four decades after the end of the Vietnam War, Vietnam–U.S. relations have greatly improved. The two former enemies entered into a "comprehensive partnership" in 2013. From Hanoi's view, the historic visit by CPV General Secretary Nguyen Phu Trong to the United States in 2015 was an important indication that Washington acknowledged the legitimacy of the CPV regime. Another indication of the close relationship was the visit by Vietnamese Prime Minister Nguyen Xuan Phuc to the United States in May 2017, which made him the first Southeast Asian leader to visit the White House under the Trump administration.

On the South China Sea disputes, Vietnamese analysts generally believe that U.S. engagement in the issue will enhance Vietnam's leverage in its dealings with China and encourage Beijing to adopt a less assertive approach to the disputes (see, for example, Hiep 2015; Tho and Khuong 2016). During President Obama's visit to Vietnam in May 2016, the two sides agreed to enhance cooperation in regional and international forums, including Asia-Pacific Economic Cooperation (APEC), ASEAN, EAS, ASEAN Defence Ministers' Meeting Plus (ADMM Plus), to support peace, stability, cooperation, and development in the Asia-Pacific region. The U.S.–Vietnam Joint Vision Statement adopted during the visit stated: "Vietnam welcomes the United States' policy of enhanced cooperation with the Asia-Pacific region" while the two countries noted their commitment to "strengthening cooperation on regional and global issues of mutual interest and concern" (The White House 2015). Against this backdrop, Vietnam–U.S. security ties have improved significantly in recent years, facilitated by the full lifting of the U.S. lethal arms sales embargo on Vietnam in 2016. Washington has also provided financial and technological support for Hanoi to strengthen its maritime capabilities. In 2017, for example, the United States transferred to Vietnam a Hamilton-class cutter (USCGC Morgenthau) and six patrol boats. Hanoi, however, has always been mindful of the pace of rapprochement with the United States as well as China's reactions in order not to overtly offend Beijing.

Apart from strengthening ties with Washington, Hanoi is also seeking to improve security partnerships with Japan, India, Australia and major Southeast Asian states to improve its strategic posture in the South China Sea. Vietnam and Japan currently enjoy a high level of trust and extensive bilateral cooperation. The two countries signed a strategic partnership agreement in 2009 which was upgraded to an "extensive strategic partnership for peace and prosperity in Asia" in 2014. In recent years, as noted by Do and Dinh in Chapter 5, Hanoi and Tokyo have frequently exchanged high-level visits and deepened both economic and strategic ties. Although Japan–Vietnam defence ties remain relatively limited, Japan is actively providing financial, technical, and training support for Vietnam to improve its maritime capacity. In 2014, Japan transferred six used patrol boats to Vietnam. In early 2017, Japanese Prime Minister Shinzo Abe promised to provide Vietnam with six more high-speed patrol boats funded by Japanese official development assistance (ODA) (Panda 2017).

Another increasingly significant security partner for Vietnam is India. The two countries signed a strategic partnership agreement in 2007 and in 2016 upgraded it to a comprehensive strategic partnership, the highest level of Vietnam's diplomatic relations. In recent years, the two countries have frequently exchanged high-level delegations, including visits to Delhi by CPV General Secretary Nguyen Phu Trong and Vietnamese Prime Minister Nguyen Tan Dung in 2013 and 2014. Indian President Pranab Mukherjee and Prime Minister Narendra Modi paid reciprocal visits to Vietnam in 2014 and 2016, respectively. Despite objections from Beijing, India's state-owned Oil and Natural Gas Corporation (ONGC) has been active in exploring for oil and gas within Vietnam's EEZ in the South China Sea for many years. Apart from helping to train Vietnamese submariners, India also provided military equipment, especially patrol boats, and offered satellite-based intelligence to Hanoi. More notably, the two countries were reportedly in talk over India's transfer of Brahmos anti-ship missiles to Vietnam (Pubby 2017). Prime Minister Modi's decision to provide Hanoi with a US$500 million credit line in 2016 to improve Vietnam's military, technological, and maritime law enforcement capabilities will contribute to the further deepening of bilateral security ties in the coming years.

Regarding relations with Australia, Hanoi has received significant support from Canberra in terms of military personnel training. With the financial assistance from the Australian Department of Defence, hundreds of Vietnamese military officers have completed training courses in Australia over the past few decades. In recent years, bilateral defence ties have been further expanded and diversified. Australia has agreed to provide training for Vietnamese officers who participate in UN-led peacekeeping missions. The two sides also maintain regular strategic dialogues and exchanges of military delegations, promote cooperation on humanitarian assistance and disaster relief, and coordinate their positions at multilateral forums, especially the ADMM Plus (*Voice of Vietnam* 2017).

Rethinking Vietnam's South China Sea Strategy after the 2014 Oil Rig Crisis

The 2014 oil rig crisis was a litmus test for Vietnam's South China Sea strategy and generated important implications for Vietnam's future management of the disputes. On 2 May 2014, China deployed the deep-water oil rig *Haiyang Shiyou* 981 to an area well within Vietnam's claimed EEZ. The rig was protected by more than one hundred Chinese fishing and law enforcement vessels and seven warships. China also banned all foreign vessels to enter within ten nautical miles around the rig.

Vietnam's multi-dimensional South China Sea strategy can be clearly traced in this incident. High-ranking Vietnamese officials first contacted their Chinese counterparts to protest against the move. Vietnamese Minister of Foreign Affairs Pham Binh Minh called Chinese State Councillor Yang Jiechi, demanding Beijing to withdraw the rig. On 13 May 2014, Vietnamese Deputy Minister of Foreign Affairs Ho Xuan Son was sent to Beijing to discuss the incident. Within three weeks after the crisis broke out, Vietnam attempted to contact China more than twenty times to protest against Beijing's move.

At the crisis zone, Vietnam dispatched several dozens of non-military vessels to monitor the situation and to prevent China from stationing and operating the rig. Although Hanoi could not directly force Beijing to withdraw the rig due to the overwhelming size of the Chinese flotilla, Vietnamese vessels deployed on the ground were creating constant pressure on China and conveyed a message about Vietnam's strong political will to resist China's encroachment.

Hanoi also informed regional and extra-regional countries about the incident and raised the issue at international forums. Minister of Foreign Affairs Pham Binh Minh had telephone conversations with his counterparts from the major powers and regional countries, including the United States, Russia, Indonesia, and Singapore, to share information about the incident. Meanwhile, Prime Minister Nguyen Tan Dung condemned China's move at the 24th ASEAN Summit in Myanmar on 11 May 2014. Hanoi also attempted to rally international support by circulating at the United Nations a diplomatic note that it sent to Beijing to protest against the rig.

On the media front, Hanoi organized several press conferences to inform international journalists about the incident. Some foreign reporters were allowed to board Vietnamese law enforcement vessels approaching the rig, which were on several occasions chased, rammed, and attacked by Chinese ships. There was also notable public outrage inside Vietnam and among overseas Vietnamese. Despite the fact that street demonstrations are rare and routinely suppressed in Vietnam, the oil rig crisis led to large scale rallies in major cities, including Hanoi and Ho Chi Minh City, unrestrained by the government. Some protests turned into violent anti-China riots when demonstrators attacked and burned many factories that they believed belonged to Chinese investors, especially in Binh Duong province. According to the Chinese Foreign Ministry, four Chinese citizens were killed and some 100 were injured, while Reuters reported at least twenty casualties.

On 15 July 2014, China withdrew the rig and escorting vessels, claiming that the rig had completed its commercial exploration operations. The withdrawal took place one month earlier that the original deadline of 15 August that China previously announced. After the crisis, although Vietnam's long-term strategy towards the South China Sea disputes has generally remained unchanged, the incident has left Hanoi with new perceptions of the future trajectory of Vietnam–China relations and the security situation in the South China Sea.

First, Vietnamese decision makers now believe that China's creeping assertiveness in the South China Sea will not stop if left unchallenged by regional littoral states as well as the international community. Since 2009, China has continuously expanded in the waters within the nine-dash line, including taking control of the Scarborough Shoal, placing the oil rig inside Vietnam's EEZ, and reclaiming land and constructing seven artificial islands in the Spratlys. These assertive moves by China deeply disturbed Vietnam as from Hanoi's perspective, they constitute a direct threat to Vietnam's sovereignty and maritime interests and bring about changes in the regional strategic balance detrimental to Vietnam.

Second, China's use of non-military vessels to chase, ram, and fire water cannons at Vietnamese ships during the incident presents a discernible risk of an armed conflict in the South China Sea. During the crisis, there was a distinct probability of miscalculation by either side that could trigger a large-scale conflict, especially given Chinese vessels' willingness to ram and sink Vietnamese ships. The incident proved to Vietnamese policymakers that despite Beijing's "peaceful rise" rhetoric, an armed conflict initiated by China in the South China Sea is a real threat, and Vietnam should prepare itself for the worst-case scenario.

Third, the crisis outcome showed that responses of other countries do influence China's behaviours in the South China Sea. Previously, some Vietnamese officials held a pessimistic view that Beijing would not change its assertive behaviours in the South China Sea just because of regional pressures. As such, they recommended Vietnam accommodate China's growing influence. However, the way the 2014 oil rig crisis unfolded challenges that conviction. Beijing initially planned to station the rig for more than three months, but eventually withdrew it one month ahead of schedule. Although China claimed that its early withdrawal of the rig was due to the completion of the rig's commercial operations, many believe that Vietnam's strong reactions and the international media glare surprised China and forced it to retreat. At the same time, some analysts point out that China's decision to withdraw the rig also derived from its consideration of regional responses, especially U.S. political and diplomatic pressures (Thayer 2014*a*). For Hanoi, the lesson learned is that international support is an important source of leverage for it to deal with Beijing, and "internationalizing" the disputes remains a relevant option in Hanoi's South China Sea strategy.

Finally, the crisis demonstrates that the South China Sea security situation has immense impact on the overall national economy and security of Vietnam (Thanh and Thai 2014). After the incident, Vietnamese scholars and the media openly debated about "thoat Trung" (exiting China's orbit). Economic commentators argued that Vietnam's heavy economic dependence on China, especially in terms of imports, prevented the former from standing up against the latter should tensions in the South China Sea intensify. As a consequence, after the crisis, as noted by Trung and Vu in Chapter 4, Vietnam has made efforts to reduce its economic vulnerabilities vis-à-vis China.

In the short term, Vietnam's approach to China and the South China Sea disputes after the oil rig crisis has been influenced by some key domestic and external considerations. Domestically, given the importance of China to Vietnam's security and economic well-being, Vietnam continues to consider maintaining good relations with China a major foreign policy task. As such, while resisting China's pressures in the South China Sea, Vietnam has tried to maintain amicable ties and comprehensive cooperation with China.

Externally, three major developments have played a role in Vietnam's handling of the South China Sea issue since mid-2016: the July 2016 arbitral tribunal ruling in the *Philippines vs. China* case,[4] and the election of Philippine President Rodrigo Duterte and U.S. President Donald J. Trump. As the tribunal ruled that China's nine-dash line claim is invalid and no features in the Spratlys are qualified islands entitled to an EEZ, the geographical scope of the South China Sea disputes have been significantly reduced. Moreover, the ruling serves as an important legal precedent for Vietnam to rely on should it decide to pursue legal options against China, especially regarding the disputes over the Paracels and surrounding waters. The ruling therefore strengthens Vietnam's position and emboldens Hanoi in its handling of the disputes with China.

However, the election of President Rodrigo Duterte in the Philippines in June 2016 has shifted Manila's South China Sea policy as the new administration decided to put the arbitral tribunal award on the back burner and adopt a more accommodative stance towards Beijing. While trying to embrace China for economic benefits, Manila also distanced itself politically and militarily from Washington. Against this backdrop, regional countries tend to respond to the ruling in a reserved manner. Beijing has taken advantage of the opportunity to expand its strategic footprint in the region. Specifically, Beijing has continued to build up its military and maritime law enforcement capabilities in the South China Sea, quietly militarize the seven artificial islands that it has completed, and strengthen its influence in Southeast Asian countries, especially Malaysia, the Philippines, and Cambodia, through economic aid and investment. By the end of 2017, China appears to have regained its strategic upper hand in Southeast Asia and in the South China Sea.

Meanwhile, the election of U.S. President Donald Trump has added uncertainty to the strategic outlook in East Asia. During his first months in power, President Trump decided to withdraw the United States from the Trans-Pacific Partnership Agreement and made a number of statements on foreign policy issues that cast doubt on Washington's commitment to its regional allies and security partners. Such developments have severely dented U.S. credibility in the region and created a strategic and economic vacuum, which China has been keen to fill. Under the leadership of President Xi Jinping, China has been promoting various mechanisms of regional economic cooperation, such as the Belt and Road Initiative (BRI) and the Asian Infrastructure Investment Bank (AIIB). On the South China Sea issue, China has reached an agreement with ASEAN on the framework for a Code of Conduct.

These developments have generated a certain level of uncertainty in the South China Sea as to how the United States as well as key claimant states, especially China and the Philippines, will handle the disputes in the coming years. As such, Vietnam has slightly adjusted its South China Sea policy since mid-2016. Although the policy of self-reliance, peaceful resolution of disputes, and diversification and multilateralization of external relations remains unchanged, Vietnam has also tried to avoid any public and direct confrontation with China. Hanoi has responded to the arbitral award cautiously. While welcoming the ruling, the Vietnamese government has to date not issued an official statement on the content of the award. It has also avoided advocating openly for dispute resolution by third parties in order not to antagonize China. In July 2017, Vietnam halted an oil exploration mission at a block in the Tu Chinh area on Vietnam's continental shelf but within China's nine-dash line after China reportedly issued threats of force (*BBC* 2017). Vietnam also tried to improve ties with China as a hedge against strategic uncertainty, especially the possibility of Washington's gradual disengagement from and China's increased strategic preponderance over the region. The visits by Vietnam's top three leaders to China within just nine months in late 2016 and early 2017 as well as Hanoi's support for Beijing's regional initiatives such as the BRI and the AIIB can be seen as indications of this policy adjustment.

Nevertheless, the adjustment may be Vietnam's temporary response to short-term shifts in the regional geostrategic landscape. While fostering better relations with China, Vietnam has also continued to build its maritime capacity and expand its security network with the major powers and other regional countries as a hedge against Chinese assertiveness.

Conclusion

The South China Sea plays a vital role in Vietnam's security and economic development strategies. Defending Vietnam's sovereignty and maritime rights in the South China Sea has been one of the key security concerns of the Vietnamese government since the end of the Cold War. Vietnam has strived to neutralize potential security threats in the South China Sea by actively negotiating with neighbouring countries to settle outstanding disputes through a series of agreements on maritime boundary delimitation. However, disputes regarding the sovereignty over the Paracels and the Spratlys as well as the rights over different bodies of waters around them remain unresolved.

In order to manage heightened tensions in the South China Sea since 2007, Vietnam has pursued a complex strategy that consists of three main elements: improving relations with China, building up domestic capabilities, and engaging regional as well as extra-regional stakeholders to manage the disputes. Hanoi has been patient in engaging China politically, economically, and diplomatically to enhance mutual trust, minimize miscommunication, and maintain the habit of cooperation. More importantly, Vietnam is investing considerably in upgrading its naval and maritime law enforcement capabilities to enhance its deterrence against hostile actions in the South China Sea. Vietnam is also deepening defence cooperation with the major regional powers to accelerate the modernization of its maritime capabilities and to create an informal web of like-minded countries interested in maintaining law and order in the South China Sea. At the same time, Vietnam encourages ASEAN to be more active in managing the South China Sea disputes to maintain peace and stability in the region.

This multi-dimensional and multi-layered approach has been instrumental in helping Vietnam protect its interests in the South China Sea while maintaining a relatively peaceful external environment conducive to its domestic economic reforms. However, new developments in the regional strategic landscape, such as China's rise and its increasing maritime assertiveness and policy shifts by some major regional countries regarding the South China Sea issue, have presented Vietnam with new challenges. As such, whether Vietnam will be able to successfully navigate the troubled waters of the South China Sea in the coming years remains to be seen.

NOTES

1. The 1977 Statement is available at <http://www.un.org/depts/los/ LEGISLATIONANDTREATIES/PDFFILES/VNM_1977_Statement.pdf>.
2. The 1982 Statement is available at <http://www.un.org/depts/los/ LEGISLATIONANDTREATIES/PDFFILES/VNM_1982_Statement.pdf>.
3. Full text of the Law (in Vietnamese) is available at <https://thuvienphapluat. vn/van-ban/Giao-thong-Van-tai/Luat-bien-Viet-Nam-2012-143494.aspx>.
4. The award made five major conclusions: (i) China's historic claims within the nine-dash line has no legal basis; (ii) none of the features in the Spratlys

are capable of generating EEZs, (iii) Chinese activities have violated the Philippines' sovereign rights in its EEZ; (iv) the Chinese government has not fulfilled its obligation to protect the maritime environment in the South China Sea; and (v) China's large-scale land reclamation activities in the Spratlys were incompatible with the obligation of a state during dispute resolution proceedings. Full text of the award is available at <https://pca-cpa.org/wp-content/uploads/sites/175/2016/07/PH-CN-20160712-Award.pdf>.

REFERENCES

Abuza, Zachary. "Analyzing Southeast Asia's Military Expenditures". *Center for Strategic and International Studies* (7 May 2015). Available at <https://www.cogitasia.com/analyzing-southeast-asias-military-expenditures/> (accessed 1 July 2017).

BBC. "South China Sea: Vietnam Halts Drilling After 'China Threats'", 24 July 2017. Available at <http://www.bbc.com/news/world-asia-40701121> (accessed 1 Ooctober 2017).

Communist Party of Vietnam (CPV). *Tai lieu hoc tap Nghi quyet Hoi nghi lan thu tam, Ban chap hanh Trung uong Dang khoa IX* [*Materials for Studying the Resolutions of the IXth Central Committee's Eighth Plenum*]. Hanoi: NXB Chinh tri quoc gia, 2003.

————. "Bao cao chinh tri cua Ban Chap hanh Trung uong Dang khoa Xi tai Dai hoi dai bieu toan quoc lan thu XII cua Dang" [Full Text of Draft Political Report of CPV of 11th Central Committee to the 12th Party Congress]. 2016. Available at <http://www.dangcongsan.vn> (accessed 1 July 2017).

Dong, Manh. *Maritime Delimitation between Vietnam and Her Neighboring Countries*. Tokyo: UN-Nippon Foundation, 2009.

Gatdula, Donnabelle. "Joint Exploration Pact Lapses". *Philstar*, 12 July 2008. Available at <http://www.philstar.com/headlines/72480/joint-exploration-pact-lapses> (accessed 1 July 2017).

Hai, Do Thanh. *Vietnam and the South China Sea: Politics, Security and Legality*. New York: Routledge, 2017.

Hayton, Bill. *Vietnam and the United States: An Emerging Security Partnership*. Sydney: The United States Study Center, 2015.

Hiep, Le Hong. "Dia chinh tri cua quan he Viet-My" [The Geopolitics of Vietnam–U.S. Relations]. *BBC Vietnamese*, 6 July 2015. Available at <http://www.bbc.com/vietnamese/forum/2015/07/150706_geo_politics_viet_us_lehonghiep_views>.

————. *Living Next to the Giant: The Political Economy of Vietnam's Relations with China Under* Doi Moi. Singapore: ISEAS – Yusof Ishak Institute, 2017.

Nguyen Hong Thao. "Maritime Delimitation and Fishery Cooperation in the Tonkin Gulf". *Ocean Development & International Law* 36 (2005): 25–44.

Nguyen Hong Thao and Ramses Amer. "Managing Vietnam's Maritime Boundary Disputes". *Ocean Development & International Law* 38, no. 3 (2007): 305–24.

Nguyen Hong Trao. "Vietnam's First Maritime Boundary Agreement". *IBRU Boundary and Security Bulletin* (Autumn 1997).

Nguyen Thi Lan-Anh. "Origins of the South China Sea Dispute". In *Territorial Disputes in the South China Sea*, edited by Jing Huang and Andrew Billo. London: Palgrave Macmillan, 2015.

Panda, Ankit. "Japan Pledges 6 New Patrol Boats for Vietnam Coast Guard". *The Diplomat*, 17 January 2017. Available at <http://thediplomat.com/2017/01/japan-pledges-6-new-patrol-boats-for-vietnam-coast-guard/> (accessed 11 May 2017).

Pedrozo, Raul. "China versus Vietnam: An Analysis of the Competing Claims in the South China Sea". *CNA Occasional Paper* (2014).

Pubby, Manu. "Indian Offer to Sell Brahmos Missiles to Vietnam Stalled". *The Print*, 30 August 2017. Available at <https://theprint.in/2017/08/30/indian-offer-sell-brahmos-missiles-vietnam-stalled/> (accessed 1 October 2017).

Stockholm International Peace Research Institute (SIPRI). "SIPRI Military Expenditure Database 1988–2016", 2016*a*. Available at <http://www.sipri.org/research/armaments/milex/milex_database> (accessed 31 May 2016).

———. "Trends in International Arms Transfers, 2015", 2016*b*. Available at <https://www.sipri.org/sites/default/files/SIPRIFS1602.pdf> (accessed 1 July 2017).

Thanh, N.D. and N.Q. Thai. *Anh huong cua su kien Gian khoan 981 den kinh te Viet Nam het 2014 va xa hon* [*CNOOC981's Incident: Its Impacts on Vietnamese Economy in 2014 and Further*]. Hanoi: Vietnam Institute for Economic and Policy Research, 2014.

Thayer, Carlyle A. "4 Reasons China Removed Oil Rig HYSY-981 Sooner Than Planned". *The Diplomat*, 22 July 2014*a*. Available at <http://thediplomat.com/2014/07/4-reasons-china-removed-oil-rig-hysy-981-sooner-than-planned/>.

———. "Vietnam's Maritime Forces". Paper presented at the Conference on Recent Trends in the South China Sea and U.S. Policy, Washington, D.C., 10–11 July 2014*b*.

The White House. "United States – Vietnam Joint Vision Statement", 7 July 2015. Available at <https://www.whitehouse.gov/the-press-office/2015/07/07/united-states-%E2%80%93-vietnam-joint-vision-statement> (accessed 23 July 2015).

Tho, L. and D. Khuong. "Vietnam 'can bang' nuoc lon, Nga khong ban re dong minh" [Vietnam "Balances" with Major Powers, Russia is Still an Ally]. *VietTimes*, 20 May 2016. Available at <http://viettimes.vn> (accessed 10 June 2017).

Tuan, Ha Anh. "The Tragedy of Vietnamese Fishermen: The Forgotten Faces of Territorial Disputes in the South China Sea". *Asia Journal of Global Studies* 5, no. 2 (2012).

U.S. Department of Defence. "Asia-Pacific Maritime Strategy", 2015. Available at <https://www.defense.gov/Portals/1/Documents/pubs/NDAA%20A-P_Maritime_SecuritY_Strategy-08142015-1300-FINALFORMAT.PDF> (accessed 10 June 2017).

Voice of Vietnam. "Day manh quan he hop tac Quoc phong Viet Nam–Australia" [Promoting Vietnam–Australia Defence Ties]", 27 July 2017. Available at <http://vov.vn/chinh-tri/day-manh-quan-he-hop-tac-quoc-phong-viet-nam-australia-652542.vov> (accessed 1 October 2017).

Zou, Keyuan. "The Sino–Vietnamese Agreement on Maritime Boundary Delimitation in the Gulf of Tonkin". *Ocean Development & International Law* 36 (2005): 13–24.

11

Vietnam's International Economic Integration under *Doi Moi*

To Minh Thu

International economic integration has been the centrepiece of Vietnam's reform programme under *Doi Moi*. Vietnam has evolved from a centrally-planned and mostly close economy before 1986 into one of the most open economies in the region. The country is now signatory or member of more than ten bilateral and regional free trade agreements (FTAs). The foreign-invested sector has become a major source of Vietnam's exports and economic growth, while its degree of openness measured by the share of exports and imports to GDP is around 160 per cent (WTO 2015).

This chapter reviews Vietnam's economic integration process by examining the contextual and ideological drivers behind its integration policy changes, as well as the issues facing Vietnam in the coming years. The chapter argues that due to its background as a command economy, Vietnam's international economic integration has been a dual process in which the integration happened alongside Vietnam's domestic transformation from a centrally-planned to a market-based economy. During this process, the economic thinking of the ruling Communist Party of Vietnam (CPV) has gradually evolved to adapt to changes in the internal and external conditions, while maximizing the benefits that international integration could contribute to the Party's domestic agenda of political stability and economic prosperity.

The chapter is divided into three sections. The first reviews the trajectory of Vietnam's international economic integration over the past thirty years, focusing on how the evolution in the CPV's thinking on international integration has led to corresponding policy changes. The second analyses the impacts of international economic integration on Vietnam, and the third discusses the new policy challenges for the country in its next phrase of expanded and deepened international integration.

Thirty Years of Economic Integration: Ideological and Policy Changes

Preparation for Integration (1986–90)

Before the launch of *Doi Moi* in 1986, the close-door policy and economic mismanagement vastly impoverished Vietnam, causing production of essential products, such as grain, foodstuff, coal, cement, or goods for export, to frequently fall below targets. Most factories only performed at half of their designed capacity. Labour productivity and product quality was diminishing. Product distribution was inefficient, prices rocketed, and living standards were extremely low (CPV 1986).

Against this backdrop, Vietnam's limited external economic relations were a function of its command economy. Trade was subject to central planning and state monopolies. Only state-owned trading enterprises were allowed to carry out import and export activities under predetermined government-to-government protocols. The government controlled foreign trade through an extensive system of licenses and quotas. The exchange rate system was also complex with different rates for different purposes, while the domestic currency was constantly overvalued. As such, Vietnam's trading partners were confined to mostly socialist countries. At the same time, Hanoi was largely isolated from the rest of the world (IMF 1996). These pre-*Doi Moi* conditions made Vietnam's international economic integration ever more challenging.

On the verge of an economic collapse, the CPV made a bold change in its economic thinking at the sixth national congress in 1986. Most importantly, the congress acknowledged the failure of the autarkic, closed economy model. It also emphasized the necessity to expand international economic relations to take advantage of the international markets and resources for domestic socio-economic development.

In terms of external economic relations, two major ideological shifts were most notable. *First*, the Party recognized globalization as an objective trend. As a result, it decided to open up the economy to expand trade, investment, science and technology cooperation with the outside world. *Second*, the Party shifted the foundations of its economic relations from political ideology to economic efficiency (CPV 1986).

Such ideological changes paved the way for the introduction of an array of new policies and measures to promote market-oriented external economic relations. Major policies included, among others, the relaxation of restrictions on foreign trade, the unification of foreign exchange rate systems, and the adoption of the Law on Foreign Investment and the Law on Import and Export Duties. Trading companies and export-oriented manufacturers were allowed to follow market rules. Remittances in cash (rather than in goods) and foreign direct investment (FDI) in various forms were encouraged. Export-promotion schemes were implemented, and export-processing zones began to spring up to facilitate investment and promote exports. Some major foreign banks were allowed to open official commercial branches in Ho Chi Minh City and Hanoi. At the same time, throughout this period, Vietnam undertook a serious stabilization programme alongside other reforms to improve the country's macro-environment, thereby promoting production and foreign investment.

These reforms brought about significant changes to the Vietnamese economy. Domestic production expanded rapidly. For example, in terms of food production, Vietnam quickly transformed itself from a net rice importer before 1986 into a major rice exporter in 1990. Its export turnover during the period 1986–90 doubled that of the previous five years. Exports to non-socialist countries also grew. Foreign investment started to flow in. By 1990, there had been more than 200 foreign investment projects with the total registered capital reaching US$1.4 billion (CPV 1991).

However, after the first five years of economic reform, the economic management system was still cumbersome and inefficient (CPV 1991; Thanh 2005). The systems of exchange rate and commodity control were complicated and restrictive. Until 1991, Vietnam imported almost all petroleum, steel, iron, cotton, fertilizers, and important machines and equipment from the former Soviet Union. While acknowledging the need to expand economic relations with other countries, the sixth national congress of the CPV still gave priority to economic cooperation under pre-agreed programme with the Soviet bloc and considered foreign aid as an important source of funding for imports and economic development. In addition, economic reform during this period was hampered by the U.S. trade embargo imposed since 1975. The embargo had damaging impacts on Vietnam's trade not only with the United States but also with other countries and greatly limited the benefits of Vietnam's reform efforts.

In brief, the wide-ranging reform measures in the first five years of *Doi Moi* were an essential part of Vietnam's economic integration process. By the early 1990s, although the overhaul of the economic system was still far from complete, important foundations for international integration had been created. As such, this initial period prepared the stage for Vietnam's entry into the next phases of deepened bilateral and multilateral economic integration.

Reconnection with Major Economic Powers and Institutions, and Accession to ASEAN (1991–95)

The initial economic achievements strengthened the CPV's confidence in the new economic policies and drew strong public support for more changes. As a result, further reforms in external economic relations were put forward. Accordingly, the seventh national congress of the CPV in June 1991 called for the "expansion, diversification, and multilateralization of external economic relations on the basis of independence, sovereignty, equality and mutual benefits". This policy direction paved the way for Vietnam to expand relations with all countries regardless of their political and social regimes. At the same time, multiple forms of external economic activities were promoted, and all domestic economic sectors (including private companies) were encouraged to take part in external economic activities.

In 1991, two major events contributed to the shaping of Vietnam's international economic integration trajectory. *First*, the dissolution of the Soviet Union was a major shock to Vietnam as the country lost its most important export and import market, as well as its main source of aid and investment. This situation urged Vietnam to look for new markets.

Second, the conclusion of the Paris Peace Agreements on Cambodia profoundly transformed the regional environment and facilitated Vietnam's rapprochement with ASEAN and Western countries. Vietnam was in a better position to speed up its accession to ASEAN as well as its normalization of relations with major economies such as the United States, China, and the European Union.

This transitional period witnessed drastic changes in Vietnam's foreign trade. For example, from early 1991, trading relations between Vietnam and the Soviet Union were forced to follow market rules, with payment made in hard currency and commodities were traded at world prices. As a result, the share of the former Soviet Union in Vietnam's total trade fell sharply from nearly 40 per cent of Vietnam's total trade in 1990 to only about 10 per cent in 1991 and less than 5 per cent in 1992 and 1993 (GSO, various years; Morley and Nishihara 1997, p. 48). At the same time, Vietnam gradually turned to Asian countries such as Japan, Singapore, Hong Kong, Thailand and Malaysia for trade. These economies quickly emerged as Vietnam's major trading partners. Specifically, by 1993, Japan, China, South Korea, Taiwan, Hong Kong, and ASEAN countries had accounted for 82 per cent of Vietnam's imports and 60 per cent of its exports. FDI into Vietnam started to increase at a faster pace after 1991. Pledged foreign investments picked up from US$1.3 billion in 1991 to nearly US$7 billion in 1995 (GSO, various years). The top three investors as of 1994 were Taiwan, Hong Kong, and Singapore, followed by Korea, Japan, Australia and Malaysia (GSO, various years).

Starting from 1992, remaining obstacles in Vietnam's relations with major trade partners and international donors were gradually removed. In 1992, Vietnam signed the textile trade agreement with the European Community, which was the first trade deal that Vietnam had with a Western partner. In 1993, Vietnam resumed its relationship with the International Monetary Fund (IMF), World Bank (WB) and Asian Development Bank (ADB) after fifteen years of suspension, enabling the country to access international credits and assistance for economic development. In February 1994, the United States also lifted its economic embargo on Vietnam.

The year 1995 witnessed three important milestones in Vietnam's diplomacy and international economic integration under *Doi Moi*: the normalization of diplomatic relations with the United States, the signing of the Framework on Economic Cooperation with the European

Union, and the accession to ASEAN. These breakthroughs in external relations significantly enhanced Vietnam's international stature and opened up new opportunities for the country to access major markets for its exports. With the accession to ASEAN and the ASEAN Free Trade Agreement (AFTA) — the first regional free trade agreement of Vietnam — the country had to fulfil its trade liberalization commitments in a concrete schedule and to reform its trade regime in line with international standards. The AFTA earned Vietnam important experiences in pursuing free trade agreements and laid the groundwork for its participation in higher-level trade liberalization initiatives in later years.

Between 1991 and 1995, Vietnam's GDP grew at an annual rate of 8.2 per cent. While industrial output grew by 13.3 per cent, exports expanded by more than 20 per cent per year. Inflation rate also dropped from 67.1 per cent in 1991 to 12.7 per cent in 1995 (CPV 1996). After ten years of economic reforms, Vietnam became a leading exporter of rice and coffee and a promising destination for foreign investment.

Several factors underlined the faster diversification and multi-lateralization of Vietnam's international economic relations during this period. Before 1991, internal economic crisis was the main driver of policy reforms, and most changes were made unilaterally to liberalize production forces and to overhaul the failed economic management model. After 1991, however, dealing with the collapse of the Soviet bloc became the more important impetus for Vietnam to accelerate the multilateralization and diversification of its economic ties. The combination of both internal and external pressures therefore served as the push factor for policy changes. At the same time, the favourable regional conditions after the conclusion of the Paris Agreements on Cambodia and the initial successful economic developments also further encouraged Vietnam to step up its reforms.

The Vietnam–U.S. Bilateral Trade Agreement and WTO Accession (1996–2006)

Following the initial economic boom and major breakthroughs in external economic integration in 1995, Vietnam was on track towards further economic integration. In 1996, the eighth congress of the CPV set the task "to build an export-oriented economy which is integrated with the region and the world" and "to accelerate the economic integration process" (CPV 1996). It was the first time a CPV resolution had used the term "international integration" instead of "international cooperation", and pointed out the need to speed up economic integration to promote national development.

After the ASEAN accession, signing a bilateral trade agreement (BTA) with the United States and accession to the World Trade Organization (WTO) became the next integration priorities for Vietnam. These goals were reflected in the CPV Central Committee's Resolution 04/NQ-HNTW in December 1997, which clearly specifies the task "to proactively prepare domestic conditions in terms of human resource, legal environment, and products that can be competitive in regional and international markets; to speed up the negotiation of the Bilateral Trade Agreement with the United States, accession to APEC and WTO, and to make concrete plans to implement AFTA commitments". The resolution indicates the strong determination of Vietnamese leaders to achieve another breakthrough in Vietnam's international integration.

The negotiation of the Vietnam–U.S. BTA was completed in July 1999. However, the ratification of the agreement was delayed for one and a half years due to some hesitation from both sides (Manyin 2002). The agreement, which eventually came into force in December 2001, led to a wide range of legal and administrative changes that went beyond the removal of tariff as well as non-tariff trade barriers. Accordingly, the two countries significantly lowered tariffs on most traded commodities. The services market in Vietnam was also opened to U.S. service providers. In many areas, such as intellectual property rights, customs, licensing, state trading, technical standards and sanitary and phytosanitary measures, Vietnam adopted WTO standards. In addition, investment protection was strengthened and policy transparency was enhanced.

The Vietnam–U.S. BTA was a "stepping stone" for Vietnam's accession to the WTO as it helped the country gain experience in trade negotiation and prepare human resources and legal frameworks for trade and trade-related areas. More importantly, the negotiation and implementation of the BTA eased concerns about institutional challenges during the negotiation on Vietnam's WTO membership. Institutional changes imposed by the BTA means that many of the WTO requirements had also been met. By the end of 2000, Vietnam had completed the trade policy transparency process to move to the next step of market access negotiation. In April 2002, Hanoi presented its first offer on goods and services. Bilateral negotiations with WTO members were started soon after that.

By the early 2000s, Hanoi's political determination to pursue WTO membership had become obvious. The ninth congress of the CPV in April 2001 introduced the new term "proactive international economic integration", which implies Hanoi's acceptance of a higher level of external economic liberalization. In November 2001, the Politburo issued Resolution 07-NQ/TW on "International Economic Integration", which called for the active negotiation on WTO accession "according to plans and schedules suitable to the country's conditions". The government also made active preparations in anticipation of the country's forthcoming WTO membership. Bilateral negotiations with twenty-eight partners took four years to complete, and Vietnam finally became the 150th member of the WTO in January 2007.

WTO accession had been the most far-reaching and profound accomplishment of Vietnam in terms of international integration by then. As a WTO member, Vietnam could enjoy an equal position in trading with other nations. It also brought Vietnam greater access to the world market and provided further incentives for the country to undertake more market reforms in line with WTO regulations.

Post WTO and WTO-Plus FTAs (2006–15)

After WTO accession, Vietnam's international integration agenda was expanded to cover not only economic cooperation but also international cooperation in other areas. As a result, at its eleventh national congress the CPV replaced "international economic integration" with "international integration" as the key concept in its foreign policy platform, implying Vietnam's wish to pursue comprehensive integration in all areas.

By the early 2010s, concluding bilateral and regional FTAs had become a prevalent trend across Asia. The fear of being left out of preferential trade deals and losing competitive advantages resulted in the proliferation of FTAs, especially in the Asia-Pacific region. Against this backdrop, Vietnam started to launch negotiations on a wide range of FTAs with various partners. Economically, Hanoi expected that FTAs would open up markets, bring in more foreign investment, and become a catalyst for further domestic reforms. FTAs would also improve Vietnam's position in the regional production networks. In addition, political and geostrategic considerations also play a role. FTAs with important partners would help reinforce bilateral economic and political relations, thereby strengthening Vietnam's strategic posture.

Over the past three decades, the CPV's thinking on international integration has been fine-tuned continuously to adapt to changes in

Vietnam's economic development, foreign policy and the external economic conditions. As shown in Table 11.1, there have been three

TABLE 11.1
Major Developments in the CPV's Thinking on International Economic Integration, 1986–2016

Events/Time	Major Developments
Sixth CPV Congress (Dec 1986)	Official launch of economic reforms and open-door policy.
Seventh CPV Congress (Jun 1991)	Adoption of the policy of "diversification and multilateralization of relations with all countries and international economic organizations".
Eighth CPV Congress (Jun 1996)	Concept change: from "cooperation" to "integration". The term "economic integration" was used for the first time in official documents.
Ninth CPV Congress (Apr 2001)	Concept change: from "economic integration" to "proactive economic integration".
Resolution 07-NQ/TW (27 Nov 2001)	Calling for negotiations on WTO membership.
Tenth CPV Congress (Apr 2006)	Expansion of the scope of integration: "Proactive and active international economic integration and expansion of cooperation in other areas".
Resolution 08-NQ/TW (5 Feb 2007)	Introducing guidelines and policies for rapid and sustainable economic development after Vietnam's accession to WTO.
Eleventh CPV Congress (Jan 2011)	Expanding the scope of international integration beyond economic cooperation: "Proactive and active international integration".
Resolution 22-NQ/TW (10 Apr 2013)	Clarifying the guideline of the eleventh congress of the CPV on international integration; specifying that international integration will be conducted broadly and deeply in all areas; emphasizing the need for economic integration to be linked with Vietnam's economic restructuring.
Overall Strategy for International Integration (Jan 2016)	Adopting the "Overall Strategy for International Integration until 2020, with vision to 2030"; setting the objective of achieving the same degree of economic integration as the four most advanced ASEAN countries by 2030.

Source: Author's own compilation.

major developments in this ideological evolution. Vietnam's concept of integration was advanced from "international cooperation" to "international economic integration" at the CPV's eighth congress (1995), followed by "proactive international economic integration" at the ninth congress (2001), "proactive and active international economic integration" at the tenth congress (2006), and "proactive and active international integration" at the eleventh congress five years later. The scope of economic integration was also expanded from regional to global, from low to high, and from limited commitments to extensive commitments beyond the standard free trade agreements.

During this period, several specialized resolutions on international economic integration were issued, including the Politburo's Resolution 07-NQ/TW dated 27 November 2001 on international economic integration, the CPV Central Committee's Resolution 08-NQ/TW dated 5 February 2007 on "some major guidelines and policies for rapid and sustainable economic development after Vietnam becomes a member of the World Trade Organization", and the Politburo's Resolution 22-NQ/TW dated 10 April 2013 on international integration. Most recently, the CPV's Central Committee issued Resolution 06-NQ-TW dated 5 November 2016 to provide guidance for economic integration in the context of Vietnam's participation in high standard FTAs. These resolutions shape Vietnam's official discourse on international economic integration and help accelerate and deepen the country's economic integration over the past two decades.

Since the mid-2000s, Vietnam has accelerated its trade liberalization. Together with other ASEAN members, Vietnam has participated in five FTAs between ASEAN and its partners, namely China (2004), Japan (2008), Korea (2006), India (2009), and Australia and New Zealand (2009).

Apart from the ASEAN framework, Vietnam has also signed or concluded negotiation on bilateral FTAs with Japan, South Korea, Chile, and multilateral FTAs with the Eurasian Economic Union, the European Union, and the other eleven members of the Trans-Pacific Partnership (TPP). These agreements, especially the TPP and those with the European Union and South Korea, are expected to have strong impacts on Vietnam's trade, production, and inward foreign investment. At the same time, they will lead to further domestic market deregulation, deeper integration of the services sector, and improvement in the investment environment of Vietnam.

Table 11.2 summarizes the status of major FTAs that Vietnam has concluded or is negotiating. It shows that most of Vietnam's trade links are now covered by FTAs. When fully implemented, these FTAs would cover about 83 per cent of Vietnam's exports and 85 per cent of Vietnam's imports,[1] which is among the highest in the Asia-Pacific region.[2]

TABLE 11.2
Vietnam's FTAs and Their Status, September 2017

Agreements	Members	Status
ASEAN FTA	Ten members of ASEAN	Effective
ASEAN–China FTA	ASEAN and China	Effective
ASEAN–Japan FTA	ASEAN and Japan	Effective
ASEAN–Korea FTA	ASEAN and Korea	Effective
ASEAN–India FTA	ASEAN and India	Effective
ASEAN–Australia–New Zealand FTA	ASEAN, Australia and New Zealand	Effective
Japan–Vietnam Economic Partnership Agreement	Japan and Vietnam	Effective
Chile–Vietnam FTA	Chile and Vietnam	Effective
Vietnam–Korea FTA	Vietnam and Korea	Effective
Vietnam–Eurasian Economic Union FTA	Vietnam, Russia, Belarus, Kazakhstan, Armenia and Kyrgyzstan	Effective
Vietnam–EU FTA	EU and Vietnam	Negotiation concluded, pending signing
Trans-Pacific Strategic Economic Partnership (TPP)	Australia, Brunei, Canada, Chile, Japan, Malaysia, Mexico, New Zealand, Peru, Singapore, the United States, Vietnam	Signed, pending ratification
ASEAN–Hong Kong, China FTA	ASEAN and Hong Kong	Negotiation concluded
Regional Comprehensive Economic Partnership (RCEP)	ASEAN, China, Japan, Korea, Australia, New Zealand and India	Under negotiation
Vietnam–Israel FTA	Vietnam and Israel	Under negotiation
Vietnam–European Free Trade Assocation FTA	Iceland, Liechtenstein, Norway, Switzerland and Vietnam	Under negotiation

Source: Author's own compilation.

In sum, Vietnam's international economic integration has both expanded and deepened under *Doi Moi*. The CPV's thinking on international integration has evolved gradually yet consistently towards further economic liberalization. During this period, Vietnam has also taken steps to build up a market-based economic system by adopting common international standards. This process is facilitated by Vietnam's participation in various international trade agreements which enables the country to get greater access to foreign market, capital and technology.

Impacts of the International Economic Integration Process

Expansion of Economic Relations, GDP, Trade and Investment

After thirty years of *Doi Moi*, Vietnam has established trade and investment relations with more than 200 countries and territories, and entered into trade agreements with all of its major trading partners. As shown in Table 11.2 and Figure 11.1, by the end of 2016, Vietnam had been a member or negotiating party of fifteen bilateral and multilateral FTAs and a member of most major FTAs in the region.

FIGURE 11.1
Vietnam in the Regional Network of FTAs

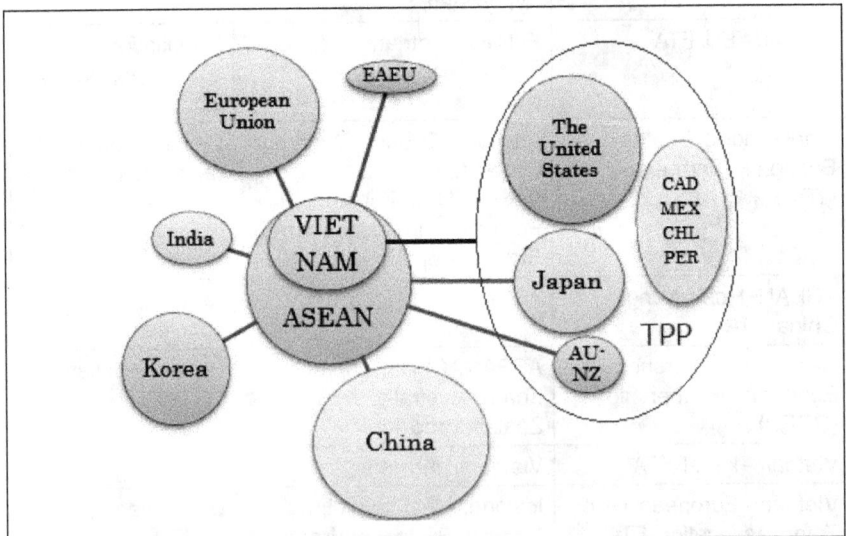

Source: Author's own compilation.

Against this backdrop, as shown in Table 11.3, Vietnam's trade and investment over the past thirty years have expanded significantly. Specifically, exports increased from US$800 million in 1986 to US$5 billion in 1995, US$32 billion in 2005 and US$162 billion in 2015. Among ASEAN countries, Vietnam currently ranks fifth in terms of total trade value, FDI stock and FDI flows, only after ASEAN-4 (UNCTAD 2015; WTO 2015).[3] More notably, in recent years, the value of announced green field FDI into Vietnam has been the highest among ASEAN countries (UNCTAD 2015).

TABLE 11.3
Trade and Investment in Vietnam, 1986–2015

	1986	1990	1995	2000	2005	2010	2015
Export value (US$ bil.)	0.8	2.4	5.4	14.4	32.4	72.2	162.4
Import value (US$ bil.)	2.2	2.8	8.2	15.6	36.8	84.8	165.6
Trade balance (US$ bil.)	−1.4	−0.3	−2.7	−1.2	−4.3	−12.6	−3.2
Trade balance/GDP (%)			11.1	2.8	−8.1	−10.9	−1.6
Openness (Trade/GDP)		53	54	94	130.3	135.4	165.0
Export per capita (US$)	13.1	36.5	76.2	184.1	390.5	830.4	1,765.6
Implemented FDI (US$ bil.)	–	–	2.8	2.4	3.3	11.0	14.5

Source: GSO (various years) and author's calculations.

Export composition has shifted from resource-based to labour-intensive manufactured goods. Some manufactured products such as electronics, telephone, and garments have emerged as major export items with their respective turnover reaching more than US$20 billion in 2015. Exports of raw materials have become less important. In 2015, crude oil only accounted for about 3 per cent of Vietnam's total exports, compared with more than 20 per cent during the period 1990–2008. However, Vietnam still has much to do to improve its exports in terms of quality, added value and domestic content.

Export and import distribution by country/region has also profoundly changed. The United States, the European Union, ASEAN, China, Japan, and Korea are now major markets of Vietnam, while traditional ones such as Russia and Eastern Europe have declined in significance. Using the share of Vietnam's top ten export partners, we calculate that the export market diversification index of Vietnam has increased over time. However, as shown in Table 11.4, while

TABLE 11.4
Vietnam's Exports and Imports Distribution by Country/Region, 1986–2015

Country/Region	Export (%)				Import (%)			
	1986	1995	2005	2015[1]	1986	1995	2005	2015[1]
ASEAN	9.0	20.4	17.7	11.1	2.5	29.2	25.4	14.4
Taiwan	0.0	8.1	2.9	1.3	0.0	11.1	11.7	6.7
Hong Kong	0.0	4.7	2.0	4.3	1.8	5.1	3.4	0.8
China	5.8	6.6	10.0	10.4	2.1	2.5	16.0	30.4
Japan	4.3	26.8	13.4	8.7	5.6	10.1	11.1	8.7
Korea, Rep.	2.6	4.3	2.0	5.5	0.3	12.4	9.8	16.7
Eastern Europe	46.7	2.8	1.5	1.0	73.5	6.1	2.9	0.6
European Union	9.8	13.4	17.0	19.1	4.5	8.7	7.0	6.2
North America	0.0	4.4	21.2	22.3	0.0	1.2	2.8	5.1
Others	21.8	8.5	12.3	16.3	9.7	13.6	9.9	10.4
Diversification Index[2]	3.5	6.4	6.7	6.7	1.8	6.4	7.0	5.9

1. Data for 2015 are preliminary data.
2. The higher Diversification Index indicates higher level of diversification.
Source: CEIC database and General Statistics Office of Vietnam for 2015.

Vietnam's import sources have generally been diversified since *Doi Moi*, the country has also become increasingly dependent on China in recent years due to the rise of China as a global manufacturing powerhouse.

In terms of trade openness, Vietnam is on par with neighbouring countries. For example, Vietnam's weighted average tariff rate is within the same range as other ASEAN countries and China. Meanwhile, in terms of trade per capita, Vietnam is equivalent to China, higher than Indonesia, the Philippines and Cambodia, but lower than Malaysia and Thailand. Most notably, as shown in Table 11.5, Vietnam's trade to GDP ratio is the highest among inspected countries.

TABLE 11.5
Regional Comparison of Selected Trade Indicators

Country	Export Value (US$ bil.)	Import Value (US$ bil.)	MFN Applied Tariff (%)		Trade to GDP Ratio (%)	Trade Per Capita (US$)
			Simple Average	Weighted Average		
Cambodia	10.8	13.5	11.2	8.0	137.5	1,393
China	2,342.3	1,959.4	9.6	4.6	46.9	3,262
Indonesia	176.3	178.2	6.9	4.4	45.7	1,656
Malaysia	234.1	208.9	6.1	4.4	157.3	16,679
Philippines	62.1	67.5	6.3	4.3	55.5	1,518
Thailand	227.6	228.0	11.6	6.6	145.2	8,141
Vietnam	150.5	149.3	9.5	5.1	164.2	3,130

Note: Export, Import Values and MFN Applied Simple Average Tariff are for 2014; Weighted Average Tariff are for 2013; Trade/GDP and Trade/Capita are average of the period 2012–14.
Source: WTO trade and tariff profile, available at <www.wto.org> (accessed 8 March 2016).

Quantitative Assessments of Trade Liberalization

Since economic integration and reforms in other areas in Vietnam were conducted simultaneously during the past thirty years, it is important to separate the impacts of economic integration from those generated by other reforms. A large number of quantitative studies have assessed Vietnam's trade reforms and liberalization. Some of these studies have attempted to distinguish the impacts of different integration policies (such as tariff and non-tariff reduction) on different economic variables. Fukase and Martin (2000, 2001), for example, estimate the impacts of the United States granting the Most Favoured Nation (MFN) status to Vietnam and Vietnam joining AFTA. The study finds that Vietnam enjoyed a 127 per cent increase in exports to the United States thanks to the bilateral BTA, in which garment export rose by fifteen times. However, only modest economic impacts are found in the case of Vietnam's accession to AFTA.

Vietnam's participation in wider regional FTAs has been considered in a number of studies. For example, Toh and Gayathri (2004) evaluate Vietnam's regional integration strategy, including trade liberalization under AFTA and ASEAN–China FTA. The study demonstrates that Vietnam has benefited from increased welfare through expanded trade and the "economies of scale" made possible by regional trade agreements, especially those beyond AFTA. Meanwhile, To (2010) assesses impacts of some current and hypothetical regional FTAs on Vietnam's welfare and sectoral output. The study finds that Vietnam's welfare would increase by 2.1 per cent in ASEAN+3 FTAs as compared to 0.6 per cent in AFTA. In addition, the study, which treats rice as a "sensitive sector", reveals that Vietnam's agricultural production would expand if rice is liberalized by all ASEAN+3 countries, but would contract otherwise. Meanwhile, Itakura (2013) evaluates the impact of ASEAN economic integration, taking into account the reduction in trading time resulting from ASEAN's regional integration. The results are positive for ASEAN countries in general and for Vietnam in particular. Vietnam's GDP is expected to increase as high as 12.1 per cent under the five ASEAN+1 FTAs, 12.5 per cent in the ASEAN+3 FTA scenario, and 13.4 per cent in the Regional Comprehensive Economic Partnership (RCEP) (ASEAN+6 FTA) scenario compared with the baseline in 2015. Improvement in Vietnam's economic welfare is also significant at 10.3 per cent in ASEAN+3 FTA and 11.2 per cent in ASEAN+6 FTA.

Impacts of Vietnam's WTO membership are analysed in, among others, Roland-Holst et al. (2002), Dimaranan et al. (2005), and Huong and Vanzetti (2006). Results from the three studies generally converge that Vietnam's gains from its WTO accession are positive for merchandise commitments, but highly dependent on the performance of the textiles and apparel sectors. Meanwhile, the potential impacts of the TPP have also been examined in several studies. Petri et al. (2012) and the Vietnam Economic and Policy Research Institute (2015), for example, find that Vietnam would have the highest GDP gain among TPP members in terms of percentage change from the baseline.

Vietnam's unilateral trade liberalization is studied in To and Lee (2015). The paper evaluates impacts of Vietnam's deeper trade liberalization, including both tariff reductions, increase in foreign investment and reforms in other trade-related areas. It finds that with unilateral trade liberalization, Vietnam's economic welfare could increase by 8.4 per cent in 2020 compared with when there is no unilateral trade liberalization. The output expansion is most significant in the textiles and apparel sectors. However, agricultural, minerals and fuel sectors would contract.

In sum, most of the quantitative studies share the same prediction that opening up the economy by joining FTAs and attracting FDI would lead to export and import expansion, higher GDP, and welfare gains, but certain uncompetitive sectors would also be hurt.

Impacts on Institutional Building and Domestic Reforms

An important aspect of the economic integration process is its impacts on Vietnam's domestic institutional building. Over the past three decades of reform, Vietnam has built up and streamlined its legal system to be in conformity with international standards. Basic laws on external economic relations such as Law on Exports and Imports, Law on Foreign Direct Investment, Investment Law, and Law on Technology Transfer have been enacted to facilitate economic integration. It should be noted that most of the current major legislations on foreign investment in Vietnam and foreign trade were passed between 2003 and 2008, when Vietnam was preparing for its WTO accession and commitment implementation. The government's international economic integration agenda obviously plays an important role in accelerating this process.

According to the Ministry of Justice, until December 2006, more than 325 normative documents were promulgated by central agencies in preparation for Vietnam's WTO accession, including 43 laws, 31 ordinances, and 102 decrees. The implementation of WTO agreements involved further revision of the legal system. More than 40 legislations, including 16 laws, were proposed for revision to be in line with WTO regulations. These do not include legal documents on the exercise of Vietnam's membership rights in its trade relations with other WTO member countries (Hiep 2006).

Vietnam's international economic integration also creates lock-in effects on domestic reforms. The progress of trade liberalization in Vietnam has so far been regarded as faster than reforms in other areas, such as those on state-owned enterprises and the banking sector. This reflects Vietnam's strategy to use global integration as a mechanism to "lock in" other structural reforms and gradually create the incentive for changes in other areas. As observed by a number of research, binding commitments to trading partners reduces the risks of backtracking (World Bank 2006, p. 50). With its expanding international commitments, Vietnam's trade, investment and industrial policy instruments will be increasingly bound by signed agreements. The country will not be able to arbitrarily change its external economic policies without risking violating WTO regulations and other trade agreements. At the same time, Vietnam has also been under pressure to open most of its services sector to international competition and strengthen its enforcement system to protect intellectual property rights. External pressures through these commitments have also forced Vietnamese businesses to enhance their capabilities to compete more effectively with foreign players. Such a proactive integration approach is expected to lead the country to a more efficient market-based economy.

Trade and FTA Efficiency

Vietnam's continuous international economic integration process has brought about significant changes to its economy in many aspects. However, whether or not Vietnam has made the most out of its many FTAs is still an open question. There is evidence that Vietnam has not fully utilized its FTAs and a gap between negotiating and preparing for FTAs still exists.

First, despite signing many FTAs, the utilization rate by Vietnamese exporters is rather low. Specifically, Vietnam's utilization rate of AFTA and most of ASEAN+1 FTA[4] ranges from as low as 7 per cent to 31 per cent (Cuong 2012). This is due to the difficulties and extra costs for exporters to meet the requirements of rules of origin. In addition, exporters are not well-informed of or not interested in trade agreements. A survey in 2015 shows that 56.8 per cent of enterprises do not know or are not interested in the ASEAN Economic Community (AEC) while 40.9 per cent is not interested in or aware of the TPP.[5] More worryingly, 33.4 per cent of the surveyed enterprises do not even know about the WTO. Vietnamese enterprises' awareness of the country's international economic integration is far lower than their counterparts in Laos, Cambodia and Myanmar (Quang 2015). This lack of awareness tends to prevent domestic enterprises from having adequate preparation to take full advantage of the new opportunities offered by Vietnam's trade agreements.

Second, trade expansion has not been very effective in terms of changing Vietnam's economic growth model. Although exports expand, imports of intermediate inputs and raw materials also increase due to the lack of domestic supplies. The lack of supporting industries causes the level of added value in Vietnam's exports to be very low, especially within the manufacturing sector. Agriculture and aqua-culture exports are mostly raw materials or simply processed products that are sold to consumers under distributors' brands. In addition, since most of the increased exports come from foreign-invested enterprises, foreign investors have been the main beneficiaries of Vietnam's export expansion.

Meanwhile, trade in services has been suffering from a widening deficit. Freight transport by sea is the main imported service. The import of other services such as finance, insurance and telecommunications is also witnessing an upward trend. Compared with trade in merchandise, Vietnam's trade in services is less competitive due to the lack of management experience, capital and technology. As Vietnam implements more liberalization commitments, its trade deficit in services is expected to further expand in the coming years.

As shown in Table 11.4, while Vietnam's trade partners have been diversified since the launch of *Doi Moi,* import markets have become more concentrated in recent years due to the burgeoning share of imports from China. Trade deficit with China reached an alarming level of US$33.5 billion in 2015, which was equal to 20 per cent of Vietnam's total exports. This trend is unlikely to change in the short term as supporting industries in Vietnam are still weak. Moreover, Vietnam's trade management is still rather incompetent, and trade policy measures available for Vietnam to narrow the deficit have become increasingly limited.

Vietnam's economic integration can therefore be seen as a combination of "active negotiation" and "passive preparation". The government has been proactive in sealing trade deals with important partners. However, such a policy has not been accompanied by a comprehensive and efficient industrial development strategy as well as adequate domestic preparation. Domestic businesses are generally not well-informed of or well-prepared for deeper liberalization. Sectors that have comparative advantages are not ready to make the most out of opportunities offered by FTAs, while disadvantaged ones are not fully aware of challenges arising from increasing foreign competition. As such, Vietnam still has much to do to improve the efficiency of the overall economy as well as the export sector.

Deepened International Economic Integration and Policy Challenges

After thirty years of *Doi Moi*, Vietnam has now reached a new stage of international economic integration. The establishment of the AEC as well as the potential conclusion of the TPP and RCEP, which represents a deepened level of economic integration for Vietnam, will bring the country both opportunities and challenges. The new economic environment that Vietnam is now facing, as well as its implications for the country's future economic trajectory, will be different from that of the past.

First, Vietnam's economic policies in the coming years will be bound to a significant extent by its international agreements. Under its current and forthcoming FTAs, Vietnam will have to eliminate most of its tariffs on imports from FTA partners. Behind-the-border issues relating to state-owned enterprises, worker's rights, environmental issues, and intellectual property rights are becoming increasingly essential parts of trade pacts. On the one hand, this trend helps improve policy transparency and predictability. On the other, many policy instruments are now no longer available to the government, which constrains its room for manoeuvrability in dealing with domestic economic challenges. Vietnamese authorities also need to be more cautious when it comes to investors' rights. Under the Investor–State Dispute Settlement regulations of the TPP, for example, they can be brought to court by foreign investors if their policy is seen as causing damages to investors' interests. Against this backdrop, it is essential for Vietnam's central and local governments to change their policy mindset to reflect the fact that even domestic or local policies now need to be in line with international commitments.

Second, liberalizing the allocation of resources is important for reaping full benefits from FTAs. Indeed, economic integration does not automatically bring in benefits. It only provides certain conditions for resources to be allocated more efficiently both within and across partner countries. An important underlying condition for a party to benefit from its FTAs is the mobility of resources across sectors, at least domestically, so that resources can be transferred from inefficient sectors to more efficient ones. Accordingly, it is important for Vietnam to further facilitate the flow of essential resources, such as land rights, labour and capital, across regions and sectors to achieve a higher level of economic efficiency and to strengthen its production forces.

Third, sectoral adjustments under newly signed agreements will pose some structural challenges for Vietnam. Most quantitative studies using general equilibrium models project large increase in exports, outputs, employment in textile, garments and footwear industries at the expense of agriculture and other manufacturing industries (see, for example, Kelly 2016; To and Lee 2015; Vietnam Economic and Policy Research Institute 2015). Kelly (2016) even warns that the Vietnamese economy is increasingly dominated by low-skilled assembly work in electronics, garment and footwear factories. Therefore, continued reliance on the current static comparative advantages could turn Vietnam into a labour-intensive manufacturing centre, not a modern economy. In order to avoid being stuck in the "low-skilled, low-value" manufacturing sector, it is crucial for Vietnam to create dynamic comparative advantages. Improving the education system and a more efficient business environment would be fundamental for the new comparative advantages to emerge. In its pursuit of deeper international economic integration, Vietnam should pay greater attention to economic restructuring to gradually transform the country into a modern industrialized economy.

Finally, after decades of global trade liberalization, tariffs have been greatly reduced across the board. The impacts of tariff reduction alone has become much lower than liberalization of other factors such as investment and non-tariff barriers to trade (To and Lee 2015). Therefore, unilateral liberalization in terms of reducing investment impediments, non-tariff barriers and other administrative and regulatory hindrances to trade should be considered to be an equally important task for Vietnam in the coming years. Reforms in these areas could help further amplify impacts of the international economic integration process on the country.

Conclusion

Since *Doi Moi* was launched in 1986, Vietnam has embraced international economic integration as a major tool to modernize its economy. During this process, the CPV and its government have undergone significant ideological changes, accompanied by corresponding policy developments to open up the economy. As a result, the expanded foreign trade, greater inflow of foreign investment as well as domestic reforms to meet international commitments have transformed Vietnam into one of the most notable economic success stories in Asia over the past three decades.

The CPV's thinking on international economic integration has continuously evolved to adapt to new developments in Vietnam's internal and external conditions. This consistent political commitment to economic integration helps enhance trust and confidence of foreign partners in Vietnam's reforms.

At the same time, Vietnam has adopted a pragmatic and gradual multilateralization and diversification approach to international integration. It started with unilateral liberalization measures to build up the necessary institutional and legal frameworks of a market-based economy. This is followed by a low level of liberalization within the ASEAN framework, then BTAs with the major partners, accession to the WTO, and finally, participation in high-level WTO-plus FTAs.

Over the past three decades, international economic integration has contributed to Vietnam's growth in trade and investment, institutional building, as well as domestic reforms. However, trade growth has been rather inefficient due to the lack of preparation at both macro and micro levels. The absence of strong supporting industries to facilitate export production and the underperforming services sector remain major obstacles for Vietnam to improve its trade balance and to reap greater benefits from trade.

Vietnam's plan to pursue deeper international integration in the coming years will present the country with multifaceted challenges that require a new approach to policy formulation to facilitate the implementation of its expanding international commitments. More profound liberalization in factor markets, and the further reduction of non-tariff barriers as well as trade-related administrative and regulatory ones, are necessary for FTAs to generate expected benefits. In addition, structural changes as a result of trade liberalization could lead to the dominance of low value-added, low-skilled labour-intensive sectors. In particular, the agriculture sector would be highly vulnerable as more than half of the work force is employed in this sector. As such, improvements in the education system and business environment are needed to promote dynamic comparative advantages. On the other hand, a more sophisticated social safety net should be developed to cover those who are displaced from contracting sectors due to the increasing level of integration.

NOTES

1. Author's calculation based on Vietnam's 2015 trade data.
2. Even when ASEAN+1 FTAs (which are not high quality FTAs) are not taken into account, FTA coverage of Vietnam's trade stands at 62 per cent (author's own calculation), while that of Japan is 37 per cent (including TPP), Korea 62 per cent, the United States 47 per cent, and Mexico 82 per cent.
3. ASEAN-4 refers to Singapore, Malaysia, Thailand and Indonesia.
4. ASEAN-Korean FTA is the only case in which the utilization rate by Vietnamese exporters is greater than 90 per cent.
5. The survey titled "Awareness of International Economic Integration of Vietnamese Enterprises" was conducted by the PACE Institute of Management. The results were released on 28 December 2015.

REFERENCES

Communist Party of Vietnam (CPV). "The Political Report of the Central Committee to the 6th Party Congress" (in Vietnamese), 1986. Available at <http://dangcongsan.vn/tu-lieu-van-kien/van-kien-dang/van-kien-dai-hoi/khoa-vi/doc-392420153571056.html> (accessed 10 March 2017).

————. "The Political Report of the Central Committee to the 7th Party Congress" (in Vietnamese), 1991. Available at <http://dangcongsan.vn/tu-lieu-van-kien/van-kien-dang/van-kien-dai-hoi/khoa-vii/doc-21012201511352246.html> (accessed 10 March 2017).

————. "The Political Report of the Central Committee to the 7th Party Congress" (in Vietnamese), 1996. Available at <http://dangcongsan.vn/tu-lieu-van-kien/van-kien-dang/van-kien-dai-hoi/khoa-viii/doc-292420154134156.html> (accessed 10 March 2017).

Cuong, Tran Ba. "FTA Utilization and How to Support SMEs". Paper presented at The Increasing of FTA Utilization by SMEs, Tokyo, Japan, 2012. Available at <http://www.meti.go.jp/policy/trade_policy/apec/about/pdf/08%5BSession2%5DTRAN_Ba_Cuong.pdf>.

Dimaranan, Betina, Le Thuc Duc, and Will Martin. "Potential Economic Impacts of Merchandise Trade Liberalization under Viet Nam's Accession to the WTO", 2005. Available at <https://www.gtap.agecon.purdue.edu/resources/download/2164.pdf> (accessed 10 July 2017).

Fukase, Emiko and Will Martin. "The Effect of the United States' Granting MFN Status to Vietnam". *Review of World Economics* 136, no. 3 (2000): 539–59.

————. "A Quantitative Evaluation of Vietnam's Accession to the ASEAN Free Trade Area". *Journal of Economic Integration* 16, no. 4 (2001): 545–67.

General Statistics Office of Vietnam (GSO). "Monthly Statistical Information" and "Statistical Data" sections, various years. Available at <http://www.gso.gov.vn> (accessed 1 July 2017).

Hiep, Hoang Phuoc. "Reforming the Legal System to Meet the Nation's WTO Commitments". *Vietnam Law Magazine* (2006). Available at <http://vietnamlawmagazine.vn/reforming-the-legal-system-to-meet-the-nations-wto-commitments-3220.html> (accessed 4 March 2017).

Huong, Pham Lan and David Vanzetti. "Vietnam's Trade Policy Dilemmas". Paper presented at the Ninth Annual Conference on Global Economic Analysis, Addis Ababa, Ethiopia, 2006.

International Monetary Fund (IMF). "Vietnam: Transition to a Market Economy". *Occasional Paper,* No. 135 (1996).

Itakura, Ken. "Impact of Liberalization and Improved Connectivity and Facilitation in ASEAN for the ASEAN Economic Community". *ERIA Discussion Paper* 2013–01 (2013).

Kelly, Ruth. "EU Free Trade Deal with Trap Vietnam in Low-Wage, Low-Skilled Cycle", 2016. Available at <https://www.euractiv.com/section/trade-society/

opinion/eu-free-trade-deal-will-trap-vietnam-in-low-wage-low-skill-cycle/> (accessed 16 March 2017).

Manyin, Mark E. "The Vietnam–U.S. Bilateral Trade Agreement". *CRS Report RL30416* (9 September 2002).

Morley, James W. and Masashi Nishihara. *Vietnam Joins the World*. New York: M.E. Sharpe, 1997.

Petri, Peter A., Michael G. Plummer, and Fan Zhai. *The Trans-Pacific Partnership and Asia-Pacific Integration: A Quantitative Assessment*, Vol. 98. Washington, D.C.: Peterson Institute for International Economics, 2012.

Quang, C. "40.9% doanh nghiep chua biet gi ve TPP" [40.9% of Enterprises Do Not Know About the TPP]. *Dan Tri*, 2015. Available at <http://dantri. com.vn/kinh-doanh/40-9-doanh-nghiep-viet-chua-biet-gi-ve-tpp-20151229093917162.htm> (accessed 15 February 2017).

Roland-Holst, David, Finn Tarp, Van An Dinh, Vo Tri Thanh, Pham Lan Huong, and Hien Minh Dinh. *Vietnam's Accession to the World Trade Organization: Economic Projections to 2020*. Hanoi: Central Institute for Economic Management, 2002.

Thanh, Vo Tri. "Vietnam's Trade Liberalization and International Economic Integration: Evolution, Problems and Challenges". *ASEAN Economic Bulletin* 22, no. 1 (2005): 75–91.

To Minh Thu. "Regional Integration in East Asia and Its Impacts on Welfare and Sectoral Output in Vietnam". *International Public Policy Studies* 14, no. 2 (2010): 97–112.

To Minh Thu and Hiro Lee. "Assessing the Impact of Deeper Trade Reform in Vietnam Using a General Equilibrium Framework". *Journal of Southeast Asian Economies* 32, no. 1 (2015): 140–62.

Toh Mun Heng and Vasudevan Gayathri. "Impact of Regional Trade Liberalization on Emerging Economies: The Case of Vietnam". *ASEAN Economic Bulletin* 21, no. 2 (2004): 167–82.

United Nations Conference on Trade and Development (UNCTAD). "FDI Outward Stock, by Region and Economy, 1990–2014", 24 June 2015. Available at <http://unctad.org/Sections/dite_dir/docs/WIR2015/WIR15_tab04.xls> (accessed 10 10 October 2015).

Vietnam Economic and Policy Research Institute. "The Impacts of TPP and AEC on the Vietnamese Economy: Macroeconomic Aspects and the Livestock Sector". *VEPR Report* (August 2015).

World Bank. *Vietnam — Aiming High: Vietnam Development Report 2007*. Washington, D.C.: World Bank, 2006.

World Trade Organization (WTO). "Trade Profile: Vietnam", 2015. Available at <http://stat.wto.org/CountryProfile/WSDBCountryPFView.aspx?Country=VN&Language=E> (accessed 10 March 2017).

12

Norm Diffusion through Trade: The Case of the EU–Vietnam Free Trade Agreement

Hoang Hai Ha

The current chapter aims to assess how the Government of Vietnam, as a norm recipient, responds to political, economic and social norms diffused through the European Union (EU)–Vietnam Free Trade Agreement (EUVFTA) negotiations.

As Manners (2009) suggests, the EU should be regarded as a normative power that works mainly through ideas and values rather than pure military or economic force. The notion of normative power in world politics indicates a separate form of engagement different from the conventional forms described by neo-realist and neo-liberal theories (Manners 2009). In this context, the concept of Normative Power Europe (NPE), which stems from a unique combination of "historical context, hybrid polity and legal constitution" of the EU (Manners 2002, pp. 240–41), could be regarded as a working approach that grasps the Union's distinctive features, determines, guides and legitimizes its international role (Diez 2005). At the same time, some scholars argue that the EU's role as a normative power should be explored in the field of trade policy because trade is an important source of EU power, and trade policy is its oldest and most "communitarized" external policy area (see, for example, De Zutter and Toro 2008; Leeg 2014; Orbie 2011; Sicurelli 2015).

Since the NPE concept has mainly been developed in the field of EU studies, analyses of the EU's normative power tend to concentrate on norm makers in Brussels, which makes it "Euro-centric" (Gerrits 2009, p. 2). Some studies suggest that apart from the EU's limited *material* and coercive *power* and institutional complexity, other countries' contexts and positions on European norms might also constrain the efficiency of European normative power (Börzel and Risse 2012; Garcia and Masselot 2015). However, these explanatory factors have been under-researched. According to Ringmar (2012, p. 19), the reaction of other countries is "far more important than the action itself and their reaction is what the exercise of power ultimately seeks to influence". This chapter thus moves beyond the existing research on NPE, which mainly focuses on the mechanisms and channels of the EU's norm export, while generally overlooking the positions of norm recipients and their strategies of norm import. It accordingly seeks to address the empirical gap in the current literature on the EU's norm diffusion, which has mostly focused on the EU's neighbourhood and Africa, by looking into how Vietnam — a Southeast Asian country — responds to the EU's norm diffusion through free trade negotiations.

The normative power concept offers an alternative approach to' study EU–Vietnam relations and to assess the EU's influence on Vietnam during the postcolonial period. Vietnam is selected as its history, cultural traditions, political particularities and emerging economy status are likely to provide a litmus test for the empirical validity of the EU's role as a normative power. Since the launch of market reforms in 1986, Vietnam's rapid economic growth and social development have altered the basic setting of the bilateral relationship. Vietnam has become one of the most important Asian partners for the EU (Rompuy 2012), and is the third ASEAN country after Singapore and Malaysia with which the EU has negotiated a comprehensive free trade agreement (FTA). The EUVFTA belongs to the third generation of EU's FTAs designed to target countries with high potential for investment and trade with Europe. In addition, the EU, as Vietnam's second largest trading partner, wields a significant level of influence over the country. These conditions turn Vietnam into a suitable case to study how the EU can use trade to diffuse its norms to recipient states.

This chapter argues that through the EUVFTA negotiations, the EU seeks to export its constitutive norms to Vietnam, but the norm diffusion process is challenged by Vietnam's reactions. The chapter begins by explaining the NPE concept and presenting a theoretical framework for analysing normative impacts. It then explores the new generation of FTAs that the EU has pursued since 2006 and its position during EUVFTA negotiations. Finally, the chapter analyses Vietnam's responses to EU norm diffusion, especially how domestic factors determine its import of EU norms.

Theorizing Local Responses to EU Norm Diffusion

The current chapter relies on the literature on NPE, Europeanization and norm diffusion to explain whether the EU's constitutive principles such as democracy, human rights, good governance and sustainable development, can be imported into Vietnam. Since Manners first introduced the concept of "normative power" in 2002, it has generated substantial interest among scholars in the debates on EU self-perception, its relevance to norms[1] as well as its identity in the international system. Manners conceptualizes the EU as a "normative power", i.e. an actor that has [...] "*the ability to define what passes for 'normal' in world politics*" (Manners 2002, p. 253). A normative power also stands for and promotes universal norms (Manners 2002, pp. 239–42). In his seminal articles, Manners (2002) identifies nine norms of the EU, namely peace, liberty, democracy, rule of law, human rights, social solidarity, anti-discrimination, sustainable development, and good governance. More recently, Parker and Rosamond (2013) and Rosamond (2014) add such principles of socio-economic organization as free trade, fair trade, and market economy to the list of the EU's constitutive norms.

A normative power tends to adopt a deliberative approach, positive conditionality or substantial incentives in order to diffuse its constitutive norms to other countries. Accordingly, the EU can exert positive influence on other countries through trade agreements with non-binding provisions (i.e. soft laws),[2] information exchange, tariff reduction, or the provision of technical assistance for capacity building (H.H. Hoang 2016, pp. 184–85). Under certain circumstances, coercive economic and military means may be employed if they conform to international standards (Diez 2005, p. 616; Diez and Manners 2007, p. 176; Tocci 2008, pp. 5–6). In the framework of trade agreements, trading obligations that are legally enforceable sit well within the group of such "hard" approaches. These legally binding commitments constrain trade partners' ability to modulate national political and economic policies at their discretion because violations would result in trade sanctions (Damro 2012, pp. 691–95). As far as the EU is concerned, the Union has used the enforcement of WTO commitments via the organization's dispute settlement mechanisms to tie market access to regulatory issues.

This chapter focuses on exploring how norms are imported into the domestic systems of EU partners, or how these norms develop in these countries. In order to judge if the EU is successful in "shaping conceptions of what is *normal*", the impact of the EU's norms on the norm recipient states' practices must be analysed (Diez and Manners 2007, pp. 175–76). Normative diffusion is expected to lead recipient states to fully adopt or copy the norms (Forsberg 2011; Manners 2002, 2008). In practice, however, problems arise during the norm diffusion process, leading to different shades of normative change. According to Flockhart (2006), a partner can share or resist some or even most of the Union's normative principles. As such, norm diffusion in international relations can be conceptualized as a two-way process: the recipient states are not only the targets of diffusion but also active agents that impact the content and outcomes of the process (Pu 2012, p. 344).

Therefore, the responses of local actors to EU norm diffusion should be considered. Such responses may be shaped by "scope conditions", including geographical proximity, historical contingency, cultural particularity, local traditions, institutions and politics, socio-economic structures, ideas and interests of the ruling elites, and power asymmetries (Börzel and Risse 2012, pp. 11–12; Malova and Haughton 2002, p. 116). Although the recipient country may adopt or imitate new norms, some pre-existing normative orders might still be strongly maintained (Acharya 2004, p. 251). In this sense, the degree of "cultural match" or "normative fit" between foreign and pre-existing domestic norms and needs (Björkdahl 2005; Björkdahl, Chaban, Leslie, and Masselot 2015; Checkel 1999) determines the depth of norm import by each state. In the same vein, Acharya (2004, p. 241) argues that whether the norm-maker is successful or not in diffusing norms is determined by the extent to which "norm-takers build congruence between transnational norms [...] and local belief and practices". Meanwhile, Strange and Meyer (1993) argue that diffusion strategies must take into account the cultural match of local contexts so that norms can be smoothly acknowledged. For instance, with regard to democracy, there should be some domestic resonance for democratic values and practices in order for democracy norms to be locally accepted. It is therefore essential for empirical studies to integrate the "scope conditions" into the analysis of normative impacts. In the case of Vietnam, the one-party political system, cultural values, historical issues and political ideology have shaped its worldview in general and its response to European norms in particular.

Norm recipients generally respond to foreign partners' norm diffusion at four different levels, namely (1) adoption or copying; (2) adaptation, socialization and localization; (3) resistance; and (4) rejection. These typical positions of norm recipients and their strategies of norm import are summarized in Figure 12.1.[3]

FIGURE 12.1
Typical Responses of Norm Recipients

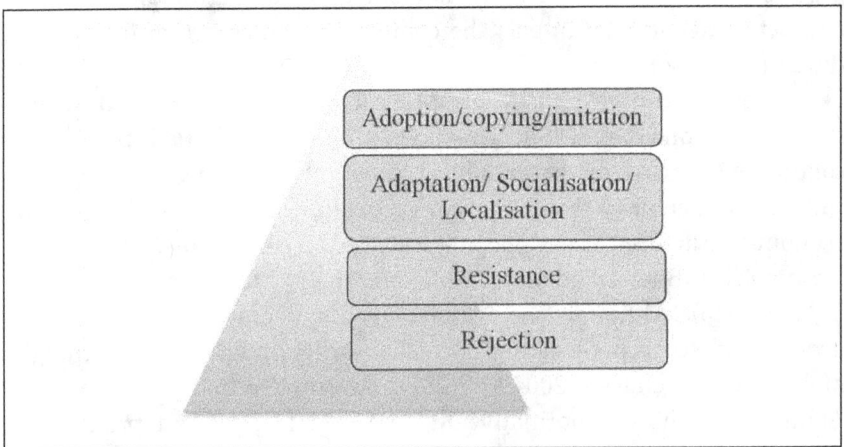

Source: Author's own compilation.

Adoption or *copying* leads to the highest grades of normative change which involve full, conscious and unambiguous transfer of norms into the domestic setting of the norm recipient (Björkdahl et al. 2015, p. 4; Lavenex and UçArer 2004, p. 422). Norm recipients thus absolutely adhere to imported norms. Meanwhile, *adaptation* involves the translation/interpretation/incorporation of norms to make them conform to the local context (Björkdahl et al. 2015, p. 4). In some regards, adaptation is similar to what is termed *localization*. Acharya (2004, p. 245; 2009, p. 21) defines localization as the "active construction (through discourse, framing, grafting, and cultural selection) of foreign ideas by local actors", who actively borrow foreign ideas to strengthen their traditions and authority. As adaptation is a generic term that refers to various kinds of behaviours and outcomes (Acharya 2004, p. 250), and is "difficult to separate from localization" (Cesari 2014, p. 20), *adaptation* and *localization* are normally used interchangeably to refer to the process of translation of norms in which the norm recipients contextualize and/or domesticate/internalize external norms. According to Risse and Sikkink (1999, p. 5), this process can also be understood as a process of *socialization* of norms, in which external and local norms need to find common ground for coexistence (Imai 2011, p. 36).

In some cases, the recipient state's pre-existing domestic norms might be divergent from or competing with those of the normative power. It could therefore *resist* the norm diffusion, which leads to the limited importation of foreign norms and the dominance of local ones (Björkdahl et al, 2015, p. 4; Solingen 2012). At the same time, local actors claim the right to formulate rules and address their own issues without intervention by any outside authority (Acharya 2011, p. 102). Under this scenario, few practices of the recipient state conform to the norms diffused by the normative power, and too much resistance will cause the norm transfer to fail. In other cases, the recipient state may even take active steps to explicitly *reject* outside ideas which they do not regard as worthy of selective borrowing or adoption in any form (Acharya 2011, p. 99).

As far as the EU is concerned, a recipient state's changes towards its norms beg the question of whether the norms have been truly internalized and contextualized, or it is merely a strategy of the recipient state to obtain the EU's reward of market access or aid that come with the "policy import" (De Zutter 2010, p. 1114). In other words, normative changes might result from the extent to which EU rewards and threats alter the strategic utility calculations of the recipient country's actors (Schimmelfennig and Sedelmeier 2005, pp. 10–11). In this case, the recipient state's socialization of foreign norms may be short-lived and "the newly adopted behaviours can be discarded once incentive structure change" (Checkel 2005, p. 813).

EU's FTA Strategy and EU–Vietnam Trade Negotiations

As a major global trade power, the EU has long used FTAs as a tool to diffuse its constitutive principles beyond its borders. At the same time, since the Eurozone crisis started in 2008, the EU has sought to consolidate its ambitious trade liberalization agenda to facilitate economic recovery (De Ville and Orbie 2011; Siles-Brügge 2014). The EU 2006 Global Europe and 2007 Single Market strategies state that the rejection of protectionism at home must be accompanied by the activism in creating open markets and fair conditions for trade abroad. Accordingly, the two core elements of the new EU trade agenda are "stronger engagement with major emerging economies and regions; and a sharper focus on barriers to trade behind the border" (European Commission 2006, p. 6). Towards these ends, EU negotiators seek to establish greater market access and stronger rules in new trade areas important to the Union, such as intellectual property, services, investment, public procurement, and competition. A new political strategy titled "Europe 2020: A strategy for European Union growth" also mentions the elimination of non-tariff barriers and fair trade as the EU's main objectives in international trade (European Commission 2010).

In addition, EU trade policy is aimed at broader objectives beyond trade and investment liberalization. As some researchers have pointed out, the EU's external trade relations are increasingly attached to its normative principles, such as freedom, democracy, human rights, rule of law, labour standards, gender equality, sustainable development, and good governance (Manners 2008, p. 23). Commitments to the external promotion of these development norms are explicitly reflected in the Global Europe Strategy: "As we pursue social justice and cohesion at home, we should also seek to promote our values, including social and environmental standards and cultural diversity, around the world" (European Commission 2006, p. 5). This document, however, also stresses that the EU will "take into account the development needs" of its trading partners. Subsequent European strategies continue to acknowledge that the EU is "committed to promoting sustainable development, international labour standards and decent work [...] Trade policy should continue to support green growth and climate change objectives" (European Commission 2010, p. 8). In 2012, the EU released an updated version of its trade and development strategy which considers trade as a powerful engine for development, in line with the EU's principles of Policy Coherence for Development (European Commission 2012, pp. 2–3). These changes reflect the EU's efforts to spread normative goals of traditional foreign policy into the realm of trade policy.

Under the framework of the 2006 Global Europe Strategy, former EU Trade Commissioner Peter Mandelson indicated that the "new generation" of FTAs should embrace "a step change" in how the EU integrates more explicit language on social issues, such as international decent work standards of the International Labour Organization (ILO) and its broader agenda of sustainable development, into bilateral and bi-regional trade agreements (Mandelson 2006). In doing so, the EU wants its FTA partners to commit to sustainable development in economic, social, and environmental dimensions, such as economic development, poverty reduction, full and productive employment, decent work for all, and the protection and sustainable use of eco-systems and natural resources (Bossuyt 2009). Furthermore, the EU also added provisions committing FTA parties to evaluating the potential political and socio-economic impacts of trade agreements through Trade Sustainability Impact Assessments (TSIAs).[4] As such, alongside Technical Barriers to Trade (TBT) and Sanitary and Phytosanitary (SPS) measures that contain environmental aspects, the EU has tried to diffuse the concept of sustainability through the inclusion of social and environmental sustainability provisions into various FTAs that it has negotiated with different partners around the world, especially those with Latin American and Asian developing countries.

In 2007, the EU launched negotiations for an FTA with ASEAN, which was then the EU's third largest trading partner after the United States and China. However, the negotiations were suspended in 2010 when the Union switched to bilateral FTA negotiations with individual ASEAN member states. These bilateral talks have been accompanied by negotiations on Framework Agreements on Comprehensive Partnership and Cooperation (PCA) which aimed to establish the normative base of the EU, including human rights, sustainability, and cooperation in anti-corruption, peace, and security. On the basis of the Commission's mandate, only ASEAN member states that had already concluded a Framework Agreement with the EU (or agreed to do so in the future) were eligible to negotiate an FTA with the EU (Garelli 2012, p. 16).

Vietnam and the EU launched their FTA negotiation on 26 June 2012, and one day later, the EU–Vietnam PCA was signed. The EU–Vietnam trade relationship is therefore embedded in the framework of the PCA (European Parliament 2014), which ensures that EU norms are to be diffused to Vietnam through FTA negotiations. Moreover, the fact that the conclusion of the PCA and the start of FTA negotiations happened almost at the same time suggests that the EU wanted to use the lure of trade to gain Vietnam's acceptance of normative principles contained in the PCA (Garcia and Masselot 2015). In other words, the PCA makes the EU's trade cooperation with Vietnam conditional upon Vietnam's compliance with the EU's normative demands.

The EU–Vietnam FTA negotiations lasted more than three years from 2012 to December 2015. The talks went far beyond the removal of tariffs and quantitative restrictions and covered a whole range of regulatory issues, such as technical regulations and standards, rights of establishment, investment, liberalization of government procurement, competition policy, state aid and trade in services, which shows the EU's explicit commitment to a broad set of liberal economic principles.

The two parties also discussed a robust and comprehensive chapter on trade and sustainable development. In contrast to the U.S. positions on the Trans-Pacific Partnership (TPP) negotiations, the EU adopted a more nuanced approach in FTA talks, signifying a preference for cooperative measures (e.g., dialogues to share information and experience, technical assistance and capacity building) rather than sanctions. The EUVFTA provides for non-binding obligations that prevent Parties from refusing to uphold labour and environmental standards based on competitiveness-related reasons.[5] In addition, the agreement prohibits the use of labour rights, such as the protection of employees, as an excuse for trade protectionism, and includes a mechanism for engaging economic, social, and environmental stakeholders in the implementation of the chapter.

The two sides concluded their negotiations on 2 December 2015 and released the agreed text of the agreement in January 2016. This text needs to be signed by both parties, then ratified by the Vietnamese National Assembly, the European Parliament as well as EU Member States before entering into force. The EUVFTA is expected to serve as a model and a template for the EU's trade agreements with other ASEAN member states (European Institute for Asian Studies 2016, p. 6).

Vietnam's Responses to EU Norm Diffusion

This section investigates how Vietnamese institutions and policies have introduced changes (if any) to deal with the norms diffused through trade negotiations with the EU. Normative changes happen if Vietnam agrees to comply with norms embedded in legal provisions of the agreement. Data and arguments in this section are based on interviews with policymakers and documentary analysis.

Very limited correlation can be observed between EU trade policies towards Vietnam and the change in Vietnam's legislation concerning human rights and democracy. Quite on the contrary, Vietnamese negotiators resisted the EU's promotion of human rights and democracy during the EUVFTA negotiations. Although human rights were mentioned in the "essential element clause" of the PCA, the Vietnamese government strongly protested the discussion of these norms within the framework of trade negotiations, despite the fact that such discussion was required by the European Parliament. Vietnam maintained that the EU's human rights requirements may undermine the economic objectives of the trade agreement and intervene in Vietnam's internal affairs.[6] As analysed below, the EU and Vietnam also showed differences over certain labour rights during their discussion of the chapter on sustainability. Given these divergences, the two parties agreed to mention their commitment to human rights norms in the preamble of the FTA only. However, under the international law of treaties, the preambles of treaties are not legally binding. Furthermore, unlike the cases of Georgia, Moldova and the Caribbean Forum (CARIFORUM), the PCA with Vietnam do not make explicit reference to the possibility of suspending mutual trade commitments in case of human rights violations. This suggests that Vietnam is unlikely to accept the entire human rights norms requested by the European Parliament's Resolution on EUVFTA (2013/2599).

Under the EUVFTA, Vietnam has committed to remove almost all of its import duties in trade with the EU and not to increase those that will remain in force as exceptions (such as in the pharmaceutical and auto industries). However, Vietnam hesitated to adopt the whole set of market liberalism norms, especially legally binding commitments related to government procurement and competition that aim to reduce the role of state-owned enterprises (SOEs) in the economy (T. Hoang 2014). By using legally binding obligations, the EU has strongly pushed for the liberalization of the government procurement market and positioned this as a crucial area for the free trade deal because Vietnam delayed the opening-up of this sector to competitive bidding (Binder 2016; H.H. Hoang and Sicurelli 2017).

However, like many other developing countries, Vietnam was not interested in negotiating the issue of government procurement due to concerns over national sovereignty and the high costs of violation given the EU's hard stance on the issue (H.H. Hoang 2016, p. 192). Moreover, Vietnamese negotiators highlighted that government procurement, competition rules, and privatization models need to be relevant with local conditions and policy objectives, and the agreement should therefore allow for adequate flexibility.[7] This was also the argument advanced in Vietnamese statements that the EU's position exhibited a superficial and limited interpretation of Vietnam's salient characteristics, such as its socialist-oriented market economy and its level of development (WTO 2013).[8]

In addition, the EU urged Vietnam to reduce control of protected sectors in the national economy, which are dominated by state-owned and state-related firms, and state intervention in markets. This is a clear case where local political and economic conditions weaken EU normative impacts. The Vietnamese side argued that in its current economic structure, SOEs not only perform business functions but also fulfil many social and political responsibilities (Vu 2014, p. 9). The government would like to ensure that SOEs are put at the centre of the national economic development strategy in order to secure the "socialist orientation". Moreover, as the private sector is still rather weak and vulnerable, it is necessary for the state-owned sector to play a major role in the economy.[9] These divergent positions on government procurement, competition and SOE privileges protracted the FTA negotiations. Although the two sides eventually agreed on principles largely in line with the Government Procurement Agreement of the WTO, Vietnam is still facing difficulties in discarding the preferences given to SOEs in order to meet the FTA requirements.

Meanwhile, Vietnam showed eagerness to adopt EU norms and standards regarding sustainable development and environment protection. There was no considerable divergence between the two sides concerning the chapter on sustainability.[10] In parallel with FTA negotiations, Vietnam and the EU also negotiated the Voluntary Partnership Agreement on Forest Law Enforcement, Governance and Trade (VPA/FLEGT)[11] which aims to ensure that Vietnamese timber exports to the EU are legally sourced and produced. Normative changes in this regard have resulted from both Vietnam's calculations of gaining access to the EU market and the relevance of these norms to the country. This means that Vietnam behaves in conformity with norms that it consider the most appropriate in a given context, and internalizes them actively (March and Olsen 1998, pp. 160–61; Risse 2002, p. 599). Through the FTA with the EU, Vietnam expects to promote its sustainable production of high-quality goods for both local and foreign markets, instead of relying on low-quality goods and outdated technology imported from China (Nguyen 2011). At the same time, Vietnamese producers and legislators recognize that they need to accept and adopt EU standards to improve Vietnamese products' competitiveness.[12] For example, when Vietnamese producers want to export their products to the EU, they are compelled to comply with relevant EU standards. In this sense, the EU uses access to their markets as a motivation to change environmental practices at the enterprise and government level of their trade partner (Bretherton and Vogler 2006). In the case of Vietnam, the sustainability norm import can also be attributed to the Trade Related Assistance (TRA) provided by the EU. Both the Vietnamese government and local producers often do not have the financial means and technology to comply with EU standards as the compliance usually requires significant investment in advanced technology and logistics. Indeed, the EU's TRA, such as the Multilateral Trade Assistance Project (MUTRAP) II and III,[13] has enhanced Vietnam's capacity to meet EU's trade-related environmental requirements, thereby improving the international competitiveness of Vietnamese products.

When it comes to social norms, the friction between Vietnam and the EU during FTA negotiations occurred over labour rights, especially the freedom of association for workers. Vietnam has not ratified ILO conventions on several core labour standards.[14] Neither are these norms included in Vietnam's 2013 Constitution, which creates legal challenges for the incorporation of relevant ILO Convention provisions into the EUVFTA. The Vietnamese government was therefore hesitant to negotiate the issue of labour rights within the context of the agreement. Vietnamese government officials interviewed for this chapter did not reject the universality of labour rights, but they stressed that labour issues are the product of a country's specific level of economic development and political conditions, and irrelevant to trade agreements/ negotiations. Such differences on labour rights, together with divergent positions on the treatment of SOEs, protracted the trade negotiations, which were not concluded until 2 December 2015.

Vietnam's resistance to EU's transfer of labour rights norms can be attributed to a number of factors. *First*, as a developing country, Vietnam prioritizes economic targets over social ones, including the protection of labour rights as demanded by trade partners in FTA negotiations. This is reflected in Vietnam's FTA strategy (Decision No. 1051/QĐ-TTg)[15] which puts economic growth before social objectives. *Second*, Vietnam is concerned that FTA labour commitments can undermine its comparative advantage of cheap labour. *Third*, the observance of labour commitments in FTAs will also present the Vietnamese government with a technical challenge as it will have to take into account the conflicting interests of different interest groups, and embark on an elaborate law-making process to internalize these regulations into the country's legal systems (T.M.H. Hoang et al. 2014, p. 50). *Finally*, the Communist Party of Vietnam and its government may be concerned that broader labour rights, especially the freedom of association, may facilitate the politicization of its workforce, which will undermine the Party's monopoly of power. As a consequent, Vietnam resisted the EU's pressures in this regard.

Nonetheless, further delays in the EUVFTA negotiations would be counterproductive as Vietnam needed greater access to the EU market as early as possible to boost its exports against the backdrop of slowing economic growth in recent years. According to the text of the EUVFTA released in January 2016, Hanoi agreed to ratify the remaining ILO Conventions while taking into account its "domestic circumstances". As of September 2017, the Vietnamese government was still working to have these Conventions ratified before 2020.[16]

Vietnam's attitude towards the labour issues therefore shows a trade-off between political autonomy and economic interests.

Conclusion

The chapter argues that Vietnam imports norms diffused by the EU through the EUVFTA negotiations at various levels, depending on its perception of national interests as well as its political, cultural and economic background. Accordingly, Vietnam selects and adapts only certain EU norms and values to serve its domestic purposes.

If the EU's Generalized System of Preferences (GSP) ends, the EUVFTA will be a significant instrument for Vietnam to get important trade benefits, including greater access to the EU markets and the recognition of its market-economy status by the EU (H.H. Hoang 2016; Sicurelli 2015). As pointed out by To Minh Thu in Chapter 11, Vietnam is undergoing major economic transformations, further advancing market reforms and integrating itself deeper into the global trade system. Therefore, although Vietnam is not an enthusiastic recipient of all EU norms, it still feels the need to selectively localize these norms, or at least search for a compromise on disputed ones in order to maintain positive trade ties with Europe. Specifically, while Vietnam tends to resist some "unattractive" norms, such as those related to human rights and democracy, it is quite active in receiving economic and environmental norms as these norms are compatible with the country's economic development agenda.

As pointed out by some scholars, the EU's huge internal market not only creates a great attraction but also skews trade relations, in particular with weak trade partners, in favour of the EU (Bretherton and Vogler 2006, p. 54). This "compliance pull" (Langbein and Börzel 2013) might be at work in Vietnam, which is required to import EU norms and standards to be eligible for greater access to EU markets. Enforcement mechanisms may also work thanks to the EU's market power, which creates incentives for Vietnam's continued compliance. This is where the evidence of the EU's economic and normative power is clearly presented, with not only Vietnam but also many other nations now seeking to enter into FTAs with the EU. However, as far as the EUVFTA is concerned, the challenge for both parties now is how to accelerate the ratification process of the agreement, which has been hindered by some EU members' concerns about Vietnam's human rights record.

NOTES

1. For the purpose of this study, "norms" are defined as constitutive principles of the EU which are codified in rules and laws (Manners 2008; Tocci 2008). They construct the EU's identity and govern its action towards its citizens as well as the wider world.

2. Hard law and soft law are two types of legal instruments. They can be distinguished by three criteria: obligation, precision, and delegation (Abbott and Snidal 2000, p. 421). Hard laws are highly legalized across three criteria, while soft ones are weakened on one or two criteria.

3. The categorization is based on the literature on NPE, Europeanization and norm diffusion (see, for example, Acharya 2004; Kavalski 2007; Kinnvall 2004; Lavenex and UçArer 2004; Levitt and Merry 2009; Rumelili 2004; Solingen 2012; Zwingel 2012).

4. Since the early 2000s, the Directorate General for Trade of the European Commission has commissioned independent studies to evaluate the potential influence of FTAs on the EU and partner states in order to integrate that knowledge into trade negotiations.

5. Interview with EU trade official, Brussels, 4 July 2014.

6. Interviews with Vietnamese trade officials in Paris (August 2013), Brussels (July 2013), Hanoi (December 2013–March 2014).

7. Interviews with Vietnamese trade officials in Paris (August 2013) and Hanoi (December 2013).

8. Also interviews with Vietnamese trade officials in Brussels (July 2013) and Hanoi (January 2014).

9. Interviews with Vietnamese trade officials in Hanoi (December 2013–March 2014).

10. Interviews with Vietnamese trade officials in Brussels (July and September 2013).

11. The negotiation started in 2010 and ended in May 2017.

12. Interviews with Vietnamese trade officials in Paris (August 2013) and Hanoi (January and Febuary 2014).

13. MUTRAP aims to support the Ministry of Industry and Trade in facilitating sustainable international trade and investment through capacity building for policymaking, policy consultation, and the negotiation and implementation of trade related commitments, particularly vis-à-vis the EU.

14. These include C.087 (Freedom of Association and Protection of the Right to Organise Convention, 1948), C.098 (Right to Organise and Collective Bargaining Convention, 1949), and C.105 (Abolition of Forced Labour Convention, 1957).

15. Decision No. 1051/QĐ-TTg on the adoption of strategies in the participation in Free Trade Agreements until 2020 issued by Vietnamese Prime Minister on 9 August 2012 outlines the main tasks of FTA participation as follows:

(1) exploiting trade preferences; (2) attracting high technology, increasing market shares and efficiency in exportation, optimal exploitation of national potentials and comparative advantages in international economic relations; (3) fostering economic transition, economic restructuring, corporate restructuring, competitiveness of products, firms and the economy, the effective participation of Vietnam in global production networks and value chains; (4) creating essential premises and factors in developing high-quality human resources, modern infrastructure system to improve growth quality, enhancing export efficiency, investment effectiveness and maximal mobilization of resources domestically and overseas for harnessing national potentials and advantages to speed up the industrialization and modernization process; and (5) implementing social objectives, creating jobs and increasing income for the people (Hoang, Phung, Tran, Nguyen, and Nguyen 2014, p. 8).

16. Interview with Vietnamese trade official in Hanoi (March 2014).

REFERENCES

Abbott, Kenneth W. and Duncan Snidal. "Hard and Soft Law in International Governance". *International Organisation* 54, no. 3 (2000): 421–56.

Acharya, Amitav. "How Ideas Spread: Whose Norms Matter? Norm Localisation and Institutional Change in Asian Regionalism". *International Organisation* 58, no. 2 (2004): 239–75.

———. *Whose Ideas Matter?: Agency and Power in Asian Regionalism*. Ithaca: Cornell University Press, 2009.

———. "Norm Subsidiarity and Regional Orders: Sovereignty, Regionalism, and Rule-Making in the Third World". *International Studies Quarterly* 55, no. 1 (2011): 95–123.

Binder, Krisztina. "Driving Trade in the ASEAN Region: Progress of FTA Negotiations". *European Parliament* (December 2016). Available at <http:// www.europarl.europa.eu/RegData/etudes/BRIE/2016/595850/EPRS_ BRI(2016)595850_EN.pdf> (accessed 3 July 2017).

Björkdahl, Annika. "Norm-maker and Norm-taker: Exploring the Normative Influence of the EU in Macedonia". *European Foreign Affairs Review* 10, no. 2 (2005): 257–78.

Björkdahl, Annika, Natalia Chaban, John Leslie, and Annick Masselot. "Introduction: To Take or Not to Take EU Norms? Adoption, Adaptation, Resistance and Rejection". In *Importing EU Norms? Conceptual Framework and Empirical Findings*, edited by Annika Björkdahl, Natalia Chaban, John Leslie, and Annick Masselot. Heidelberg: Springer, 2015, pp. 4–25.

Börzel, Tanja A. and Thomas Risse. "From Europeanisation to Diffusion: Introduction". *West European Politics* 35, no. 1 (2012): 1–19.

Bossuyt, Fabienne. "The Social Dimension of the New Generation of EU FTAs with Asia and Latin America: Ambitious Continuation for the Sake of Policy Coherence". *European Foreign Affairs Review* 14 (2009): 703–22.

Bretherton, Charlotte and John Vogler. *The European Union as a Global Actor*. London: Routledge, 2006.

Cesari, Jocelyne. *The Awakening of Muslim Democracy*. New York: Cambridge University Press, 2014.

Checkel, Jeffrey T. "Norms, Institutions, and National Identity in Contemporary Europe". *International Studies Quarterly* 43, no. 1 (1999): 83–114.

————. "International Institutions and Socialization in Europe: Introduction and Framework". *International Organisation* 59, no. 4 (2005): 801–26.

Damro, Chad. "Market Power Europe". *Journal of European Public Policy* 19, no. 5 (2012): 682–99.

De Ville, Ferdi and Jan Orbie. "The European Union's Trade Policy Response to the Crisis: Paradigm Lost or Reinforced?" *European Integration Online Papers* 15, no. 1 (2011).

De Zutter, Elisabeth. "Normative Power Spotting: An Ontological and Methodological Appraisal". *Journal of European Public Policy* 17, no. 8 (2010): 1106–27.

De Zutter, Elisabeth and Francisco Toro. "Normative Power is in the Eye of the Beholder: An Empirical Assessment of Perceptions of EU Identity at the WTO". *UNU-CRIS Working Paper Series, W-2008-074* (2008).

Diez, Thomas. "Constructing the Self and Changing Others: Reconsidering 'Normative Power Europe'". *Millennium — Journal of International Studies* 33, no. 3 (2005): 613–36.

Diez, Thomas and Ian Manners. "Reflecting on Normative Power Europe". In *Power in World Politics*, edited by Felix Berenskoetter and Michael J. Williams. New York: Routledge, 2007, pp. 173–88.

European Commission. "Global Europe: Competing in the World", 2006. Available at <http://trade.ec.europa.eu/doclib/docs/2006/october/tradoc_130376.pdf> (accessed 1 July 2017).

————. "Trade, Growth and World Affairs: Trade Policy as a Core Component of the EU's 2020 Strategy", 2010. Available at <http://trade.ec.europa.eu/doclib/docs/2010/november/tradoc_146955.pdf> (accessed 1 June 2017).

————. "Trade, Growth and Development: Tailoring Trade and Investment Policy for Those Countries Most in Need", 2012. Available at <http://trade.ec.europa.eu/doclib/docs/2012/january/tradoc_148992.pdf> (accessed 1 June 2017).

European Institute for Asian Studies. "The EU and Vietnam: Taking (Trade) Relations to the Next Level", 2016. Available at <http://www.eias.org/wp-content/uploads/2016/03/EIAS_Event_Report_EU-Vietnam_Trade_Relations_27.04.2016.pdf> (accessed 3 June 2017).

European Parliament. Resolution of 17 April 2014 on the State of Play of the EU–Vietnam Free Trade Agreement, 2014. Available at <http://www.europarl.europa.eu/sides/getDoc.do?pubRef=-//EP//TEXT+TA+P7-TA-2014-0458+0+DOC+XML+V0//EN> (accessed 1 June 2017).

Flockhart, Trine. "'Complex Socialization': A Framework for the Study of State Socialization". *European Journal of International Relations* 12, no. 1 (2006): 89–118.

Forsberg, Tuomas. "Normative Power Europe, Once Again: A Conceptual Analysis of an Ideal Type". *Journal of Common Market Studies* 49, no. 6 (2011): 1183–204.

Garcia, Maria and Annick Masselot. "The Value of Gender Equality in the EU–Asian Trade Policy: An Assessment of the EU's Ability to Implement its Own Legal Obligations". In *Importing EU Norms? Conceptual Framework and Empirical Findings*, edited by Annika Björkdahl, Natalia Chaban, John Leslie, and Annick Masselot. Heidelberg: Springer, 2015, pp. 191–210.

Garelli, Serena. "The European Union's Promotion of Regional Economic Integration in Southeast Asia: Norms, Markets or Both?" *Bruges Political Research Papers, No. 25* (2012).

Gerrits, Andre. "Normative Power Europe: Introductory Observations on a Controversial Notion". In *Normative Power Europe in a Changing World: A Discussion*, edited by Andre Gerrits. The Hague: Netherlands Institute of International Relations Clingendael, 2009, pp. 1–8.

Hoang, Ha Hai. "Normative Power Europe through Trade: Vietnamese Perceptions". *International Relations of the Asia-Pacific* 30, no. 2 (2016): 176–205.

Hoang, Ha Hai and Daniela Sicurelli. "EU's Preferential Trade Agreements with Singapore and Vietnam: Market vs Normative Imperatives". *Contemporary Politics* (2017): 369–87.

Hoang, Thi Minh Hang, Yen Thi Phung, Huong Thi Lien Tran, Lan Thi Nguyen, and Linh Hoang My Nguyen. "Labour Provisions in Preferential Trade Agreements: Potential Opportunities or Challenges to Vietnam?" *SECO/WTI Academic Cooperation Project Working Paper Series, 2014/02* (2014).

Hoang, Tu. "Viet Nam dang tien gan den FTA voi EU, TPP" [Vietnam Comes Close to FTA with the EU and TPP]. *Thoi bao Kinh te Sai Gon* (2 April 2014). Available at <http://www.thesaigontimes.vn/112874/Viet-Nam-dang-tien-gan-den-FTA-voi-EU-TPP.html> (accessed 1 June 2017).

Imai, Kohei. "Turkey's Norm Diffusion Policies toward the Middle East: Turkey's Role of Norm Entrepreneur and Norm Transmitter". *The Turkish Yearbook of International Relations* 42 (2011): 27–60.

Kavalski, Emilian. "Partnership or Rivalry between the EU, China and India in Central Asia: The Normative Power of Regional Actors with Global Aspirations". *European Law Journal* 13, no. 6 (2007): 839–56.

Kinnvall, Catarina. "Globalization and Religious Nationalism: Self, Identity, and the Search for Ontological Security". *Political Psychology* 25, no. 4 (2004): 741–67.

Langbein, Julia and Tanja A. Börzel. "Introduction: Explaining Policy Change in the European Union's Eastern Neighbourhood". *Europe-Asia Studies* 65, no. 4 (2013): 571–80.

Lavenex, Sandra and Emek M. UçArer. "The External Dimension of Europeanization: The Case of Immigration Policies". *Cooperation and Conflict* 39, no. 4 (2004): 417–43.

Leeg, Tobias. "Normative Power Europe? The European Union in the Negotiations on a Free Trade Agreement with India". *European Foreign Affairs Review* 19, no. 3 (2014): 335–55.

Levitt, Peggy and Sally Merry. "Vernacularization on the Ground: Local Uses of Global Women's Rights in Peru, China, India and the United States". *Global Networks* 9, no. 4 (2009): 441–61.

Malova, Darina and Tim Haughton. "Making Institutions in Central and Eastern Europe, and the Impact of Europe". *West European Politics* 25, no. 2 (2002): 101–20.

Mandelson, Peter. "Trade Policy and Decent Work Intervention". Paper presented at the EU Decent Work Conference, Brussels, 2006.

Manners, Ian. "Normative Power Europe: A Contradiction in Terms?" *Journal of Common Market Studies* 40, no. 2 (2002): 235–58.

———. "The Normative Power of the European Union in a Globalised World". In *EU Foreign Policy in a Globalized World: Normative Power and Social Preferences*, edited by Zaki Laïdi. New York: Routledge, 2008, pp. 23–37.

———. "The EU's Normative Power in Changing World Politics". In *Normative Power Europe in a Changing World: A Discussion*, edited by Andre Gerrits. The Hague: Netherlands Institute of International Relations Clingendael, 2009, pp. 9–24.

March, James G. and Johan P. Olsen. "The Institutional Dynamics of International Political Orders". *International Organisation* 52, no. 4 (1998): 943–69.

Nguyen, T.T. "Hiep dinh thuong mai tu di voi EU — Kinh nghiem tu nhung nguoi di truoc" [Free Trade Agreement with the EU — Experiences from Previous FTAs]. *Vietnam Chamber of Commerce and Industry* (28 March 2011).

Available at <http://www.trungtamwto.vn/vn-eu-fta/hiep-dinh-thuong-mai-tu-do-voi-eu-kinh-nghiem-tu-nhung-nguoi-di-truoc> (accessed 1 June 2017).

Orbie, Jan. "Promoting Labour Standards through Trade: Normative Power or Regulatory State Europe?" In *Normative Power Europe Empirical and Theoretical Perspectives*, edited by Richard G. Whitman. London: Palgrave MacMillan, 2011, pp. 161–86.

Parker, Owen and Ben Rosamond. "'Normative Power Europe' Meets Economic Liberalism: Complicating Cosmopolitanism Inside/Outside the EU". *Cooperation and Conflict* 48, no. 2 (2013): 229–46.

Pu, Xiaoyu. "Socialisation as a Two-Way Process: Emerging Powers and the Diffusion of International Norms". *The Chinese Journal of International Politics* 5, no. 4 (2012): 341–67.

Ringmar, Erik. "Performing International Systems: Two East-Asian Alternatives to the Westphalian Order". *International Organisation* 66, no. 1 (2012): 1–25.

Risse, Thomas. "Constructivism and International Institutions: Towards Conversations Across Paradigm". In *Political Science: State of the Discipline*, edited by Ira Katznelson and Helen V. Milner. New York: W.W. Norton, 2002, pp. 597–623.

Risse, Thomas and Kathryn Sikkink. "The Socialization of International Human Rights Norms into Domestic Practices". In *The Power of Human Rights: International Norms and Domestic Change*, edited by Thomas Risse, Kathryn Sikkink and Stephen C. Ropp. Cambridge: Cambridge University Press, 1999, pp. 1–38.

Rompuy, Herman V. "Statement by President of the European Council Herman Van Rompuy Following His Meeting with President of Vietnam Truong Tan Sang", 31 October 2012. Available at <http://www.consilium.europa.eu/uedocs/cms_data/docs/pressdata/en/ec/133266.pdf> (accessed 1 July 2017).

Rosamond, Ben. "Three Ways of Speaking Europe to the World: Markets, Peace, Cosmopolitan Duty and the EU's Normative Power". *The British Journal of Politics & International Relations* 16, no. 1 (2014): 133–48.

Rumelili, Bahar. "Constructing Identity and Relating to Difference: Understanding the EU's Mode of Differentiation". *Review of International Studies* 30, no. 1 (2004): 27–47.

Schimmelfennig, Frank and Ulrich Sedelmeier. "Introduction: Conceptualising the Europeanization of Central and Eastern Europe". In *The Europeanization of Central and Eastern Europe*, edited by Frank Schimmelfennig and Ulrich Sedelmeier. Ithaca: Cornell University Press, 2005, pp. 1–28.

Sicurelli, Daniela. "The EU as a Norm Promoter through Trade: The Perceptions of Vietnamese Elites". *Asia Europe Journal* 13, no. 1 (2015): 23–39.

Siles-Brügge, Gabriel. "EU Trade and Development Policy beyond the ACP: Subordinating Developmental to Commercial Imperatives in the Reform of GSP". *Contemporary Politics* 20, no. 1 (2014): 49–62.

Solingen, Etel. "Of Dominoes and Firewalls: The Domestic, Regional, and Global Politics of International Diffusion". *International Studies Quarterly* 56, no. 4 (2012): 631–44.

Strang, David and John W. Meyer. "Institutional Conditions for Diffusion". *Theory and Society* 22, no. 4 (1993): 487–511.

Tocci, Nathalie. "Profiling Normative Foreign Policy: The European Union and Its Global Partners". In *Who is a Normative Foreign Policy Actor?*, edited by Nathalie Tocci. Bruxelles: Centre for European Policy Studies (CEPS), Belgium, 2008, pp. 1–23.

Vu, T. hanh Tu Anh. "WTO Accession and the Political Economy in Vietnam". *GEG Working Paper* 92 (2014).

World Trade Organization (WTO). "Trade Policy Review: Viet Nam". Minutes of the Meeting 17 and 19 September 2013. Available at <https://www.wto.org/english/tratop_e/tpr_e/tp387_e.htm> (accessed 1 June 2017).

Zwingel, Susanne. "How Do Norms Travel? Theorizing International Women's Rights in Transnational Perspective". *International Studies Quarterly* 56, no. 1 (2012): 115–29.

Index